Primal Dream and Primal Crime

Primal Dream and Primal Crime

Orwell's Development as a Psychological Novelist

Richard I. Smyer

University of Missouri Press
Columbia & London
1979

Copyright © 1979 by The Curators of the University of Missouri
University of Missouri Press, Columbia, Missouri 65211
Library of Congress Catalog Card Number 79-4840
Printed and bound in the United States of America

Library of Congress Cataloging in Publication Data

Smyer, Richard I   1935-
    Primal Dream and Primal Crime.

    Bibliography: p. 176
    Includes index.
    1.   Orwell, George, 1903–1950—Criticism and
interpretation.   I.   Title.
PR6029.R8Z789   823'.9'12   79-4840
ISBN 0-8262-0282-9

To my parents,
my children,
and Nancy

Preface

During the last fifteen years or so there has been a steady stream of books and articles on George Orwell, and as the year 1984 draws nearer interest in the man and the writer will surely increase. Indeed, there is reason to believe that he is edging his way into the gilt-lettered ranks of the English classics. For years almost routinely included in freshman English essay anthologies, he is now making a first appearance in *The Norton Anthology of English Literature* (fourth edition)—perhaps signifying a shift in emphasis away from Orwell the isolated spokesman for human decency toward a recognition of his place within the context of important literary and intellectual traditions.

In dealing with the psychological dimension of Orwell's fiction, I have stressed the relationship existing between his vision of reality and those of other writers and thinkers, not only British but also European and, to some extent, American. Although there can be no doubt that Orwell's imagination was greatly influenced by extra-literary experiences, I am convinced that to appreciate most fully his unique contribution to twentieth-century literature we must note the vital connection between Orwell the reader and Orwell the writer. Determining the nature of this relationship is especially important in charting the course of his development as a novelist. As I shall argue, frequently he relied on thematic and technical elements derived from other writers. However, in pointing out the extent of Orwell's indebtedness—the creditors range in time from Swift to Freud, in space from the Americans Poe and Jack London to the Russian Zamyatin, in style from Wells to Joyce—I am not questioning his right to a position among the prominent figures of British literature. If in some cases Orwell's failure to assimilate such borrowings resulted in thematic vagueness and stylistic awkwardness, we should regard these flaws as marking the trial-and-error process by which a serious writer constantly struggled to comprehend the violent and irrational forces shaping the age—forces also at work within himself—and to communicate his insights with honesty and artistic skill. The fact that *1984* seems as imaginatively intense and disturbingly truthful now, as we move into the 1980s, as it did in the fifties, suggests to me that Orwell has settled his literary and intellectual accounts.

My own indebtedness starts with Profs. S. Dale Harris, Wilfred Stone, and Richard Scowcroft, whose encouragement and sound advice during my postgraduate years at Stanford University enabled me to formulate ideas basic to the present study. For invaluable assistance in acquiring material on Orwell, I am grateful to the staffs of the Stanford University and the University of Arizona libraries. I am obligated to Harcourt Brace Jovanovich, Inc., for permission to reprint the poem in Volume 1, p. 118, of *The Collected Essays, Journalism and Letters of George Orwell*, edited by Sonia Orwell and Ian Angus, copyright 1968, and for permission to use brief quotations from the four volumes of *The Collected Essays* and from

Animal Farm, *Burmese Days*, *A Clergyman's Daughter*, *Coming Up for Air*, *Homage to Catalonia*, *Keep the Aspidistra Flying*, *1984*, and *The Road to Wigan Pier*. In a somewhat revised form, chapters of this study have appeared in the following journals, to which I wish to make grateful acknowledgment: *Arizona Quarterly* 27:1 (Spring 1971), copyright 1971; *English Language Notes* 9:1 (September 1971), copyright 1971, Regents of the University of Colorado; *Modern Fiction Studies* 21:1 (Spring 1975), copyright 1975, Purdue Research Foundation; and *South Dakota Review* 8:4 (Winter 1970–1971), copyright 1970, University of South Dakota.

R. I. S.
Tucson, Arizona
January 1979

Contents

I. Introduction, *1*

II. From Blair to Orwell, *9*

III. The East as Waste Land, *24*

IV. Orwell and Joyce, *41*

V. From Rebel Poet to Common Man, *59*

VI. Questioning the Past, *76*

VII. Politics and the Imagination, *94*

VIII. The Age of Unreason, *111*

IX. The Golden Country, *136*

X. Conclusion, *160*

Notes, *165*

Bibliography, *176*

Index, *183*

Primal Dream and Primal Crime

Chapter I

Introduction

One can imagine the tight grin with which Eric Blair might have greeted the idea that in creating a public identity for himself, in becoming George Orwell, he would be presenting the world with a handy, sometimes all-too-handy, adjective, or that in writing his last novel, *1984*, he would be adding to the vocabulary of contemporary polemics. The political terrorism of any present-day police state almost automatically becomes an "Orwellian nightmare"; it is a rare advance in computer technology that is not viewed by some journalist as one more step in the direction of 1984—the social dystopia, not just the year; and lest we forget about the voyeuristic tendency of government bureaucracies, we are constantly reminded that Big Brother is watching us.

These terms have become very much a part of our consciousness: besides being used to characterize and judge aspects of modern society, they have at times hardened into the very conceptual categories by which we experience reality. Orwell belongs to that small group of twentieth-century writers whose fictional works have influenced the thinking of readers who are only slightly interested in imaginative literature (others who come to mind are H. G. Wells and Solzhenitsyn). Jeffrey Meyers's claim that Orwell "is more widely read than perhaps any other serious writer of the twentieth-century" is undebatable.[1] Indeed, Orwell has become something of a public institution—the community property of sociologists, editors, political scientists, journalists, and many others besides literary critics.

The resulting diversity of opinion regarding the merits of Orwell's works is, of course, healthy, for it indicates that critical judgments have not solidified into critical dogmas, that there is still room for debate about his standing as a writer. His aims and stylistic modes, his relationship to various intellectual and literary traditions, his strengths and weaknesses as both thinker and artist, the personal and public factors influencing his development are all matters still open to discussion.

This work will trace Orwell's development as an imaginative writer, primarily as a novelist, from the early 1930s until the late 1940s and the appearance of his last major work, *1984*. I shall argue that the writings of these two decades chart Orwell's struggle to transform personal attitudes into aesthetically and intellectually satisfying works of art. I hope to show that these works are the collective expression of Orwell's striving to earn the right to voice the important concerns of his generation.

1

Throughout his career, Orwell wrestled with the complexities of human existence. Strain, tension, and conflict are the enduring characteristics of the man and his works. If we suspect that Cassandra is Orwell's muse, it is because he is a man of the twentieth century, too exposed to the demonic powers threatening the moral and cultural integrity of his society. The fact that Orwell's sense of crisis is a deeply felt personal experience explains that grim, sometimes feverish, intensity of his writings. Rarely do we find here the Olympian irony of Thomas Mann or Conrad. It is just this personal intensity that gives to Orwell's vision of reality its vividness and, it must be admitted, its occasionally confusing ambiguity.

As I shall point out, Orwell's earlier major works are thematically and structurally disjointed. In them we detect a narrative disunity and blurred focus, and we feel that the writer's need to cope with a private disturbance is interfering with the examination of some political or social crisis. Too often the effort to diagnose the ills of society becomes a shadowy struggle to exorcise some personal demon. So insistent is this psychological dilemma that at times we wonder if the fictional characters of the early works are much more than the collective projection of an unresolved private conflict. As a result, the depiction of society at a certain point in history is vaguely related, even irrelevant, to the personal lives of his characters.

Although flawed, the earlier novels do indicate that Orwell was, at least, partly aware of his shortcomings. As we move into the late thirties and forties, we find increasing evidence of a more conscious interest in the general significance of psychological experience and a more systematic effort to establish a convincing link between the dilemmas of the fictional characters and the political, social, and cultural dilemmas of the age.

A glance at some of the criticisms on Orwell may help to define more clearly my approach. For example, Orwell is most frequently dealt with in social and political terms. His primary themes, it is claimed, are politics and poverty.[2] He has been called a late-born nineteenth-century liberal who is opposed to modern corporate-state socialism;[3] an heir to the English tradition of radicalism represented by such men as Langland, Bunyan, Cobbett, Dickens, and Chesterton;[4] and a reactionary because of his skepticism about technological progress and the classless society.[5] On the other hand, Stephen Spender tells us that Orwell "was really classless, really a Socialist."[6]

Positive and negative judgments on Orwell often relate to the sociopolitical accuracy and validity of his works. *Nineteen Eighty-four*, the most Orwellian of his novels, is praised as much for its vivid description of existing abuses as for its vision of future evils.[7] Orwell's treatment of contemporary totalitarianism has been compared favorably to that of Kafka, Camus, and Koestler.[8]

Other critics are less enthusiastic. Not only is Orwell's view of twentieth-century England regarded as naively simplistic[9] but also his general ideas about politics and history have been questioned. His awareness of the past limited by too intense a focus on the contemporary, Orwell could think of the future only as an extension of the present.[10] Several critics consider *1984*, with its vision of an invincible and changeless totalitarian state, as based upon wholly unrealistic assumptions about politics and history.[11]

However, what we need to question is whether Orwell is primarily a political or sociological novelist. There is evidence that what we ordinarily think of as public problems and issues are really indicative of more private modes of experience. By reorienting our perspective we can see that he is not the narrowly sociopolitical novelist some critics make him out to be, that sociopolitical categories are only partially applicable to his fiction. Although Orwell's remark in "Why I Write" (1946)—since 1936 the aim of his serious writings has been to combat totalitarianism and defend "democratic Socialism"—indicates a political concern,[12] several people have suggested that his works exhibit contradictory tendencies. During the late thirties and early forties, there appears in Orwell's writings a disgust with politics coinciding with the development of a personal interest in quietism.[13] The claim is made that his involvement with the struggle for economic justice and against political tyranny in time gives way to a more contemplative and psychological approach to life.[14] In the view of John Atkins, Orwell passed from a stage in which he stressed the improvement of social institutions to one in which the most important reforms were personal and psychological.[15] We would do well to bear in mind the opinion of Orwell's friend Richard Rees that he "was a good deal nearer to the other-worldly Tolstoy and Gandhi and a good deal further from the average humanistic progressive than he himself was prepared to recognize" (p. 114).

I shall also discuss those critics who overlook the complexity of Orwell's style in stressing its clarity and directness, traits associated with realistic prose.[16] They regard Orwell as being a pre-modern, even old-fashioned, novelist, his style being most closely linked to that of the Victorians and Edwardians.[17] *Naturalistic* is a term frequently applied to his writings. Orwell's concern with giving a clear picture of external reality is evidence, George Woodcock claims, that "naturalism permeated every aspect of his outlook."[18] Keith Alldritt maintains that despite some experimentation with symbolism during the 1930s, by temperament Orwell's true allegiance lay with the naturalistic tradition of Dickens, Gissing, and Wells (pp. 19–20). Another writer considers the attempt to apply to Orwell's works the modern tools of critical exegesis as doomed to failure: "His novels [are] direct and fairly simple narratives in an old tradition. Their meanings are mostly on the surface. Orwell posed no riddles, elaborated no myths, and manipulated no symbols."[19]

David Lodge's elaborate and sophisticated version of these ideas is worth summarizing.[20] Drawing upon the writings of Roman Jacobson and upon the concepts associated with structuralism, Lodge argues that twentieth-century British literature alternates between two stylistic poles—the metaphoric and the metonymic. Metaphor he defines as a substitution, one thing being substituted for (and identified with) something else even though these two things are obviously dissimilar. Thus in symbolic art there is a wide gap between an image and what it means. Metonymy, under which Lodge includes synecdoche, involves a process of deletion. Of all the spatially contiguous objects one might describe, some are actually presented while the rest are omitted. The part stands for the whole. Since spatial contiguity implies physical reality, the external world, metonymy is the predominant stylistic mode of conventional realism, as well as of informational prose. Although metaphors inevitably appear in a realistic prose narrative, they are tightly controlled by the metonymic context and prevented from diverting the reader's attention away from the realistic level toward a surrealistic mode of experience. On the basis of these ideas, Lodge finds a "definable continuity in technique" between Orwell (as well as other writers of the thirties) and the "Edwardian realists" (p. 46).

Some critics regard Orwell's supposed simplicity as a sign of imaginative impoverishment. Facts, the raw material of reality, prove too tough for his imagination to break down and remold into fiction.[21] As a consequence of this imaginative poverty, he was unable to grasp the importance of such irrational forces as religious feelings and unconscious impulses.[22] As a political novel, *1984* cannot rank with *The Possessed*, *The Magic Mountain*, and *The Red and the Black* primarily because Orwell, more rationalistic than imaginative, was not able to embody within his novel those "inexplicable and subterranean" forces at play in the works of Mann and his predecessors. Hampered by a naturalistic method uncongenial to symbolism, Orwell never managed to fuse history and literature, fact and fiction; he could not transform political ideas into artistically satisfying visions. This weakness is reflected in his tendency to portray the modern individual's nightmarish sensation of entrapment in a pre-modern manner. He defines his characters' dilemmas in "social and economic terms, not psychologically."[23]

While granting that Orwell's novels at times fall short of being artistically unified wholes, we need not accept the charge of imaginative weakness as the final word in this matter. The fact that in recent years Orwell's novels and nonfiction have been closely studied as more or less autonomous constructs to which are applicable the methods of modern criticism may suggest a belief among some that these works do possess an imaginative vitality.[24]

It is, I think, a mistake to regard Orwell's style as nothing more than leadenly naturalistic. A close examination of his novels reveals that they are at times heavily metaphoric in Lodge's sense of the term. Patterns of events take on symbolic meanings to suggest psychological forces at work below the visible contours of a naturalistic terrain. For this reason, we must define Orwell's characters by two different modes, the realistic and the symbolic. Like those designs that alternate between concave and convex before our eyes, the realistic scenes and events of the novels sometimes produce a surrealistic effect. A shift in perspective changes the realistic and external into the symbolic and psychological.

Furthermore Orwell's literary allegiance is not confined to the social realism of the Victorian and Edwardian periods. In the fiction of the 1930s, he uses modernist literary methods to deal with modernist themes. These earlier novels are deliberately experimental to some extent, showing the influence of Dostoevski, T. S. Eliot, Joyce, Henry Miller, and Proust. Although Orwell's interest in some of these writers waned during the forties, he did not simply become a born-again realist. Determined to anatomize the horrors of a totalitarian decade, Orwell turned to those writers who, in his view, communicated a grotesque and savage vision of reality, such as Swift, Poe, Dickens, and Zamyatin.

Those who fault Orwell for lack of psychological insight and an inability to handle the complexities of human motivation will not be enthusiastic over my approach, which is based on the assumption that psychological, and even psychoanalytic, formulations can tell us something about Orwell's works. Since Rees claims that he has no recollection of his friend "ever once mentioning the name of Freud, or Jung" (p. 8), one objection might be that Orwell was unaware of such ideas. Another objection might be based on the grounds that Orwell was disinclined to agonize over verbal subtleties, being more interested in the clear, direct message than in the labyrinthine ambiguities associated with the modern psychological novel.[25] Finally, it could be asserted that Orwell's obvious concern with the urgent social and political problems of the age makes it unlikely that he would turn his attention away from the crucial events taking place on the stage of history and would spend valuable time and energy tracing out the convolutions of the individual's inner life.

These objections can be disproved in several ways. For instance, Orwell, like any other writer, may have resorted to writing as a means of expressing his own personal feelings, disguising in the form of social commentary a complex of intimate feelings understandable in more or less psychoanalytic terms.

Stating that Orwell was unable to wear a mask, Mander claims that each of his works is a "didactic monologue," always in Orwell's own voice, with the result being that there is a "peculiarly direct relationship" between Orwell, his works, and the reader.[26] On this assumption, some critics have unhesitatingly used Orwell's oeuvre, including the novels, as a reliable guide to his personal life.

Perhaps reacting against exaggerated claims regarding Orwell's objectivity and honesty, some have called attention to subjective distortions in his writings. According to Kingsley Amis: "No sooner have you established [Orwell] in your mind as a fearlessly honest critic of society than you come up against little bits of journalistic fudging in his reportage and big bits of subjective fantasy where, whatever is being criticized, it is something far larger and more dimly apprehended than society."[27]

Critics have often tried to show that Orwell's ideas were influenced by his personal experiences and attitudes. Relative poverty was responsible for Orwell's emphasis on society's avarice;[28] and his suspicion that Roosevelt, Stalin, and Churchhill were scheming to divide the postwar world into oppressive superstates resulted from a "persecution mania."[29] Much of Orwell's pessimism has been attributed to the childhood experiences described in "Such, Such Were the Joys."[30] Anthony West's reference to some "hidden wound" responsible for Orwell's outlook (p. 176) calls attention to the critics who claim to have discovered within Orwell a veritable rats' nest of personal disorders: sadism, masochism, sexual anxiety, and a crypto-Nazism.[31] Supposedly Orwell distrusted, even loathed, humanity.[32] Some critics detect in Orwell a connection between a malicious need to foresee social doom and a suicidal impulse.[33] Alldritt relates Orwell's "intense revulsion from the human body" to a "thoroughgoing disgust at life" (p. 70).

Although some of these judgments may be valid, we should bear in mind a very important point: the same works that reveal these personality traits also express Orwell's struggle to free his imagination from a stultifying fixation on personal and idiosyncratic disturbances. One example is Orwell's conservatism. Combined with his nostalgia for the past, an affection for the days prior to World War I, is his hostility toward those who reject or distort the past.[34] For him the Great War was a wall separating modern man from times of relative decency and innocence, and his pessimism about the future sprang from a conviction that the prewar vision of progress is no longer credible.[35]

In Orwell's works, the past presents itself in several ways. In addition to being a completed segment of public history, the past is a mental reality. Interiorized, it may exist as a remote, longed-for, and dimly perceived world of peace and vitality, or it may express itself as a guilt- and anxiety-provoking presence, immanent and threatening. In the earlier works, the past is to be either revered or eluded, but not confronted. It is a sacred precinct, a taboo area, and to penetrate it may be a dangerous violation. However, in the forties, when Orwell's focus on English society expands to include a concern for Western civilization and culture, his historical perspective broadens. Paralleling this is his greater willingness to explore into the primitive irrationalities of the human mind. This confronting of the interiorized past, this hazardous journey into the darker regions of the self, is an activity symbolizing the release of Orwell's imaginative power for further development.

Orwell may not have been so psychologically unsophisticated as Rees's remark suggests. Apart from the fact that he does refer to Freud and psychoanalysis (see 2. 45, 193, and 3. 224), such essays as "Benefit of Clergy: Some Notes on Salvador Dali" and "Raffles and Miss Blandish" clearly indicate Orwell's interest in the psychosexual aspects of literature. Also, we should not forget that for over four months in 1935 Orwell rented a room from a psychology student, Mrs. Rosalind Obermeyer, who attended University College London and was well-enough acquainted with him to introduce him to Eileen O'Shaughnessy, another student majoring in psychology in the same institution and to whom he was married from June 1939 until her death in March 1945. Even if Orwell had learned nothing about psychology from his landlady, it is hard to believe that none of his wife's academic interests would have influenced him over a period of six years. Of course, almost as unlikely is the possibility that a man with Orwell's curiosity would be insensitive to the intellectual atmosphere of the times, particularly to the interest in psychoanalysis that became so widespread during the 1920s and later.

Finally, we have no right to assume that, were Orwell interested in making use of such ideas in his fiction, he lacked the diligence and dedication to stylistic intricacy necessary to accomplish his aim. Although his writings may not exhibit the sustained scrupulous artistry of Henry James or Virginia Woolf, we must at least recognize that Orwell was a conscientious craftsman. Comparing his rather slapdash writing during the early days of World War II with his usual practice, he states: "Nowadays, when I write a review, I sit down at the typewriter and type it straight out. Till recently, indeed till six months ago, I never did this. . . . Virtually all that I wrote was written at least twice, and my books as a whole three times—individual passages as many as five or ten times."[36]

As for the objection that Orwell was single-mindedly devoted to writing about the public crises of his time, I can only present my own interpretations and let the reader judge their validity. However, I might point out again that the unearthing of psychological meanings in the novels is not an end in itself but rather part of an attempt to determine the extent to which he was able to integrate various modes of reality into an artistic whole. In itself the existence of a symbolic style expressing private types of experience is neither more nor less significant than a realistically conveyed sociopolitical content. At issue is their organic relationship.

In emphasizing the psychological dimension of Orwell's works, I am, of course, aware that conclusions about the author's private life based on his writings, especially the fiction, are necessarily somewhat speculative. Our present knowledge of the way in which almost any verbal utterance, oral or written, may be a mythmaking act involving the creation of an anti-self should check any tendency to mistake inference for fact. Certainly nothing is lost by heeding the words of Orwell's biographers Peter Stansky and William Abrahams, who warn against the automatic assumption that the personal experiences Orwell used as the "raw material" of his writings and the writings themselves are identical, even though the latter may give this impression. The creation of the illusion that art and life are one is part of Orwell's strategy in his autobiographical works as well as in his novels.[37] Therefore, I have tried to exercise restraint in noting parallels between Orwell's private life, including the psychological factors at work during various stages of his personal growth, and, on the other hand, his development as a writer. I have called attention to Orwell's personal attitudes only when they might throw light on his intentions as a writer.

Although I have used, throughout, various psychoanalytic insights and concepts in interpreting Orwell's fiction, I have chosen not to indicate extensive parallels between the fiction and specific psychoanalytic works, especially Freud's, until my discussion of *1984* (Chapter IX). As I shall argue, it was not until the middle or late forties that Orwell was able to both confront his own psychological complexities and subject them to the ends of his art. Frequently Orwell's earlier fiction is the compulsive expression of private obsessions; however, by the time he was writing *1984* he was able to envision the broadly cultural implications of these obsessions. It is a sign of his personal liberation that in his last novel he was able to use psychoanalytic material in a much more conscious and systematic manner to convey general truths about the inner condition, spiritual as well as psychological, of society.

Chapter II

From Blair to Orwell

It is a mark of Orwell's nondogmatic attitude that in his essays he appears as a clear-sighted observer who shows the reader specific aspects of reality rather than simply telling the reader what to think.[1] To a large extent, the vigor of the essays, especially those recounting Orwell's personal experiences, stems from his ability to enter into the events being described. As one critic notes, the Orwellian "I" is not that of traditional essay, the "I" who conveys the impression of being at ease with his material, but rather one who is even now, as essayist, caught up in events. The Orwellian "I" is a dramatically presented participant. For the time in which they were written, Orwell's essays were "virtually a new genre—a revision of the neat structural closures of the conventional essay into the looser but more adhesive representations of fictional prose."[2]

Although one might question Orwell's originality by pointing to the essays of Montaigne, unabashedly personal in their revelation of the Frenchman's inner self, we rarely find in the *Essais* that atmosphere of crisis, that quality of conflict and struggle, present in, for example, "Shooting an Elephant" or "How the Poor Die." In Montaigne's essays, inconsistencies, doubts, and moments of outrage at the devastation wrought during the religious wars are all elements that enable us to see Montaigne the man speaking out of his own experiences. Yet these revelations of self always seem the confidences of a provincial gentleman comfortably seated in his book-lined study, far enough removed from the outer world's irrationalities to regard his own with an amused indulgence. By contrast, the Orwell of the essays is usually out in the world, immersed in its follies and indignities.

Perhaps nothing distinguishes the two essayists more clearly than their experiences with books. For Montaigne, literature was a refuge, a consolation; nothing was so restorative as a volume of one of his beloved classics lying open before him. Turning to Orwell's "Confessions of a Book Reviewer" (1946), we find: "In a cold but stuffy bed-sitting room littered with cigarette ends and half-empty cups of tea, a [book reviewer] in a moth-eaten dressing-gown sits at a rickety table, trying to find room for his typewriter among the piles of dusty papers that surround it. He cannot throw the papers away because the wastepaper basket is already overflowing, and besides, somewhere among the unanswered letters and unpaid bills it is possible that there is a cheque for two guineas which he is nearly certain he forgot to pay into the bank" (4. 181). Even if there were a Jowett translation of Cicero about, it is doubtful that the reviewer could locate it.

These are the characteristics of Orwellian reality, in the essays as in the novels: the insecurity of a "rickety table," the physical distastefulness of cigarette butts and lukewarm tea, the decay of an old bathrobe, the sense of events—the overflowing wastebasket, the missing check—getting out of control, the mounting tension as a day of reckoning for unpaid bills and unanswered letters approaches, and above all the struggle to write, to bring some order out of this chaos.

Sometimes Orwell's wrestling with the material of his art pays off, and sometimes not. Many of his works are indicative of inner struggles, expressions of personal conflicts; we can measure the success of these works by the extent to which he fuses the conflicting elements into a unified whole. At other times, what we measure is dissonance, the dispersal of imaginative energies.

To pass from the abstract to the concrete, we might examine two early works—one, the essay "A Hanging" (1931), as an example of Orwell's skill; the other, *Down and Out in Paris and London* (1933), an example of disunity. In "A Hanging," Orwell describes his awakening to an awareness of what death means, and at the same time exposes the ways in which men involved in the death of another human being attempt to protect themselves from the full knowledge of what they are doing.[3] Throughout this essay, one can sense a line of tension between ritual, the more or less formal procedure by which the men engaged in the execution of a malefactor overlook the implications of their deed, and the breaking of ritual, the intrusion of disturbing elements—the announcement that the other prisoners' breakfast is late because of the slowness of the execution, the dog that suddenly leaps up to lick the prisoner's face, the latter's cries as the noose is tightened around his neck—that force upon the officials the fearful truth that a human life is being ended forever.

In the few pages of this essay, we find some of the elements important to Orwell's later work. Basic to his reality is the circumstance that something is amiss. Something *is* that *should not be*: capital punishment is wrong. However, implicit in this statement is its reverse: what *should be*, what *should exist*, *does not*—"one mind less, one world less." The right order of things has been violated. In fact, what is thought to be the right order of things—the stern letter of the law, the ceremonial implementation of the law, the proper observance of meal times, the informal rituals of camaraderie and good-fellowship—is itself a means of shielding the executioners from the violating awareness of two very uncivilized realities—violence and death. Beneath their public and official roles as agents of punitive authority lies the human (and subhuman) urge to destroy, and beneath their conscious minds exists the frightening knowledge of their own mortality. The orderliness of ritual and ceremony is, in effect, a talisman to keep these two beasts at bay. Yet these atavistic reminders are not easily suppressed. The very assertion of a rational order implies its opposite: the story of the prisoner's panicked urinating, an anecdote meant to dispel anxiety, makes us realize the irrationality of the demand for breakfast on schedule—for presumably some of the prisoners to be fed on time are themselves destined for execution. And at the risk of overinterpreting, one might suggest a connection between Orwell's flash of conscious outrage at the proceedings and two images mythically associated with death and dissolution—the dog that seems to be welcoming the condemned man and the puddle, the mud, which he tries to avoid.

Whether or not one wishes to pursue the implications of this or that image, the important point is that all the elements of the narrative work together to produce a unified effect. As a matter of fact, what Orwell omits is almost as important to the total effect as what he includes. The scarcity of proper names, the lack of a date, and the unexplained nature of the prisoner's crime not only call our attention to the internal organization of the essay as an autonomous work of art but also emphasize the universality of the experience.

In "A Hanging" loss produces gain. The subtraction that takes place— the removal from the world of a sentient, thinking being—is balanced by the addition of another, the observer abruptly transformed from a condition of diminished awareness ("I had never realised what it means to destroy a . . . man") to a sense of the "mystery" of sudden death. Balance becomes profit when the "unspeakable wrongness" of capital punishment is verbalized, turned into the written word that will outlast the participants in the execution. In a sense, the Hindu's death is a sacrifice that calls into existence Blair the essayist. In *Down and Out in Paris and London*, we learn of another creative loss, a violation that brings into existence the Orwell whose development this study will trace.

Blair's childhood friend Jacintha Buddicom recalls that even as a young-ster he was determined to be an important writer.[4] To this end, Blair lived in the Coq d'Or working-class quarter of Paris from the spring of 1928 to the end of 1929. But progress was slow. Two novels written during this period were rejected and destroyed. The few articles that were accepted for publication and some private tutoring apparently did not relieve the financial pinch, for in *Down and Out* he says that he finally had to start looking for a regular job, perhaps as a tourist guide or interpreter. However, before Eric Blair the none-too-successful writer can follow the predictable occupational course of the educated expatriate, chance alters his life. A man occupying the same hotel surreptitiously enters Blair's apartment and steals most of his money.

The initial effect of this violation and loss is to undermine Blair's identity. Suddenly wrenched out of the stereotypic role of struggling novelist and prevented from mechanically assuming the obvious alternatives open to the Englishman abroad, Blair is plunged into the unfamiliar world of the poor, an existence "too difficult to leave much time for anything else."[5] And if the Hindu's death gives life to Eric Blair the essayist, the victimization of Blair brings into being George Orwell, the persona who eventually turns the mind-numbing life of the poor into literature: "Poverty is what I am writing about" (p. 9).

Birth is, of course, no guarantee of maturity. The first work to bear the name *Orwell* is not the thematically concentrated exposition the above quotation suggests. To better understand the nature of this work, we need to determine the extent to which it does or does not conform to that genre which during the thirties was used for purposes of sociological description and analysis—the documentary.

John Mander states that the documentary is a genre occupying a middle ground somewhere between the "public, political world of the historian and the private, psychological world" of the modern artist who makes use of external reality to express his subjective feelings. However, even though the documentary writer may communicate personal judgments and interpretations of events, the documentary should direct our attention primarily toward the concrete details of observed reality and away from the writer's private reactions. By this definition, Mander considers Orwell's *Down and Out in Paris and London* (1933) an effective documentary.[6]

Although *Down and Out* does not fit into this definition so snugly as one might think, Orwell's first book certainly exhibits some of the characteristics of a documentary. Implicit in Orwell's circumstantially detailed account of his experiences among French workers and English tramps is the disturbing truth that below the comfortable world of middle-class life exists a shadowy republic of the poor and oppressed. The writer does, after all, become tour guide and interpreter, but in a way far different from that anticipated by Blair in 1929. He is now a cicerone who, by guiding his readers through these subterranean regions of squalor, brings them face to face with harsh realities of which they might otherwise be happily unaware—thus the basic strategy of such earlier works as "The Spike" (1931), "Clink" (1931), and "Common Lodging Houses" (1932).

What makes *Down and Out* interesting for the purposes of this study is the presence of factors that divert our attention away from the documentary toward what one suspects to be more subjective elements. In reading *Down and Out*, one begins to notice that embedded in the narrator's recollections is a pattern of experience that is unrelated to the documentary aim.

As an example of how personal attitudes may color the documentary, we might look first at an earlier classic of social reportage, Jack London's *The People of the Abyss* (1904), a grim exposé of living—and dying—conditions in the London East End around the turn of the century. Before entering into the life of the poor in the East End during the summer of 1902, London puts on frayed secondhand clothes, an act that he claims with the dauntless confidence of an American pioneer in the wilderness of industrial England immediately prepares him for the task at hand: "Presto! in the twinkling of an eye, so to say, I had become one of [the lower-class English]. . . . I now shared with them a comradeship."[7] So garbed, he visits a local spike, a public dormitory for the poor, and also gains access to apartments, or rather fetid dens, into which several families must pack themselves, living without privacy.

However, in reading London's exposure of the murky depths of this social pit, we begin to suspect that the narrator is subtly emphasizing his own superior position in life. Beneath the American's documentary observations is an implicitly Darwinian view of reality in which the East Enders are the hapless losers in a fierce struggle for survival: "There is no place for them in the social fabric, while all the forces of society drive them downward till they perish. At the bottom of the Abyss they are feeble, besotted, and imbecile" (p. 40). These people are not just unfortunate individuals but rather a defeated species on the way to extermination—"a weak-kneed, narrow-chested, listless breed, that crumples up and goes down in the brute struggle for life with the invading hordes from the country" (p. 47). Constantly hovering over London the socialist critic of industrial society is the dark, contemptuous bulk of London the Nietzschean *Übermensch* taking what one suspects to be a grim comfort from the knowledge that these ill-fed, diseased, and debased wretches are "the quickest to die" (p. 109).

So personally upsetting is the abyss, this vision of social and biological defeat, that the narrator must implicitly stress the difference between himself and these dying breeds. Symbolic of this insistence on his identity as one determined, if not destined, to survive is the fact that instead of living in the heart of the abyss, London chooses as his base of operations a fairly decent apartment on the fringes of the district, his intention being "to have a port of refuge, not too far distant, into which I could run now and again to assure myself that good clothes and cleanliness still existed." More than a refuge, this apartment is a kind of fortress offering protection against a threatening world of decadence, a stronghold from which he can "sally forth" (p. 19).

The "new and warm" underclothes worn beneath his ragged outer garments (p. 10), the emergency money sewn into the lining of his slumming singlet (p. 12), the flight, after only one night's stay in a tramps' public dormitory, to a Turkish bath to steam the germs out of his skin (p. 112)— these all suggest that *The People of the Abyss* is, in addition to being a documentary account of East End living conditions and an indictment of the modern city, an attempt on the part of the narrator to preserve a self-image in sharp contrast to the puny and debased creatures he walks among. The result is an intriguing combination of social outrage and pitying contempt, the former springing from London's socialist principles, the latter deriving perhaps from a mixture of Darwinian and Nietzschean attitudes.

Turning to Orwell's work, one can find another example of a double message, as it were, although here the components of the message are not quite the same as those in *The People of the Abyss*. In addition to being a more or less chronologically arranged record of a middle-class Britisher's journey through modern society's lower depths, *Down and Out* is a guilt-burdened expression of lost sexual innocence, a symbolic statement of the narrator's anxiety regarding sensual experience. In other words, this work functions at two different levels, the social and the personal, and the existence of these different layers of meaning increases the possibility that the narrative itself may be fragmented.

The narrator's re-creation of his earlier experiences among the French and English poor exhibits a somewhat puzzling bipolar design at both the sociopolitical and psychological levels. Critics have correctly perceived the marked tonal difference between the Paris and London sections of the book; and although there is some bitterness in the Paris half and humor in the London account, the narrator's remarks seem much less overtly oppressed by the knowledge of evil in the first part than in the second.[8]

The effect of poverty on the lower-class Parisians usually excites Orwell's innocent curiosity, rarely his moral indignation. He calls the Paris slums a gathering place for eccentrics, for people who have given up trying to be normal and respectable. Rather than oppressing, poverty liberates, freeing people "from ordinary standards of behaviour, just as money frees people from work." The narrator's sense of wonder is aroused by the realization that poverty is the condition for human variety. Thus, he can claim that "some of the lodgers in our hotel lived lives that were curious beyond words" (p. 7).

Curiosity, not bitterness, is Orwell's habitual response to life in Paris. Working as a dishwasher, he reacts to being the object of his superiors' curses simply by counting "from curiosity" the number of times he is called a pimp (p. 58). Another dominant reaction is humor. Speaking of the various eccentrics in the slums, Orwell remarks that "it would be fun to write some of their biographies" (p. 9), and the description of his own lodgings mixes mock-heroic humor with farce: "Near the ceiling long lines of bugs marched all day like columns of soldiers, and at night came down ravenously hungry, so that one had to get up every few hours and kill them in hecatombs. Sometimes when the bugs got too bad one used to burn sulphur and drive them into the next room; whereupon the lodger next door would retort by having *his* room sulphured, and drive the bugs back" (p. 6). Rather than eliciting censure, the disparity between the glittering life of the French upper classes and the day-to-day existence of the toiling workers serves as background for a wryly humorous observation that gains point from the physical proximity of these groups. Working in the scullery of a respectable Paris hotel, he finds amusing the fact that only a door separates the luxurious dining room, filled with splendidly dressed diners, from him and his fellow workers, who are surrounded by "disgusting filth" (pp. 67–68).

Moreover, this life possesses a fairy-tale quality. No matter how dire the circumstances, something always happens to save Orwell from calamity. Paris is a fabulous world in which Orwell, penniless and sinking into black despair after a sixty-hour fast, need only glance down at the pavement to discover, "as though by a miracle," enough money to keep him going (pp. 42–43).

As I have already suggested, Orwell's account of his English experiences is quite different. Two anecdotes, one from each section, neatly exemplify this shift in mood. The first deals with a starving, out-of-work French waiter who, helplessly lying in bed, prays to a portrait that he thinks represents a female saint. Although an atheist, he promises to buy a votive candle for her if she will send him money. Soon afterward, he discovers in his room an old kettle for which he had paid a refundable deposit. The story ends in a manner reminiscent of O. Henry: learning that the portrait is, in fact, that of a notorious prostitute, the waiter can, without guilt, use the pledged money to buy himself cigarettes (pp. 83–88). In the second anecdote, Orwell, describing the men who drift into the London spikes, recalls an experience with a miserably jobless and loudly blasphemous clerk. Orwell first observes the man as the latter is hysterically proclaiming his ability to get a job without resorting to the futile act of prayer. Orwell's next encounter with him, within a small reading room, presages no wryly amusing conclusion: "As I opened the door I saw the young clerk in there all alone; he was on his knees *praying*. Before I shut the door again I had time to see his face, and it looked agonised. Quite suddenly I realised, from the expression on his face, that he was starving" (p. 156). Orwell is left with an acute sense of guilty embarrassment at having caught sight of the man's pitiful condition.

The tonal difference between these two anecdotes draws our attention to a significant structural difference. Although throughout the second part of *Down and Out* one is constantly aware that the tramps exist in a society callously insensitive to their physical and emotional needs, we note in the Paris section the idea of poverty as a social evil is not stressed, and the sociological generalizations are confined to a single chapter (22). But if the first part is characterized by a segregation of Orwell the amused observer from Orwell the social critic, within the second part exists a more interesting split, one between the narrator's eyewitness account of the socioeconomic abuses in England and the indirect expression of personal misgiving about sensual experience.

In this regard, it may be helpful to examine the speaker's recollections of the filth and decay of lower-class life. Orwell's descriptions of the dirt and squalor to be found in Paris have been quoted too often to need repeating here. However, it should be noted that these descriptions are primarily of nonhuman filth. Even in the well-known passage about a cook's careless habit of pawing the meat with his brilliantine-stained fingers and allowing spittle to fall into the dinners, we are disgusted with the condition of the food, not with the man. Furthermore, our revulsion is somewhat diluted by our ironic amusement that this is the kind of meal for which the middle-class Frenchman is probably being overcharged. Also, Orwell half-playfully defends the cook's behavior by claiming that "dirty treatment" is integral to the man's artistry in preparing a smart-looking meal (p. 80). On the few occasions in the Paris section when Orwell does draw attention to the less pleasant aspects of human physiology, such as the effect of extreme hunger on the color and consistency of one's spittle, he is calmly scientific (p. 38).

On the other hand, the London section of *Down and Out* stresses human physical decay, and the tone is pure disgust. Describing the nocturnal coughing of a lodging-house inmate, Orwell writes: "It was an unspeakably repellent sound; a foul bubbling and retching, as though the man's bowels were being churned up within him. Once when he struck a match I saw that he was a very old man, with a grey, sunken face like that of a corpse" (p. 131). Undressed the tramps are a revolting sight: "Naked and shivering, we lined up in the passage. You cannot conceive what ruinous, degenerate curs we looked, standing there in the merciless morning light. A tramp's clothes are bad, but they conceal far worse things; to see him as he really is, unmitigated, you must see him naked. Flat feet, pot bellies, hollow chests, sagging muscles—every kind of physical rottenness was there" (pp. 147–48).

On the attitude of superiority betrayed by Jack London's reaction to the East Enders, Calder notes that London's tendency to stress the gap existing between himself and the slum dwellers results in descriptions of these people which indicate that he is not really interested in them as individuals. His habit of resorting to striking similes instead of giving circumstantially specific details and his use of plural and generalizing nouns (such as "miserable multitudes") produces a hazy, impressionistic picture, more indicative of London's emotional attitude than of a desire to re-create the original scenes with a documentary objectivity.[9] In line with this observation one might note that when London turns his attention to the physical condition of the poor, we rarely get a particularly vivid description, a close-up shot, of bodily deterioration. The one really horrifying description of this type—that of a putrescent, vermin-covered corpse discovered in a tenement—relates to a scene that London only reads about, not one that he himself has witnessed (pp. 215–16).

If Jack London's generalizing tendency, with its distancing effect, reveals a certain aloofness toward the suffering human beings he has observed, I am inclined to suspect that a slightly different, and perhaps more intense, attitude is revealed by the narrator's tendency in the second part of *Down and Out* to focus attention on the revolting details of bodily deterioration, the same kind of repellent details that appear in such earlier works as "The Spike" and "Clink"—the "horrid, greasy 'toe-rags,' " the "physical rottenness" of bloated bellies, sunken chests, and watery eyes, and the "nasty faecal stench" of a jail cell (1. 37, 39, 92).

These Struldbruggian descriptions of the English tramps' bodily decay are indicative of Orwell's loathing of the corruptible flesh per se. Moreover, the contrast between this response and the more indulgent attitude evident in the first half of the book suggests the presence of two conflicting states of mind regarding the body. The abrupt shift in the narrative from what appears to be an innocent joy and lighthearted curiosity to a sort of memento mori gloom becomes particularly marked in the speaker's retrospective account of the two cities' sexual atmospheres.

"Sooner will you find a cloudless sky in winter, than a woman at the Hôtel X who has her maidenhead." These words, carved into the wall of a Parisian hotel, might stand, with some qualification, as the motto of the French poor, at least as the narrator recalls them. For him the remembered Paris slums are a libidinal Eden, a world of at least superficially uninhibited sexuality. For example, the working-class bistro that Orwell frequents is the scene of "extraordinarily public love-making" (p. 10).

Orwell's Paris possesses an extremely important characteristic: it is a place of innocent sexuality. Typical of the sexually innocuous atmosphere is the case of an old married couple who make a living by selling sealed packets supposedly containing pornographic postcards but which actually contain pictures of châteaux on the Loire (p. 7). And despite its frenetic appearance, the "public love-making" in the bistro is remarkably harmless. Charlie, a young Englishman whom Orwell earlier describes as looking like a baby, busies himself with reciting poetry and pinching the girls' breasts; meanwhile a woman performs a dance with an Arab who wields a "painted wooden phallus the size of a rolling pin." Erotic ardor increases as the drinking continues: "The girls were violently kissed and hands thrust into their bosoms and they made off lest worse should happen" (pp. 93–95). Significantly, these recollections are like the amorous scenes in a slightly naughty music-hall entertainment—the sexuality is unconsummated and, all things considered, relatively innocent.

On the other hand, England is a libidinal dystopia, a world in which sex is shameful and implicitly threatening. Orwell can tell he is in London when he finds that someone has taken pains to scratch out an obscene word from a humorous graffito (p. 132), and later he observes a group of Mormon preachers violently denounced as polygamists by their audience (p. 135). Bozo, a pavement artist whom Orwell meets during his vagabondage, tells of once drawing a copy of Botticelli's Venus on the sidewalk before a church when a churchwarden ran out and, announcing that such an obscenity must not appear near the house of God, made him wipe it out (p. 171).

We should be aware that Orwell's crossing of the channel is more than a movement from one geographical location to another, for *Down and Out* is as much an expression of the narrator's state of mind as it is a documentary, as much the expression of a personal vision of reality as a retrospective factual account. It is, of course, a psychological truism that an individual's past experiences are not necessarily identical to the later recollected experiences. The imagination, conditioned by the general mental state of the person engaged in remembering, not only adds some details and omits others but also transforms past incidents into new experience. Personal history frequently becomes personal myth. Orwell himself admitted that he had exercised selective control over the material on which *Down and Out* is based, the chronological order of some events having been altered.[10] We may, therefore, justifiably regard the speaker's account, whatever may be the degree of its autobiographical accuracy in terms of Eric Blair's life, as a metaphorical representation of his, the narrator's, sensibility as it exists in the narrative present of the work. From this perspective, we may look upon the passage from France to England as an implicit indication of the speaker's feeling of having passed from a condition of relative innocence to one of guilt.

Such interpretation may explain Orwell's somewhat curious presentation of Paris life—the paradox that although the French metropolis is supposedly a world of unfettered sexuality, the instances of sexual behavior that the speaker recalls are de-eroticized and given a make-believe quality. Charlie is a playful infant, not the jaded rake he pretends to be while in his cups; and the young women escape their wooers. The reason for this make-believe quality may be directly related to the speaker's temporal position. Between his experiences in Paris and his current memory of them lies his trip to London. In other words, his mind freighted with the disturbing knowledge that sexual behavior is somehow sinful, the more primitive memories are bereft of any erotic quality lest Orwell the observer be guilty of a reprehensible voyeurism.

By paying close attention to the position the speaker's recollections occupy in the narrative, we can better understand why, symbolically speaking, he has had to leave Paris. Toward the end of the French section, Orwell states that he finally left that country because he was tired of being a *plongeur*. One might add that the unfolding of the innocence-guilt pattern makes his departure symbolically inevitable, for at this point in the speaker's recollections there are signs that the element of shame is eroding the ties of Orwell the *plongeur* with the state of being represented by Paris. It is noteworthy that in recalling his own experiences in the Paris slums, he is almost silent regarding his relationship with women. In his account of the workers' sexual activity, he is simply an observer.[11] Only once does he refer to his personal romantic inclinations: "I remember once asking [a young parisienne] to come to a dance, and she . . . said that she had not been further than the street corner for several months. She was consumptive, and died about the time I left Paris" (p. 112).

This statement has a dual significance. First, the speaker explicitly mentions that the girl's death occurred at about the same time as his departure from Paris, a juxtaposition of events that is emphasized by the fact that this recollection appears at that point in the narrative when Orwell the *plongeur*, the speaker's remembered self, is shown preparing to leave for England. Second, this quotation contains another revealing juxtaposition of ideas: Orwell's proposal is mentioned in conjunction with statements about the girl's death and his own departure. Although there is no indication of any temporal contiguity between the invitation and the two later occurrences, the fact that in his account the speaker groups them together suggests that these events—the invitation, the girl's death, and the abandonment of Paris—are significantly related in the speaker's present state of mind.

The deeper implication of this statement becomes clearer when we recall Orwell's earlier observation regarding one of the curiosities of his Paris lodging house. In one apartment "a widower shared the same bed with his two grown-up daughters, both consumptive" (p. 7). It seems that so long as Orwell is remembered as the observer of the Parisians' sexual, or at least sexually suggestive, behavior, he can maintain a link with their world. They may act, but he must only watch—and see no evil. But the recording of his own attempt to approach a woman, to assume an active, albeit ceremonial, sexual role, marks a turning point in the narrative. The woman Orwell desires dies; the period of sexual innocence is undermined by the implicit acknowledgment of his own sexual aspirations; and as a result Orwell must move to a new environment, a new stage of being, in which the knowledge of the flesh is the knowledge of evil. One might add that in quitting his job Orwell is disavowing a covert sexual role that even in disguised form is no longer tolerable—for the occupational title *plongeur* (literally 'plunger') connotes sexuality as well as a descent into a lower social milieu.

From about this point in the narrative to the end of the first section the speaker's attitude toward Paris—an attitude indirectly expressed through the quality of his recollections—sheds its lightheartedness. His memories are unpleasant, bitter. In an uncharacteristic fit of rage, Orwell the dishwasher vilely abuses a female fellow worker, and he soon stops speaking to Boris, his closest friend.

As already suggested, Orwell's movement to England represents a new stage of awareness, one in which the onerous knowledge of evil, sexual as well as social, weighs heavily upon the speaker's mind. But the pattern is not yet complete. In addition to examining the emotional implications of Orwell's departure from the Paris working-class quarter, we must look more closely at the description of his life among the English tramps.

The speaker's explanation concerning his descent into vagrancy is not convincing, as several critics have pointed out.[12] B., a friend in London, sends Orwell the money necessary to return to England and promises him a job. Finding upon arrival that the position is not yet available, Orwell, for reasons unknown, forgets to borrow more money, even though his funds are nearly exhausted; and a short while later, suddenly aware of his oversight, he refuses to approach B. on the grounds that it would be improper to ask for another loan too soon. Then deciding that he must live in "some hole-and-corner way," he procures the filthiest, shabbiest clothes he can find and becomes a tramp. However, one is not convinced that Orwell becomes a vagrant solely because of economic necessity. When he finally does go back to B. for a loan, B. not only gives him a greater sum than he asked for but also tells him to return whenever he needs more. Orwell's response is to go right back into vagabondage (p. 158).

If Orwell's decision to become a tramp is, with its rejection of middle-class status, a means of purging himself of socioeconomic guilt, it is also a means for sexual self-denial. Dressed as a tramp, Orwell finds women inaccessible: "For the first time I noticed . . . how the attitude of women varies with a man's clothes. When a badly dressed man passes them they shudder away from him with a quite frank movement of disgust" (p. 129). This may explain Orwell's haste to assume the tramp's attire. The beggar's rags are a talisman against guilt, a wall that makes him sexually inviolate.

Insofar as the linear, chronologically sequential structure of this account is, taken as a whole, an expression of the narrator's frame of mind, the statements he makes about his past self become even more significant in relation to the narrative as a kind of symbolic gesture in the present. This being the case, we can begin to see traces in the narrative of a conflict within the speaker between exposure and concealment. Whatever may have been the motives of the real-life Eric Blair in dressing up as a hobo, there is reason to believe that in calling our attention to such a transformation at this particular point in his story the narrator is describing an Orwell who actually anticipates sexual deprivation in dressing in this fashion—or who, in any event, is placed in a situation that makes sexual assertiveness all but impossible. For earlier in the book, despite the above quotation, the narrator recalls noting during his stay in France that his dingy working-man's garb repelled Parisian women (p. 90). In other words, the narrator is engaged in a subtle game with the reader, a game the implications of which escape the former. He would have us believe that his re-created self, Orwell the vagabond in England, has unwittingly stumbled into a mode of existence precluding involvement with women; yet, strangely enough, the narrator ignores the fact that his central character, as it were, already knows the consequences of his actions. This discrepancy cannot be explained simply by claiming that the phrase "for the first time" is the narrator's observation, not that of his earlier self. The speaker has made a slip of the pen that betrays a covert aim beneath the documentary surface of *Down and Out*.

In terms of the narrator's retrospective view, an outlook expressive of his current consciousness of evil, sensual experience is tolerable so long as it is not his own. The termination of Orwell's seemingly idyllic existence in Paris is linked to his expression of interest in the consumptive girl. There-fore, it is not surprising that in the narrator's re-creation of his adventures in England the only type of sensual encounter to which he is exposed, a tramp's homosexual advances, is obviously unacceptable.

In different ways, both parts of *Down and Out* hint at an uneasiness regarding the flesh. In the section dealing with Paris, this attitude is obliquely revealed not only in the innocuous, somewhat fanciful, quality of the remembered sexual scenes but also in the narrator's tendency to present himself as an uninvolved reporter, an innocent observer. The state of mind suggested by the latter half of *Down and Out* differs only in degree: the narrator's re-creation of his experiences in England bespeaks a sharper, less veiled awareness of guilt and anxiety and a more urgent need to shield himself from this particular realization. The negative references to sensual experience in the second part—the instances of national priggishness, the women's disgust, the homosexual overture, the decaying bodies of the tramps—underscore the narrator's personal uneasiness.

It seems, therefore, that within *Down and Out* there are two narratives, two levels of meaning, the interrelation of which is not at all clear. On the one hand is the documentary narrative with its revelations about the subcultures of the French workers and English vagabonds; on the other, the personal narrative of the central character, whose wanderings represent a psychological fever chart of increasing guilt and anxiety. The unconvincing and discrepant statements made by the narrator about his earlier activities and observations call our attention to the fact that the book has several movements that do not mesh, messages that divide our attention. Orwell the *plongeur* and tramp has a puzzling dual relationship to the scenes and events of the narrative. His physical presence in Paris and England, that is, his function as a concretely rendered character within a circumstantially described setting, provides the general comments of the narrator with that element of eyewitness authenticity that is so important to the documentary. However, these documentary experiences take on a configuration which suggests that the narrative has some private meaning for the narrator. Along with the different levels of meaning we find two styles—the realistic mode of documentary reportage and a symbolic mode by which the narrator's past is turned into a personal myth.

Two related factors may be responsible for the unity of "A Hanging" and the structural and thematic confusion of *Down and Out*. Explaining the effectiveness of the former as a documentary, Mander points out that because in such a short work characters need not be developed psychologically, there is nothing to distract us from the sociological content.[13] Lodge argues that this essay gains much of its force from the author's ability to maintain a consistent realism. The few metaphoric-symbolic elements are carefully prevented from interfering with the documentary aim of the essay (pp. 13–15).

This is not the case with *Down and Out*. However disguised and indirect, there is a psychological dimension to the documentary. It is worth noting that one reason for Jonathan Cape's rejection of the original (and no longer extant) version, which probably dealt with the Paris experiences, was its brevity. The addition of material to the revised version, presumably consisting mainly of the author's later experiences among the London tramps, would have called for greater emphasis on the "I" who was to bind the two sections together.[14] This in turn would make more likely the appearance of personal and subjective elements—which is exactly what happens. Since Blair was struggling to create for himself a public identity, the literary persona Orwell, we may assume that the private self went underground, surviving covertly through the psychologically symbolic implications of the narrative. Consequently, in reading *Down and Out* we find our attention divided between sociological documentary and personal, even inadvertent, revelation.

This discrepancy between private myth and public realities appears in Orwell's novels and gives rise to a number of important questions. To what extent is the psychological complexity of the central character related to the society around him? What thematic and structural difficulties are suggested by the dual nature of the protagonists—partly realistic characters existing within a recognizable social milieu and partly key figures in some psychodramatic ritual? And what means does Orwell employ to broaden the narrowly personal into a more comprehensive vision of reality?

Chapter III

The East as Waste Land

One might suppose that the temporal and geographical setting of Orwell's *Burmese Days* (1934) would direct a reader's attention to the social and political aspects of the central character's dilemma. The year is 1923 or 1924, a period when Burmese nationalism was beginning to strain against the system of cautious reforms instituted by the colonial government. The dyarchy status granted to India in 1919, by which the native population gained some degree of elective representation in the national legislature, was extended to Burma in 1923. However, the age of relatively harmonious relations between the Burman and white population had passed. The whites and natives alike resented the British governor's order that only a few Burmese officials, as a token, were to be admitted to the exclusive European social clubs. Having never accepted British rule, Burmese peasants engaged in sporadic uprisings, and the brutal suppression of the peasants made the opposition to the imperial government even more extensive. Burmese university students, rejecting the liberal view of their elders regarding dominion status, began rioting for complete independence.[1]

John Flory, depicted as a sensitive and thoughtful figure in *Burmese Days*, seems well suited to represent the conflict between the struggle of the natives to regain their dignity and the desperate attempt of the white population to preserve the empire. Toward both the English and the Burmans Flory has mixed feelings. He is fond of Burmese life, but he thinks he has in some way been corrupted by it. Although hostile to the modernization introduced by the British, he is emotionally dependent on the good opinion of the whites, the members of the local European Club. Flory's predicament becomes more painful when his Burmese friend Dr. Veriswami, vilified by U Po Kyin, a malicious official of minor status, seeks to bolster his position by having Flory sponsor him for membership in the Club. Already fearful of the prejudiced Englishmen's reactions, Flory finds that his connection with the natives also alienates the recently arrived Elizabeth Lackersteen, a priggish and anti-Oriental Englishwoman with whom he is infatuated. By the end of the novel, U Po Kyin has triumphed over Veriswami, and Elizabeth, learning that her suitor has had a native mistress, rejects Flory, who then kills himself.

Although the plot of *Burmese Days* is set in motion by U Po Kyin's rivalry with a fellow Burman, we soon get the impression that Orwell is emphasizing the perils awaiting the imperialist himself, the corrupting effect of colonialism on the English. Colonial Burma is a moral waste land where the old-style rulers, such as Deputy Commissioner Macgregor, shamelessly exploit the bodies of native women while an even more vicious type, represented by Ellis, vents its siege-mentality hysteria through acts as well as fantasies of unrestrained violence.

The main emphasis in the novel is on Flory's intolerable dilemma as a man apparently caught between the conflicting demands of East and West, between his sense of decency and friendship for the Burmans and his need to remain on good relations with his fellow whites, especially Elizabeth. The bind in which Flory is caught grows tighter when, in helping his native friend he runs afoul of U Po Kyin, who for reasons never made entirely clear, sees his path toward power and prestige within the imperial administration blocked by Veriswami. The ambitious and sinister U Po Kyin, a sort of Oriental Count Fosco, plans to ruin Veriswami by discrediting him in the eyes of the Europeans. It appears that only Flory can save Veriswami (for reasons unknown), but as U Po Kyin suggests Flory is a coward. Disgusted by the idleness and bigotry and intellectual deadness of the local whites, Flory becomes insecure because he sees himself as an outsider. At the same time, he lacks the moral strength to reject openly the Club or to defy its prejudices. To emphasize their refusal to lower the membership requirements, several of the Club members sign a protest notice. Explaining why he, too, has signed, Flory confesses to Veriswami: "'There's no law telling us to be beastly to Orientals. . . . But—it's just that one daren't be loyal to an Oriental when it means going against the others. It doesn't *do*. If I'd stuck out against signing the notice I'd have been in disgrace at the Club. . . . So I funked it, as usual."[2]

The events of the narrative seem to move toward an unavoidable climax, an obligatory scene, as it were, in which Flory must confront the Club members and act either courageously or fecklessly. In fact, Flory does finally propose Veriswami for membership in the Club, and, as might be expected, there is great protest. But, at this point, there occurs a curious turn of events. It is now, when Flory is in utter disgrace, that his hostile compatriots are attacked and besieged by enraged natives trying to get at Ellis, who—driven by a rage fueled, one suspects, by more than ordinary bigotry—has thrashed and blinded a Burmese youth. After making a heroic dash for a nearby police camp, Flory personally leads the law-abiding officials against the rebels, disperses them, and instantaneously becomes the beloved champion of the whites. Flory can now assert that all his past difficulties with them have been resolved; and Orwell, perhaps echoing Flory's thoughts, tells the reader that there will no longer be any obstacles in the way of Veriswami's election to the Club—"the others would eat out of [Flory's] hand until the absurd riot was forgotten" (p. 258). Even more surprising is the disastrous reversal of fortune that befalls Flory. At the height of his success, when there is no doubt that Elizabeth is ready to marry him, Ma Hla May, acting upon orders from U Po Kyin, enters the local church and, in the presence of the white community, proclaims herself Flory's cast-off mistress. Utterly revolted, Elizabeth rejects Flory's offer of marriage, and soon afterward Flory commits suicide.

This summary leads one to expect a thematic polarity similar to that of Forster's novels—the uneasy tension between the personal and social imperative of "Only Connect" and, on the other hand, isolation and estrangement. We might assume that the sympathetic Flory and the embittered Ellis (also a timber merchant) embody these opposing attitudes. Ellis calls attention to this polarity in expressing his own revulsion at the idea of racial mixing and social equality in contrast to Flory's hobnobbing with Veriswami. Moreover, on the basis of Maung Htin Aung's recollection of Eric Blair having angrily caned a Burmese youth who had accidentally caused him to fall down a flight of stairs at a Rangoon train station (p. 24), we might suppose that these two characters represent the author's polarized selves—the Orwell who asserts the value of community and the earlier Blair whose fictional surrogate's vituperative condemnation of any form of interracial closeness bespeaks a radical insularity.

There is, however, reason to doubt that the central action of the book is the struggle, both within Flory and between him and others, to lower the barriers separating race from race, and more generally, one human being from another. However different they may appear on the surface, Ellis and Flory are in at least one respect quite similar. The loathing for the East that complements Ellis's fanatical determination to preserve his racial purity is matched by Flory's romantic primitivism and his hatred of modernization. Despite an occasional criticism of the British for exploiting Burma and stifling its domestic industries, what really angers Flory is his fear that Burma is changing, that Western technological progress will erase all traces of the Oriental past. Arguing with the pro-British Veriswami, Flory cries out: "Where's it going to lead, this uprush of modern progress, as you call it? Just to our . . . swinery of gramophones and billycock hats. Sometimes I think that in two hundred years . . . all this will be gone—forests, villages, monasteries, pagodas all vanished. And instead, pink villas fifty yards apart; all over those hills, as far as you can see, villa after villa, with all the gramophones playing the same tune. And all the forests shaved flat— chewed into woodpulp for the *News of the World*, or sawn up into gramophone cases" (p. 42).

Like Ellis, Flory thinks and feels in terms of separation, not connection, the separation of East and West, of past and present. The contrast that Veriswami insists on between nineteenth-century Burma under Thibaw (the last king, whose removal resulted in the loss of national independence), with its squalor, ignorance, and brutality, and contemporary

Burma, with its schools, hospitals, and laws, makes no impression on Flory, who prefers a "septic" Burma, a "Burma in the days of Thibaw." And looking at an aged, mentally retarded native seemingly untouched by European progress, Flory hopes that the old Burman will drink himself into degeneracy—"it all postpones Utopia" (pp. 43–44).

One suspects that Flory's hatred of Western civilization, at least as it affects the East, is shared by Orwell. Given the nature of the European Club, a microcosmic society of spite, priggishness, snobbery, and violence, the fact that Veriswami does not gain entry into it is as much an indication of Orwell's desire to keep his fictive Burma apart from the spiritually pollut- ing world of white civilization as it is an indictment of European insularity. Viewed in this light, what appears to be the key issue in the story, whether or not Flory will have the guts to cast the one vote needed to break the Club ban against natives, loses its dramatic centrality, for by nominating Veris- wami the unwitting Flory is symbolically exposing the Burman not to the whites' cruel rejection but to a morally calamitous acceptance. This cir- cumstance leads to the further irony that Flory's downfall, his puzzlingly sudden loss of face at the end of the novel, is the very event that keeps the decent Veriswami separated from the corrupt whites and, appropriately enough, results in the evil U Po Kyin becoming a member of their Club.

The fleeting instances of intimacy in Forster's India become assertions of human meaning in a universe that denies all meaning. Amid the prejudice, misunderstandings, and pettiness of this society, some of Forster's charac- ters can break free from a constrictive egotism and attain that degree of self-detachment necessary for friendship. In *Burmese Days*, the waste land world of Anglo-Burmese civilization mocks detachment and perverts human closeness into suspicion and hostility.

It is important to note that Orwell's setting is itself split in two. One part is colonial Burma tainted by the encroachment of the West. It is a realm of moral debasement peopled by sadistic bigots, unscrupulously ambitious native bureaucrats, mean-spirited Englishwomen, and corrupt Burmese girls. Here intimacy is thought to be criminal, and love reduces itself to sex. Looking back at his ten years wasted on whores and alcohol, Flory feels himself "drifting, rotting, in dishonour and . . . futility" (p. 73).

The other Burma is that of nature, the nonhuman world of flora and fauna, where Flory (whose name indicates a closeness to the green world) finds some measure of peace. This jungle is a sacred grove that must be kept inviolate.[3]

The significance of this precivilized Burma will become clearer if we take note of several important aspects of Orwell's colonial society. First, it is to some extent a preadult world. Flory's servant Ko S'la, although the same age as his master, regards him as a "boy still" (p. 50), and Ma Hla May is several times likened to a doll. At one point, Flory, depressed by

Elizabeth's coldness toward him, consoles himself by pillowing his head on the shoulder of a motherly whore and weeping—"a thing he had not done since he was fifteen years old" (p. 223). Elizabeth's remark that Burmese women look like boys and her uncertainty upon running into the almost contourless Ma Hla May as to whether she is male or female (p. 87) suggest the British public-school atmosphere of Orwell's Burma—an adolescent world in which comradeship and romantic "crush" are not always distinguishable. Every school has at least one bully who lives only to torment the vulnerable, and in this case it is Ellis, who baits Flory with the nickname "nigger's Nancy Boy" (p. 199). And every English schoolboy has stood uneasily before a teacher resembling Deputy Commissioner Macgregor, whose air of forced amiability reminds one of a "schoolmaster twiddling a cane behind his back" (p. 28).

The real Burma of the 1920s was beginning to enter, however hesitantly, modern history. It was changing, gathering its strength for the struggle that would in time lead to political independence. There is, however, a curiously static quality to the activities of Orwell's Burmans. The young men preparing themselves for the approaching liberation struggle, the U Nus and Ne Wins, in *Burmese Days* appear to be little more than troublesome schoolboys. Orwell's Burma is strikingly similar to the school life described in Kipling's *Stalky and Co.*, a stable world where youthful rebellion is never anything more than an exercise in mischief that changes nothing. Although the natives may agitate in behalf of nationalism, although Dr. Veriswami may long to be recognized by the whites as an equal, and although Flory may rage at the imperial system, the power structure still remains stable.

It is significant that those activities disapproved of by the white rulers are often associated with some form of sexual disorderliness. Trying to describe what it feels like to be an Englishman carrying on a friendship with a native, Flory compares his meetings with Veriswami to a minister's assignation with a "tart" and a "Black Mass on the sly" (pp. 37, 43). In their private talks, Flory and Veriswami jokingly refer to the British Empire, toward which the latter shows an exaggerated respect, as an "aged female patient of the doctor's" (p. 37). Significantly, in his attempts to thwart the doctor's bid for membership in the Club, U Po Kyin anonymously accuses Veriswami of, among other things, "sleeping by force with [his] female patients" (p. 78). To Mrs. Lackersteen, Elizabeth's aunt, the thought of rebellion calls up only one image, that of "herself being raped by a procession of jet-black coolies"; and according to another one of U Po Kyin's slanderous accusations, rebellion is just what Veriswami is wishing for (pp. 137–38). As I shall point out later, the sexual element plays a key part in Flory's ruination.

Opposed to the colonial Burma of alienation and guilt is the precivilized world of nature. To gain relief from the "suicidal" ennui that comes upon him at the end of a day, Flory strides off into the forest, thick with trees and flowers, and washes away the smell of his public existence in the cooling waters of a jungle pool, a ritual that leaves him peaceful and satisfied. More importantly, almost the only passages in the novel that do not generate menace, frustration, or sordidness are those in which Orwell describes Flory's moments of closeness to the jungle. And just as the sight of a forest pigeon fills Flory with an awareness of beauty, his relationship with Ma Hla May, usually marked by anxiety and tension, takes on a certain fleeting tenderness when he notices her feline teeth and begins stroking her throat as though she were a mere kitten (p. 53).

While observing nature's beauty, Flory, at least for short periods, is removed from time; here he loses himself in a prehistoric Eden. His final expulsion from the Garden back into narrative time takes place with a mythic inevitability. Not satisfied with being the sole human beneficiary of the jungle's beauty and tranquillity, he yearns for an Eve with whom to share the Garden, someone to "halve his loneliness" (p. 57).

As a preadolescent Adam, Flory does in fact have his Eve, the bitch Flo that tags along after him throughout the novel. But the inner imperative of Orwell's story presses on toward a rupturing of Flory's ties with the world of animal innocence and simplicity. The appearance of Elizabeth only accelerates this process. Ending his guilt-provoking liaison with his Burmese mistress Ma Hla May, Flory turns to the Englishwoman like a repentant sinner to the church: as Flory puts it, "only by marrying [Elizabeth] could his life be salvaged," and their life together would be a "paradise" (pp. 178, 180). Orwell wastes no time in letting the reader in on the truth that Flory never learns: Elizabeth is a violating, not regenerative, force. Elizabeth's excitement over a bird she has just killed makes it abundantly clear that her presence in the jungle is the introduction of eroticism and violence into the Garden: "She could hardly give it up, the feel of it so ravished her. She could have kissed it, hugged it to her breast. All the men . . . smiled at one another to see her fondling the dead bird. . . . She was conscious of an extraordinary desire to fling her arms round Flory's neck and kiss him; and in some way it was the killing of the pigeon that made her feel this" (p. 167). Later, Flory, attempting to impress Elizabeth with his manliness by displaying his spearing prowess on horseback, takes a bad fall that leaves him helplessly supine, looking up at circling vultures. The woman's only response is to gaze past him, "as though he had not existed," in the direction of the cemetery and coolly walk by, treating him as though he were a "dead dog" (pp. 187–88).

It seems that in setting up this connection between Elizabeth and death Orwell is trying to suggest the spiritually devitalizing effect of European civilization. Elizabeth's perversely excited fondling of the slain bird could be interpreted as a grotesque example of the pathological intensity with

which the imperialist carries out his work of destruction. Culturally, imperialist expansionism, by introducing the serpent of modernization,
heralds the loss of the Garden, the old Burma. In line with this, we see that
Flory's public self, his official role as agent for a timber firm, directly
involves him with the destruction of this Edenic world of uncivilized
nature. His occupation taints him with the same spiritual decay he attributes to the other whites. It is clear, then, that in longing to marry
Elizabeth, Flory is only moving farther away from the primitive simplicity
of the past. However, what is not so clear is the relationship between this
cultural Fall and the sexual anxieties of Orwell's central character.

Although Flory's sense of being "dirtied . . . beyond redemption" because of his many encounters with Burmese women may reflect a more or
less conscious awareness of the culpability he must bear for the sexual
exploitation of the native population, there are indications that in addition
Flory suffers from the effects of a more personal form of guilt, one not
directly linked to his social position as a member of the ruling class.
Something else is hinted at by the fall he takes in attempting to arouse the
admiration of Elizabeth, a fellow white, not a subservient native, by
showing off his prowess as a mounted lancer, a thinly veiled assertion of
sexual potency. Interestingly, just after this fall, as Elizabeth walks uncon-
cernedly in his direction, Flory rapidly claps a hand over his cheek to
conceal a large birthmark. Mentioned repeatedly in the novel, this facial
discoloration is closely linked to Flory's sexual anxiety. Stricken with
shame after his intimacy with Ma Hla May, Flory nervously attempts to
cover up the stain (p. 54). In the daylight, when the mark is all too visible,
his desire to embrace Elizabeth suddenly wanes (p. 168), whereas at night
it seems safe for him to kiss her (p. 177). After Elizabeth's final rejection—
brought on by the exposure during a church service of his sexual laxness—
he concludes that "it was . . . the birthmark that had damned him" (p.
278). And after his death, the mark fades.

In *Down and Out*, the tramp's clothes barring Orwell from women are
transformed in *Burmese Days* into a more lasting form of alienation, a
primal sinfulness beginning "in his mother's womb, when chance put the
blue birthmark on his cheek" (p. 64). And despite the suggestion that his
flights into the jungle represent a return to prelapsarian innocence, this
none-too-subtle token of Flory's fallen condition proclaims his enduring
guilt, just as at one point in the story we see that the scars on a native
suspected of theft—scars indicating that he is an "old offender"—serve as
proof that he is presently guilty (p. 75). And if the crescent shape of Flory's
birthmark is related to the crescent-horned water buffalo that menaces
Elizabeth on the occasion of their first meeting,[4] we may conclude that a
return to the past, to an inner realm of primitive innocence and simplicity,

is now only a false hope; for even the animal world, the Edenic condition, is burdened with the mark of guilt.

At the same time, Flory's unavoidable moral dilemma is in some way mixed up with his curiously schoolboyish predicament. Scandalized by his sympathetic attitude toward Burmans, Ellis wonders aloud that Flory's birthmark might be a sign of his Oriental blood (p. 34). Biologically incorrect, since we are told that Flory was born in England of English parents, this statement indicates that his sexual guilt links him to what appears to be the preadult, libidinally rebellious world of colonial Burma. Consequently, his wooing of the white woman, a member of the adult world, assumes the proportions of a reprehensibly defiant act. Approaching the European Club to propose to Elizabeth, Flory is prompted by "some instinct, which he did not understand," to make his bid before the other whites arrive (p. 183); and seeing the woman surrounded by Club members, he dares not "accost" her. Before Elizabeth he becomes an adolescent frightened at his own temerity: "She looked . . . so adult . . . that he feared her more than he had ever done. It was unbelievable that he had ever kissed her" (p. 192).

Verral, a cavalry officer who is Flory's romantic rival, plays an important part in the Flory-Elizabeth relationship. We should note first that the two men are almost exact complements. Flory is sickly, hapless, and a bumbling equestrian; fearful of the Europeans yet dependent on their good opinion; especially in need of a woman's love but a feckless wooer. In contrast, Verral is healthy and a skilled horseman, openly scornful of the local European community and indifferent to its judgment of him, even more indifferent to women yet at the same time brazenly aggressive in pursuing Elizabeth. Suspecting Flory of sexual misbehavior with Ma Hla May, Elizabeth eagerly turns to Verral, whose title *Honourable* indicates his social status while suggesting that he, unlike Flory, is not cursed by disabling sexual guilt. Flory's awkward wielding of the lance results in a portentous fall; but Verral, sitting in the saddle "as easily as a centaur," plunges his lance into the target with faultless skill (p. 185).

The presence of Verral suggests that in addition to conveying his story in a realistic mode Orwell is revealing a fantasy world where opposition implies identity. Verral is Flory's double, and his presence throws light on Flory's dilemma. Verral is Flory's other self, at once the person he cannot and must not be. Flory cannot be like Verral because the latter is immune to punishment—"Verral had earned many kicks in his life, but he had never received one and probably never would" (p. 209). And by abruptly leaving the village at the height of his affair with Elizabeth, Verral demonstrates his ability to free himself from her, whereas the obsessed Flory must pursue her to the end, with fatal consequences.

It is perhaps more important to understand why Flory must not be a

Verral. Verral (virile) is the sexually aggressive male, the centaurlike spearman, a figure of that libidinal assertiveness that, one might conjecture, Flory must reject if he is to regenerate himself and gain the woman's care and attention.[5] Since it is Verral who stands between Flory and Elizabeth, the absence of Verral (and what he represents) seems to be the necessary condition for Flory's success with the woman: Verral "was only amusing himself with Elizabeth. Presently he would desert her, and she would return to . . . Flory" (p. 260). Throughout the various states of the Flory-Elizabeth relationship, one senses a veiled message that the longing for the woman must not be translated into possession. Although Orwell tells us that Flory is not aware how his repeated attempts to interest the English-woman in Burmese life only arouse her indignation, Flory's reaction to her ire indicates that it is safe to desire her only when she is emotionally distant: "It was as though he had never truly loved her till this moment, when he walked behind her in disgrace" (p. 133). What appears in terms of Flory's personal psychology as a masochistic link between love and the pain of rejection is, in terms of the total design of the narrative, a statement that the fact of their alienation constitutes the very condition that allows Flory to think of himself as a wooer.

Symbolically, Orwell's introduction of Verral represents the irruption into the narrative of that physical desire that explains the central character's failure to gain the longed-for woman. And Verral's sudden disappearance is both a sign that sexual consummation must be avoided and a portent of Flory's own fate. Perhaps echoing Flory's own thoughts as he broods over Elizabeth's infatuation with the recently arrived Verral, Orwell tells us: "Once he had loved Elizabeth spiritually, sentimentally indeed, desiring her sympathy more than her caresses; now, when he had lost her, he was tormented by the basest physical longing" (p. 226). Read another way, the narrator's words imply that the existence of this "physical longing" is the reason he has lost her.

Flory seems to think that merely by rejecting a physical relationship he can gain what he thinks of as Elizabeth's healing love. After Ma Hla May's denunciation, he begs the white woman to marry him, promising never to lay a "finger" on her (p. 277). However, the burden of sin cannot be so easily lifted. If Flory's relationship with Burmese women makes him guilty of social exploitation, the desire triggered by the appearance of Elizabeth is linked both to his inability to recapture a mental paradise of childlike innocence and to his subjection to death. The young man's hubris, his defiant quest for the forbidden woman, symbolically expresses the loss of the past and the entry into a condition marked by a tormenting conscious-ness of his lasting guilt.

In the figure of U Po Kyin, Orwell gives us clues to Flory's internal and external problems. If the Oriental is the realistic embodiment of colonial corruption, the rapacious minor official who ruins Flory's career, he is also an emblem of lust. "The girls he has ruined," exclaims Dr. Veriswami, "raping them before the very eyes of their mothers!" (p. 45). Even his meals are sexual outrages—"orgies, debauches" (p. 14). A more or less realistically described example of political villainy at the beginning of the novel, U Po Kyin eventually becomes a nightmarishly hermaphroditic symbol of unbridled sexuality and its punishment: "In the . . . heat of the living-room . . . U Po Kyin was marching slowly up and down. . . . From time to time he would put a hand under his singlet and scratch his sweating breasts, huge as a woman's with fat. . . . Through the open door of the bedroom one could see the corner of [his] huge square bed, . . . like a catafalque, on which he had committed many and many a rape" (pp. 134–35). In time, U Po Kyin—"swollen with the bodies of his enemies" (p. 14), he reminds us of some grotesque creature out of myth, fairy tale, or dream, perhaps the destroying goddess Kali—turns on Flory. At both the realistic and symbolic levels, the lustful, threatening Oriental stands between Flory and Elizabeth even more effectively than does the sexually aggressive Verral. In encouraging Ma Hla May to denounce her ex-lover, U Po Kyin is in effect setting the stage for the guilt-burdened Flory's execution. Several times U Po Kyin is referred to as a crocodile that will strike at one's "weakest spot"; and although at first scorning the idea that he might become the Burman's victim, Flory eventually realizes that by sending Ma Hla May to reveal their liaison, U Po Kyin has, "like the croc-odile, . . . struck at his weakest spot" (p. 274). But the punishment inflicted by U Po Kyin has been hanging over Flory's head (and within his mind) even before the Burman turns on him. Early in the narrative, Flory, dolefully reviewing his decadent existence in colonial Burma, recalls the money squandered on "aged . . . whores with the faces of crocodiles" (p. 65).

The threat to Flory's "weakest spot" may be linked to the vague references to mutilation that appear repeatedly in the novel. Dozing around Veriswami's hospital, with its "sluttish and decaying air," are curs, pariah dogs, who are said to eat "amputated limbs; while within the hospital Veriswami practices medicine in a disconcerting fashion—patients shocked at being questioned about venereal diseases are still more upset by the suggestion that they may be operated on (pp. 144–45). One of the local curs, taking a dislike to Flory's residence, habitually bays at it (p. 61), and in the midst of her fatal exposure of Flory's sexual misdeeds Ma Hla May likens herself to a pariah dog (p. 273).

Since the distinction between the narrative voice and Flory's thoughts is so frequently blurred, we may assume that the physical reality external to the protagonist is at the same time a symbolic representation of his inner state. Orwell creates a reality outside of Flory that reflects the latter's personal guilt and anxiety. Thus, the externalized reminders of mutilation correspond to what appears to be Flory's unconscious, or at best vaguely felt, castration anxiety. However, it is just as important to realize that the fear of sexual mutilation itself figuratively represents an escape from guilt through the rejection of sexuality. Begging Elizabeth not to turn away from him because of his past relationship with Ma Hla May, Flory cries out, "I'd sooner cut my hand off than offend you" (p. 193). This exclamation is indicative of the protagonist's need to dissociate flesh from mind, to reject physical desire from consciousness, if he is to merit the Englishwoman's love, the granting of which would signify his moral acceptability and serve as proof that he is an unfallen Adam completed now by the presence of his Eve. But the fact is that all signs point toward his enduring sinfulness. Verral may be gone, but U Po Kyin still demands a sacrifice—and the birthmark remains. The guilt lasts and not only puts Elizabeth out of reach but also condemns Flory to death. Immediately before committing suicide, Flory torments himself with a mental picture of Elizabeth's marriage: "And then her wedding day approaching, her bridal night—ah, not that! Obscene, obscene. Keep your eyes fixed on that. Obscene" (p. 280). Flory's death is a self-inflicted punishment for a sexual misdeed, mental voyeurism. At the same time, suicide is Flory's final, all-too-effective attempt to abolish sexual craving from consciousness. Tormented by his irrepressible erotic fantasy of Elizabeth's wedding night, Flory finds in suicide both a punishment and an escape. If the Western Old Testament God demands a retributive death, the Eastern Kali, with her skirt of dismembered limbs, grants final peace.

In general, critics have directed their attention toward the sociopolitical significance of *Burmese Days*. Some see the novel as a satire on the myth of racial superiority fostered by the white rulers or an exposure of the ways in which imperialism contributes to the white man's dishonesty and reinforces a destructive ethnocentricity.[6] Flory is either a tragic hero, a rebel against the pettiness and immorality of colonialism who is plagued by an inability to defy white society, or himself an object of satire, a man whose misanthropy is a symptom of the evil surrounding him.[7]

However, some question the validity of the assumption that *Burmese Days* is a straightforward attack on colonialism. It has been argued that the main character is too abnormal to serve adequately as a critic of imperialism. The cause of Flory's bitterness is too personal to be a convincing indictment of colonial rule. Stemming from his disfigurement and private sense of isolation, his anger is so egotistical as to undercut the force of his criticisms of the empire. Thus, Orwell creates the impression that Flory's hatred of imperialism is without any objective basis.[8] Another critic regards the novel as little more than Orwell's masochistic fantasy in the guise of a fictional narrative. Motivated by an unconscious need for punishment,

Orwell here, as elsewhere, depicts a threatening social environment against which his persona Flory "engages in pseudo-aggressive acts" in reality designed to result in his own martyrdom.[9] These remarks are helpful in calling our attention to the possibility that the social reality shown in *Burmese Days* must be viewed in terms of the subjective vision of the narrator and the inner condition of his central character.

If we view Flory's fallen, post-Edenic discontent as a microcosmic counterpart to the cultural malaise dealt with in the novel—the decadent atmosphere of colonial life—then we might conclude that the intrusion of European civilization (and the values associated with it) into the green world of the East, the machine in the garden, stands for the Original Sin marking Western man's exile from nature, his alienation from that primal wholeness and guiltless simplicity of the prelapsarian state. Flory's sexual anxiety might represent the cultural guilt springing from the rape of nature committed in the name of progress and civilization.

Such an interpretation is, however, not as satisfying as it appears at first sight. Although there is a metaphoric link between Flory's sense of being exiled and the social fragmentation produced by the expansion of Western civilization, Flory's career exhibits singular, atypical features. For one thing, the facial discoloration that physically sets him apart from the other whites figuratively severs the bond between Flory's personal dilemma and the broader social meaning of the novel. For Flory, the stain is a vague reminder of a primal sinfulness that must be punished, of an inborn sexual guilt, something rooted within him prior to the acquisition of a specific sociocultural identity. And the fact that this guilt torments him beyond endurance puts him in sharp contrast to other whites who enjoy a scatheless libidinal freedom. Openly accused of fathering numerous bastards, Deputy Commissioner Macgregor eventually marries Elizabeth, the very woman who recoils in disgust from Flory's far less spectacular lapse from respectability; and despite his wife's jealous scrutiny, Elizabeth's uncle, another member of the Club, not only engages in numerous sexual escapades with native girls but also repeatedly accosts his niece with impunity.

Nothing more clearly reveals Orwell's early reliance on the conventions of the Victorian novel than his use of biblical parallels—the Adamic Flory alone in his Edenic Burma, his fall, the mark of Cain this exile bears on his face—to invest events with a broad moral significance. Equally traditional is Flory's attempt to regenerate himself through the pure love of a good woman. One might add that these elements are forced onto the narrative. One senses Orwell straining to pump mythic significance into a character whose dilemma is too idiosyncratic; and equally unconvincing is that character's rather showy efforts to transform his life from a rake's into a pilgrim's progress. It is hard to take seriously Flory's remorseful—and covertly boastful—claim to have defiled himself with an "endless proces-

sion of Burmese women, . . . a full hundred at the least" (p. 196). Given
his lackluster performance as a sexually aggressive male, we are more
inclined to agree with the description of Flory as being "thin as a rake" (p.
230). As a "rake" he is very "thin" indeed. It is not Flory but the other
Englishmen, Macgregor and Lackersteen and Verral, who are the sexual
athletes.[10]

Flory's cry of "Alone, alone, the bitterness of being alone" succinctly
states the central character's irrelevance to the other members of Orwell's
fictional Burma. The final chapter, dealing with the fates of the other
characters after Flory's death, reflects this discontinuity. We learn that
Veriswami's modest aspirations have been thwarted, that U Po Kyin fulfills
his worldly ambitions, and that Elizabeth gains from her marriage to
Macgregor the social status she has always wanted. In other words, the
fortunes of these characters have scarcely been affected by the presence of
Orwell's central figure, with all his inner torments and vain longings.
Conversely, so summary is Orwell's account of the other characters' fates
that the last chapter, inappropriately modeled on the epilogue of the
conventional Victorian novel, seems more like an afterthought than a
conclusion organically related to Flory's career.

However, what appears to be one of the novel's more serious
weaknesses—the failure to present Flory as a mimetically conceived
character within a realistic social context—suggests that Orwell is moving
away from Victorian social realism toward more modern themes and technical devices. As previously indicated, Orwell's colonial Burma is a less
cosmopolitan version of Eliot's bleak waste land of twentieth-century
Europe, and a glance at certain passages in *Burmese Days* allows us to
suspect that Orwell had rummaged around in Eliot's poetry to discover
some means for turning Flory's troubled soul into a mirror of imperialism
declining into its final stage of decadence. With his past debaucheries
parading across his consciousness, Flory could be the "You" of the "Preludes" who lies staring at the ceiling across which flit the "thousand sordid
images/Of which your soul was constituted." That famous Prufrockian
image of enervation, the "patient etherized upon a table," reappears in the
supine figure of Flory gazing up at vultures after his decidedly unheroic fall
from the horse, the potential amputees in Dr. Veriswami's hospital, and
the empire itself as an "aged female patient." Flory's agonizing indecisive-
ness regarding the proposal of Veriswami to the Club and marriage to
Elizabeth are tediously drawn-out versions of Prufrock's "Do I dare?" Also,
like the personae of Eliot's poems, Flory exists within a symbolic landscape. Between his bungalow and the Club (and Elizabeth) lies the cemetery, a physical placement that, in suggesting the futility of Flory's life and
aspirations, evokes "death's twilight kingdom" of "The Hollow Men"
where the "Shadow" separates motion from act, conception from creation,

and desire from spasm. The references to eyes in *Burmese Days*—eyes suspiciously watchful for any sign of rebellious behavior, eyes deprived of sight as a punishment for evil—remind one of those mysteriously vanishing and reappearing eyes that in "The Hollow Men" contribute to a hallucinatory atmosphere of guilt, paranoid anxiety, and dementia.

Although these parallels suggest Orwell's interest in employing the allusively and ambiguously symbolic techniques of modern literature, one feels that the symbolism of *Burmese Days* lacks the broadly cultural resonance present in the works of Eliot and his contemporaries. Orwell's symbolism (and the meanings generated by it) are narrowly psychological. Flory is the protagonist of an interior drama that is only remotely relevant to the world outside him, a drama perhaps more expressive of Orwell's personal obsessions than of the modern world's spiritual malaise.

In *The Road to Wigan Pier* (1937), Orwell explains that he wrote *Burmese Days* to free himself from the "hauntingly" persistent "nightmare" of the Burmese landscape (p. 141). Certainly the Burma of the novel is at times claustrophobically dreamlike. Thus, the sudden earthquake interrupting what portends to be Flory's successful marriage proposal—the ground sways as though "some enormous beast" were rocking it—is, from the standpoint of realism, an absurd coincidence, but psychologically meaningful since it is at this stage of the narrative that Verral, the sexually aggressive double, appears (pp. 181–84). Similarly, Flory's role in the suppression of the native riot that breaks out just after the nomination of Veriswami to the Club is intrusive only at the surface level of the narrative. Symbolically it is a ritual cleansing—in the course of his heroic adventure Flory swims a river—that is supposed to wash away any sign of his preadult and libidinally rebellious self (pp. 250–55). The interconnections are so relevant to Flory's personal dilemma that at times it seems we are inescapably locked into the solipsistic prison of his subconscious mind, with social conflicts transformed into the shadowy struggle between desire and guilt, between the secret wish and the need to escape the anxiety it provokes, taking place deep inside him. The kittenish Ma Hla May who self-abasingly stretches out facedown at her master's feet (p. 155) is the leopard shot by Flory (it looks like a "dead kitten") that also lies stretched out at his feet (p. 173). Flory's birthmark, a sign of the obscure guilt frustrating his pursuit of Elizabeth, ties him not only to the dead leopard, the stinking and "discoloured" hide of which disgusts the white woman (p. 217), but also to the crescent-horned buffalo that frightens Elizabeth. If the Ma Hla May who is linked to the devouring curs baying around Flory's house, both are aspects of Flory himself, the "dead dog" who sprawls on the ground after his fall from the saddle, a position that reinforces the tie between himself, his sometimes subservient mistress, and the dead leopard. And if in his sudden arrival and equally sudden departure Verral embodies the sexual aggressiveness that Flory must suppress within himself, Ellis, the sadistic timber merchant who directs his near-hysterical rages at Flory and thrashes one of the young natives whom he biologically links to the central character, is the latter's double, a savage conscience ever ready to lash out at the sexually rebellious urges covertly expressed in the narrative. Ellis's beating of the native youth, an assault resulting in the boy's loss of sight (p. 246), is a symbolic mutilation that foreshadows the destructive consequences of Flory's mental voyeurism.[11] And this tie between the sightless Burman and the Flory who eventually plunges into permanent darkness suggests a connection between his inner fears and longings and other characters who, their vision apparently faulty, need glasses—Veriswami, whose simple goodness must be preserved from contact with the morally debased Club; Macgregor, a curious mixture of cane-wielding authority figure, pansyish scoutmaster type (p. 77), and a sexually potent male who finally wins Elizabeth; and Elizabeth herself, frigid and secretly revolted by sex.

The nature of the interior drama enacted in *Burmese Days* becomes somewhat clearer when we take note of the covertly incestuous quality of Flory's relationship with women. As Freud and others have pointed out, an individual's sexual preference for someone socially or racially dissimilar may spring from a need to rid oneself of the guilt and anxiety of unconsciously incestuous longings.[12] This may explain Orwell's insistence on Flory's history of exogamous relationship with Burmese women. The birthmark is, however, a sign that his desire cannot be entirely repressed: this facial stain, which convinces Ellis that Flory is partly Burmese, symbolically indicates that Ma Hla May and her predecessors are not so safely different as they might seem. In fact, whatever the direction of Flory's romantic interest, whether toward a white-skinned or brown-skinned woman, his symbolically mixed identity unavoidably forces him into sexual uneasiness, which is rooted in an unacknowledged incestuous wish.[13]

To the extent that other characters reflect Flory's inner state (and possibly that of Orwell at this time), we can better understand Ellis's violent rejection of social and racial integration with people he calls "incestuous children of pigs"—an epithet that sounds curiously unBritish—and Elizabeth's special distaste for "all foreign men" (p. 93). This combination of xenophobia and sexual distrust implies its opposite—the nexus between sexual desire and a type of kinship.

Moreover Freud's claim that a male child's fantasy of rescuing his parents from some danger expresses a desire to replace the father in the household and to sexually possess the mother may clarify the underlying significance of Flory's rescue of the whites, specifically Elizabeth.[14] Given the incestuous nature of this apparently praiseworthy act of heroism, we can see why Flory's deed does not free him from his guilt-provoking past: the faceless ghosts of his previous sexual partners continue to haunt him; the birthmark continually asserts itself; and in the end the maternal presence, Flory's "Ma," breaks up his engagement to Elizabeth, the woman whose physical nearness in church momentarily restores Flory to his happy childhood existence in England (p. 271).

If, as Orwell claims in "Why I Write," the desire to "get your own back on grown-ups who snubbed you in childhood" is one of a writer's motives (1. 3), then *Burmese Days* may serve an analogous purpose. Concealed behind the sexually ambiguous portrayal of several male authority figures may be a symbolic emasculation of the potent father. The sexually vigorous Deputy Commissioner Macgregor who finally marries Elizabeth is described as dressed "like one of those . . . middle-aged scoutmasters, homosexual almost to a man" (p. 77). Mr. Lackersteen, no less a sexual fox among the Burmese chickens, is in one scene shown drunk and held upright by some native girls (p. 21)—a *tableau vivante* that calls to mind the tipsy and bisexual Alcibiades supported by a young woman as he lurches into Plato's "Symposium."

Conversely the writing of *Burmese Days* may have allowed Orwell to identify himself with another role, that of the adult settling old scores with real or symbolic juniors. Ellis's caning and blinding of one of the "incestuous children of pigs" may have a two-fold purpose, that of the author's harsh suppression of the disturbing child within himself and that of the unrestrained retaliatory attack Blair the offended white man was unable to unleash against the Burmese youth he must have felt was purposely harassing him. Maung Htin Aung notes that during this contretemps Blair checked the impulse to strike the boy on the head and instead caned him on the back (p. 24). The fictional Ellis can do what Blair, for reasons of prudence or conscience, could not.

If any more evidence is needed to indicate the narrowly subjective quality of *Burmese Days*, we may contrast it with Forster's *Passage to India*. Although both works deal with the tragic inability of human beings to make contact, to break down the isolating walls of misunderstanding and mistrust that separate one person from another, one culture from another, we feel with Forster's novel that even when characters, events, and settings reflect deep-seated and highly personal attitudes of the author, there does exist in the book a "real" world possessing that degree of autonomy and generating that convincing illusion of "thingness" that transforms personal vision into general statement. In *Passage to India*, the private and psychological level of meaning contributes to the public and cultural significance of the narrative.

If, therefore, *Burmese Days* seems a less satisfactory examination of the twilight period of colonialism, it does at least give some indication of the psychological factors for which we must account in interpreting Orwell's fiction. Despite the suspicion that the abrupt disappearance of Verral and

Flory (a vanishing act repeated in later novels) betrays Orwell's refusal or inability to look more closely into what are personal and insistent obsessions, the symbolic density of the narrative does indicate that Orwell was potentially capable of expanding the perimeters of a private uneasiness to encompass—as does Eliot's poetry—the spiritual anxieties of a whole culture.

Chapter IV

Orwell and Joyce

In early 1933, Eric Blair wrote a poem in which—although of little intrinsic merit—we can see the same attitudes and themes that were developed in *A Clergyman's Daughter* the following year.

Sometimes in the middle Autumn days,
The windless days when the swallows have flown,
And the sere elms brood in the mist,
Each tree a being, rapt, alone,

I know, not as in barren thought,
But wordlessly, as the bones know,
What quenching of my brain, what numbness,
Wait in the dark grave where I go.

And I see the people thronging the street,
The death-marked people, they and I
Goalless, rootless, like leaves drifting,
Blind to the earth and to the sky;

Nothing believing, nothing loving,
Not in joy nor in pain, not heeding the stream
Of precious life that flows within us,
But fighting, toiling as in a dream.

O you who pass, halt and remember
What tyrant holds your life in bond;
Remember the fixed, reprieveless hour,
The crushing stroke, the dark beyond.

And let us now, as men condemned,
In peace and thrift of time stand still
To learn our world while yet we may,
And shape our souls, however ill;

And we will live, hand, eye and brain,
Piously, outwardly, ever-aware,
Till all our hours burn clear and brave
Like candle flames in windless air;

So shall we in the rout of life
Some thought, some faith, some meaning save,
And speak it once before we go
In silence to the silent grave. (1. 118)

In this poem, we can detect some of those late-Victorian tensions that Orwell apparently experienced within the context of a more modern state of mind. Most prominent is the vision of a world lacking God's vivifying presence ("windless days," "windless air") and a society that, having lost its faith in a supramundane order of reality, is unable to commit itself to a full-bodied acceptance of this life ("Blind to the earth and to the sky"). It seems that what prevents man from becoming aware of the "precious life" flowing within him and what keeps him from experiencing life with the natural spontaneity of the now-absent swallows is the dispiriting awareness of death. So insistently oppressive are the repeated reminders of death that the final stanzas are less a bold assertion of vitality than a rather pathetic sigh of weariness and despair masking itself behind the uplift rhetoric of a sham existential heroism.

This poem is in some respects typical of Orwell's response to the world around him; for even though he is somewhat optimistic, he is more inclined to nourish his imagination on the ills of society than on its potentialities for a richer existence, and he often seems too greatly alarmed by the sense of present deterioration to be able to envision a more humanly rewarding future. "This age," he exclaimed in 1934, "makes me so sick that sometimes I am almost impelled to stop at a corner and start calling down curses from Heaven like Jeremiah or Ezra."[1] What complicates Orwell's Old Testament fury is that his disgust at the spiritual deadness of the age does not spring from a secure faith in the existence of a supernatural reality or a divinely inspired certainty regarding his own righteousness, for he himself is unable to believe. Working at a private school in Middlesex in 1932, Orwell complains of the need to attend church services and receive communion in order to stay in the good graces of his only friend, a High Anglican curate. Most annoying is the knowledge of his own dishonesty: "It seems rather mean to go to HC [Holy Communion] when one doesn't believe, but I have passed myself off for pious & there is nothing for it but to keep up the deception."[2] It is perhaps because of this feeling of moral vulnerability that in *A Clergyman's Daughter*, on which Orwell began working a year or so later, there are fewer signs than one might expect of Jeremiah-like denunciations of modern society and a greater emphasis on exploiting the pathetic aspects of the central character's inner turmoil.

In *A Clergyman's Daughter*, Orwell's central character is Dorothy Hare, daughter of an Anglican rector, who loses her religious faith after wandering through an England where Christian belief and practice have been replaced by materialism and class exploitation. Although Dorothy's personal religious dilemma is described in a straightforward manner, the novel is somewhat vague regarding what has sparked the conscious recognition of her disbelief. Toward the end, Dorothy, returning home after her adventures in London and the countryside of southern England, points out that her recent trials—she has experienced toil, poverty, and callous exploitation—are irrelevant to her loss of faith: "Even when you're practically starving—it doesn't *change* anything inside you." In fact, she cannot explain to herself or to others why she has lost her faith (pp. 294–95). This is a curious statement coming from a character whose misadventures in society comprise over half the narrative. Even more puzzling is the fact that Orwell nowhere indicates that we are to doubt the validity of her statement. At the literal narrative level, we are given no clear reason to believe that she refuses to accept the fact that her experiences with a materialistic society have resulted in a conscious loss of faith.

There is, perhaps, less vagueness surrounding Dorothy's rejection of her suitor Warburton, a neighbor who, with what appears to be the sincerity of a man grown tired of playing the rake, offers a comfortable, even emotionally rewarding, marriage as an alternative to a life of drudgery and loneliness. A confirmed atheist, Warburton can enjoy earthly pleasures without demanding immortality or any transcendent justification for human life; there are signs that despite his godlessness and scandalous reputation Dorothy is fond of him. Side by side with the life-affirming Warburton, Dorothy can calmly meet the menacing gaze of the local butcher (p. 46); at the end of the novel, Dorothy seems on the verge of accepting Warburton's offer of marriage, only to recoil in disgust at his attempt to kiss her, a revulsion that turns her toward the emotional impoverishment of a lonely spinsterhood.

Dorothy's recoil from Warburton's touch results from a deeply rooted sexual anxiety. Reflecting on her fears, Dorothy recalls "dreadful scenes" between her parents that she witnessed as a child, as well as steel engravings of nymphs being pursued by satyrs with "furry thighs." Now the thought of being approached by sexually aroused men becomes repulsive: "They were dreadful when they kissed you—dreadful and . . . disgusting, like some large, furry beast that rubs itself against you" (pp. 91–94 passim). In *Burmese Days*, the stain imprinted on Flory within the womb, coupled as it is with the dire consequences of his sexual assertiveness, causes the reader to raise a Freudian eyebrow. In *A Clergyman's Daughter*, the facial mark of the earlier novel expands into the portrait of a clothed Maja lying on the analyst's couch, an Anglo-Indian Oedipus transformed into a rural Electra, for the text coyly suggests that Dorothy's rejection of Warburton stems from a seemingly unconscious incest anxiety. Dorothy's upsetting vision of being assaulted by furry animals becomes more meaningful in view of the fact that her father's surname is Hare.

The narrator's attitude toward the central character's sexual troubles is somewhat confusing. After describing Dorothy's disgust at erotic experience, Orwell archly states, "It is . . . a thing too common nowadays, among educated women, to occasion any kind of surprise" (p. 94). This remark, on which the narrator does not explicitly elaborate, fails to clarify whether or not he regards his great commonplace about modern womanhood as a key factor in Dorothy's religious crisis. It seems to be important only in terms of Dorothy's reaction to Warburton's attempt to seduce her early in the novel, which takes the form of amnesia and which results in her wanderings through England. On the other hand, as mentioned above, there is reason to doubt that these wanderings have any effect on Dorothy's inability to believe.

A number of critics consider Orwell's apparent failure to relate either Dorothy's sexual neurosis or her experiences in the hop fields and in London to her loss of religious faith to be a major flaw in the novel. Dorothy's neurosis, the incestuous nature of which is always overlooked by the critics, is regarded as irrelevant to her religious difficulties; the description of the hop-picking, the London poor, and Mrs. Creevy's wretched school, where Dorothy is treated with calculated inhumanity, are looked upon as documentaries inserted into the narrative for their own sake. It is judged that the protagonist's emotional turmoil does not throw light either on her apostasy or on the more general spiritual crisis in society at large.[3]

Although such criticisms have some validity, there are certain aspects of *A Clergyman's Daughter* that deserve closer inspection, especially regarding the relevance of Dorothy's personal crises to Orwell's vision of history. However, before delving into the latter, we should focus our attention on the technical experimentation by which Orwell attempts to explore the mind of his heroine. Instead of emphasizing the documentary realism of Orwell's style, one might examine the psychologically symbolic meaning of the various events and situations so concretely described in this novel.

At about the time when Orwell was working on *A Clergyman's Daughter* he expressed great interest in Joyce's *Ulysses*, a work that, he claimed, "sums up better than any book I know the fearful despair that is almost normal in modern times."[4] In a letter long enough to call for an apology (the "fact is that Joyce interests me so much that I can't stop talking about him"), Orwell points out his reasons for admiring *Ulysses*. For one thing, Joyce's work is realistic in the sense that it represents "events and thoughts as they occur in life and not as they occur in fiction"—an example of this realism being the flow of ideas through Leopold Bloom's mind during Paddy Dignam's funeral. Particularly appealing to Orwell was Joyce's ability to expose the inner workings of more or less common types of humanity, such as the thoughts of Gerty MacDowell or, again, Bloom, "an ordinary uncultivated man described from within."[5]

There is an interesting similarity between Orwell's paraphrase of a passage relating to Leopold Bloom and events described in *A Clergyman's Daughter*—Bloom's recollection of an erotic encounter, the disgusting sight of a man eating, subsequent mental images of a butcher's stall, and the memory of a night at Bella's brothel. And, as Orwell notes, Bloom has certain sexual abnormalities.[6] The parallel between Bloom and Dorothy is not accidental, for to a certain extent *A Clergyman's Daughter* exhibits a shift away from some of the more traditional features of plot and characterization (as found in greater measure in *Burmese Days*) and toward a style closer to that of *Ulysses*. Thus, Orwell's favorite section in *A Clergyman's Daughter* (chapter 3, part 1) is the Trafalgar Square scene, an obvious imitation of the Circe episode in *Ulysses*.[7] And what Orwell criticizes in his own novel, its disconnected quality, elicits his mild disapproval in regard to Joyce's work.[8] The intensity of Orwell's self-dissatisfaction when comparing *Ulysses* to *A Clergyman's Daughter* further indicates the extent to which he was measuring himself against Joyce: "When I read a book like [*Ulysses*] and then come back to my own work, I feel like a eunuch who has taken a course in voice production and can pass himself off fairly well as a bass or a baritone, but if you listen closely you can hear the good old squeak just the same as ever."[9]

Even though it is not likely that anyone would ever think of *A Clergyman's Daughter* as an English *Ulysses*, Orwell's strong interest in Joyce's novel at this time should alert us to the significance of the parallels between the two works. Both are structured on journeys, those of Bloom and Stephen Dedalus through Dublin and Dorothy's wanderings through Kent and London. And just as the Joycean interior monologue reveals the deeper layers of his characters' minds, Orwell, using a somewhat different method (which I shall examine in a moment), also probes the hidden areas of his heroine's mind.

Shortly after completing *A Clergyman's Daughter*, Orwell complained of a structural flaw within it which he was unable to correct: "I was aware of it when I wrote the book, & imagined that it did not matter, because I did not intend it [*A Clergyman's Daughter*] to be so realistic as people seem to think it is."[10] Exactly what structural flaw he is talking about is not plainly described; however, his reference to the novel's nonrealistic quality may provide a hint as to the technical problems engaging his attention. To be more precise, we need to be aware of the extent to which realism of detail is used in this novel to produce a surrealistic effect, the result being that the traditional linear plot, by which we expect to be shown the interactions of the characters with their social and physical environment, becomes a series of interior adventures, a psychodrama performed within a mental landscape. And as I shall indicate, what goes on within this psychological space has, or is meant to have, some bearing on the state of modern civilization.

The broader implications of the heroine's troubled sexual life may become clearer if we direct our attention away from the documentary realism of Orwell's style and pay heed to the symbolic import of the narrative, keeping in mind the possibility that the apparently realistic, even naturalistic, treatment possesses a surrealistic dimension through which is objectified Dorothy's inner condition. *A Clergyman's Daughter* can be divided into three more or less distinct sections. Chapter 1 describes Dorothy's unhappy life at Knype Hill, an existence marked by dunning notices, a tiresome round of parish activities, and an unrewarded devotion to the needs of an emotionally frigid father. The next section (chapters 2 through 4), which begins at some unspecified time after Dorothy's lapse into amnesia, records the girl's experiences in the Kentish hop fields and in London, first as a tramp and later as a schoolteacher. In the third section (chapter 5), Dorothy returns home and, after rejecting Warburton, throws herself back into the narcotizing existence of parish drudgery. However, another way of looking at these stages of the narrative is to regard the opening section as primarily dealing with the heroine's conscious feelings of discontent; the second (and longest) section as being, for the most part, an interior drama, a descent into a subconscious mis-en-scène where an obscure struggle between guilt and a longing for innocence and peace takes place; and the third, a return to the daylight world of emotional isolation and a life spent trying to muffle an anxiety-burdened consciousness.

What drives Dorothy from Knype Hill is the circumstance that despite the girl's attempt to erect around herself a fortress of unassailable righteousness through obsessive acts of filial self-denial and religious piety, her protective redoubt transforms itself into a hall of mirrors reflecting back the shadowy dimensions of her incest fantasy, which takes on an alarming solidity in the figure of Warburton.[11] If Reverend Hare is the cold, emotionally unresponsive father, Warburton is his sexually threatening complement. The two men are doubles, halves of a single paternal entity. Deaf to the outcries of his creditors, Hare shamelessly allows his debts, such as the butcher's, to go unpaid; Warburton, deaf to the townspeople's censure, has lived openly with his mistress (pp. 31, 45). To the symbolic equation of behavioral similarities can be added the revealing coincidence that a Van Dyck portrait looks down from a wall in the rectory, while next door to the libertine lives the ever-watchful town scandalmonger, Mrs. Semprill, whose face has the "appearance of a Van Dyck portrait" (pp. 19, 50). The same panic that, triggered at the end of the novel when the suitor hugs Dorothy "pseudo-paternally" (p. 288) and precipitates the severance of their relationship, operates earlier as Warburton, alone with Dorothy in his house, prefaces a seduction attempt with the curious remark that he is "old enough to be [her] father" (p. 88).

Doubling is not, however, limited to Hare and Warburton, for Mrs. Semprill is like a fragmented part of Dorothy, an omniscient conscience relentlessly poisoning the girl's mind with reminders of evil: "No indiscretion, however small, escaped [Semprill's] vigilance." Given the nature of Dorothy's sexual anxiety, it is grimly appropriate that the scandalmonger's stories usually bear "some monstrous tinge of perversion"; within a fictive world marked by the breakdown of social unity, it is not surprising to find that Semprill's rumormongering has disrupted relationships between men and women: her tales, we learn, have brought about the dissolution of engagements and quarrels between spouses (pp. 51–54).

Within such an atmosphere—and, to some extent, with such an atmosphere within Dorothy—the flesh must be mortified, kept in check, punished. The girl forces herself to take cold baths, thrusts pins into her arm to ward off "sacrilegious thoughts," and in church kneels on bare stones "in penance for some sin of yesterday" (p. 11). But this "sin of yesterday" comes alive in the form of Warburton and frightens her beyond endurance. At the end of the first section, Dorothy, having fled in panic from the would-be seducer's house to the sanctuary of the rectory, where she futilely tries to quell her panic by working on the costumes for a church pageant, lapses into a fugue condition.

We next see Orwell's heroine, ignorant of her identity or her past, standing bewildered on a London street. This shift in geographical location is, in a way, also a shift in time. Without a past, she is now a newborn person, and in fact she behaves like a child. At first, she is not conscious of the meaning of words, of time or space, or even of her own existence. Later, like an infant learning about its world, she begins to associate words with the objects she sees around her. She becomes aware of herself as a separate entity, and by running her hands over her breasts, she discovers significantly that she is a woman (pp. 96–98). Despite this revelation of her adult femininity, she starts out on a journey into her "past," to Kent, which, not consciously known by the amnesiac, is her birthplace.

Dorothy's return to Kent, to the place of her origin, is, however, a return to a special form of the past, for hers is an interior journey, a trek into the mind where traces of the past may still exist. Thus, on the road south, Dorothy enters into a kind of dreamworld: she "seemed almost to be sleeping as she walked," and she arrives at her destination "in a dreamlike state" (pp. 110, 119).

It is important to note that the Kentish hop fields are in some way a duplicate world to that from which Dorothy has fled. Life on the road with Nobby, her male companion, is much like her life with Reverend Hare. Here, as at the rectory, Dorothy and Nobby, like Dorothy and Hare, exist on the edge of destitution (p. 118); and as in her former existence, Dorothy is kept busy cooking the man's meals (p. 122). At the rectory, the narrator tells us facetiously, there is a kitchen table that has the habit of "banging you on the hip-bone" (p. 6); on the road Dorothy carries a sack of supplies that chafes her hip until it bleeds (p. 110).

What lends importance to these similarities is the circumstance that Nobby is a combination of Warburton and Hare (the two sides of the fragmented father) who seems not to call forth the girl's incest anxiety. Nobby is a grubby version of Warburton in that both men resort to a falsehood to lure Dorothy into accompanying them—one to his house, the other to Kent—and neither man loses his composure when his sexual advances are rebuffed (pp. 89, 112). And like Hare, who refuses to pay his creditors, Nobby is a "bold thief" (p. 108). But beneath these similarities lies what would seem to be a crucial difference: Nobby is the good father. Unlike the improvident Hare, who cannot manage his own household finances, Nobby is an "expert in small economies"; in contrast to the insistently lecherous Warburton, the laborer prefers pilfering orchards to making love (p. 129).

In effect, the Kentish hop fields constitute a fantasy world, a recaptured pastoral condition seemingly untouched by the guilt and anxiety burdening the adult Dorothy. Dorothy's return to Kent is like one of those fairy-tale reversals in which an evil old life magically vanishes as a happy new one suddenly opens up. Shopping for her father during her old life, Dorothy was constantly plagued by the shame of dealing with merchants whom the rector has refused to pay, but now she has an easy conscience: "All of [the hop pickers] begged, Dorothy with the others; she had no remembered past, no standards of comparison to make her ashamed of it" (p. 108). Furthermore scandal no longer affects her. The newspapers have taken up Mrs. Semprill's story that Dorothy, flimsily attired, drove off with Warburton on the night of her visit to his house. But her newspaper photograph conveys "absolutely nothing to her mind," and she reads the headline "Passion Drama in Country Rectory" without comprehension or interest (p. 137).

Entry into Kent, her childhood home, seems to be a deliverance from time: "More and more she had come to take her curious situation for granted, to abandon all thoughts of either yesterday or to-morrow." Moreover the long, hard work in the hop fields, leaving Dorothy in an animallike torpor, narrows the range of her consciousness and renders her unable to "struggle with nebulous mental problems." In general, hop-picking is a life that, in using up all her energy, keeps Dorothy thoroughly happy (p. 135). Living with Nobby in the Kentish countryside, she regains the Edenic peace and wholeness for which the protagonist in *Burmese Days* futilely longs.

However, Dorothy can enjoy this guiltless happiness only because Orwell has made of her a dream figure, as it were, whose sexual self appears to be fragmented away. From the start of the novel, Dorothy is two persons—it is her custom to exhort herself in the second person (p. 5). She can enjoy a blissful existence in the hop fields, in the world of her childhood, because this disreputable other, less sexually innocent self becomes a tabloid phantom sinning its way, as the newspapers suggest, through the bordellos of Europe (pp. 116, 142).

But Dorothy's idyll does not last, for guilt cannot be masked forever.

Nobby's orchard raiding, a primal transgression that, as in the hunting scenes of *Burmese Days*, may be a disguised sexual violation, leads to his arrest. Thereupon Dorothy is reminded of her sexuality: we learn that her fellow pickers regard her as Nobby's lover (p. 140, 145), and it is now that Dorothy realizes that she is the rector's daughter referred to in the headlines. Her past life up to her return home from Warburton's comes painfully back to her. Despite her adamant refusal to believe the newspaper accounts—the headlines of which unintentionally suggest incest (PASSION DRAMA IN . . . RECTORY—PARSON'S DAUGHTER AND ELDERLY SEDUCER—WHITE-HAIRED FATHER PROSTRATE WITH GRIEF)—the restoration of her memory, the consciousness of her recent past, turns the hop-field existence into an intolerable ordeal. Appropriately, her last experience before leaving Kent represents the resurrected link between sex and retribution. On the night before her departure, she allows a young man to kiss her, after which she dances around the fire, "one hand clasped by a . . . butcher-boy" (p. 155).

Dorothy's predicament is made more grievous by her father's apparent refusal to answer her explanatory letter, a refusal that convinces the girl that she cannot return home. Physical separation stands for the emotional separation, the sense of being alienated from a possible source of affection and security associated with the personal past, brought about by Dorothy's deeply rooted feeling of guilt.

Dorothy's return to London after getting no response from the Reverend Hare represents the irrepressibly insistent guilt and anxiety tormenting the girl. The realistic urban setting, the subworld of London tramps, is transformed into a purgatorial nightmare of cold and dirt and hunger. The world outside of Dorothy becomes a large-scale reflection of her inner turmoil—"the world, inner and outer, grows dimmer till it reaches almost the vagueness of a dream" (p. 202). The hallucinatory Trafalgar Square chapter is a crystallization of the whole novel. Tallboys, a rector defrocked for his sexual misconduct with a local spinster (p. 175), recalls the days when he would sport among the parish Girl Guides, "in loco parentis pinching the girls' backsides" (p. 183). Later in this chapter, he suggests that Dorothy aid him in performing a Black Mass (p. 191), an obvious parallel, by the way, with the Circe episode in *Ulysses*. (One might point out, too, that in this section of Joyce's novel Leopold Bloom's hyperactive sexual fantasizing is exposed by, among others, a Mrs. Mervy Talboys, who accuses him of sending her an obscene picture.) The Trafalgar Square episode also reveals how, by splitting off Dorothy's sexual self and confining it to the supposedly erroneous headlines, Orwell tries to rid her of sexual guilt. Kept awake by the freezing night air, the tramps swathe themselves in newspapers to get a little warmth. "There is some furtive fondling of the women under cover of the paper. Dorothy is too far gone [with fatigue] to care" (p. 195).

Similarly, Dorothy's own sexual self operates "under cover of the paper" in Europe, while the Dorothy in England remains, at least at first, seemingly immune to feelings of guilt because she is, in terms of the novel's dreamworld geography, "too far gone to care."

However, reminders of sexual evil cannot be escaped. In addition to being repeatedly taken for a fallen woman while in London (pp. 100, 159, 163), Dorothy finds that her first lodging in the city is in a refuge for prostitutes (p. 164). The ineradicable obscenity carved into a wall of this establishment is one more sign of her failure to shake off the incubus of guilt (p. 158).

Before examining the connection between Dorothy's incest anxiety and the novel's treatment of broader cultural matters, we must realize that it is necessary to regard the events of the narrative as the projection of the main character's inner state, as a mental allegory. To view the novel as just a realistic presentation of external reality leads to a serious problem in regard to the plot itself. Because Hare believes Semprill's story about Dorothy and Warburton, he doesn't allow Dorothy to return home. As a result, she must go to London and experience suffering and degradation. However, toward the end of the novel Warburton informs Dorothy that her father will now receive her back because Semprill has been discredited. Sued for libeling one of the townsmen, Semprill can no longer find people willing to believe her rumors, including the one about Dorothy, and the scandalmonger has fled the scene. In addition, Warburton, who has been in Europe during Dorothy's wanderings and apparently has only recently learned of her misfortunes, assures the girl that she did not run away with him during her period of amnesia, which is still a mental blank to her (p. 273). In short, Dorothy seems to be exonerated of any sexual impropriety.

Still, the reader cannot be certain that Dorothy has been calumniated. We are told that Semprill is no longer believed, not that her story is demonstrably false. Moreover, the fact that Semprill's fall has also made "spotless" the reputation of Warburton (p. 291), a man whom Orwell clearly indicates to have been a sexual adventurer, casts doubt on the validity of Dorothy's exoneration. It would be to Warburton's advantage to convince Dorothy, whom he wishes to marry, that in fact he never did lure her away to the Continent nor desert her there. Finally, it is important to note that the narrator never indicates to the reader what really happens to Dorothy between the time of her return home from Warburton's and her appearance in London prior to the journey to Kent. This crucial interval remains a complete blank to both Dorothy and the reader. We are confronted by what appears to be an inexplicable gap in the realistic level of the narrative.

But, if it is unclear whether or not Dorothy, as a character depicted realistically, has committed an indiscretion, there can be no doubt that as the inhabitant of a fantasy world she is guilty. In Kent, she finds brief happiness with Nobby, an apparently asexual and solicitous "father," but because her guilt is inescapable she is ousted from this world into the nightmare of London. Within the fictional present, the supposed peace of the hop-field life is only a thin wash beneath which lies the dark pigment of ineradicable guilt and anxiety. It is only Dorothy's ability to live in a world of self-protecting illusions that gives to her Kent the misleading appearance of innocence and peace. In fact, from the very start of the novel she has been exiled in her private London. In the first section, Semprill functions as Dorothy's own inexorable conscience, a voice that poisons the girl's sensibility by insisting on the smuttiness of love relationships. For Semprill, and consequently for Dorothy, every form of emotional attraction becomes tinged with a reprehensible perversity. As a result, her relationship with Nobby, the girl's prototypical love object in disguised form, is doomed from the start; her Kentish idyll, corresponding to the recollected Paris in *Down and Out* and the jungle of Flory's Burma, must give way to the miserable London existence, where, as I have suggested, the punitive conscience continues to assail the girl.

Dorothy's fantasy of innocence cannot be maintained because she carries a sense of sin with her into Kent, just as Flory's stain undermines his relationship with Elizabeth. Early in the novel we are told that Dorothy, performing her morning chores, "could hear the antiphonal snoring of her father and of Ellen [Millborough], the maid of all work" (p. 6). In the ambiguous world of fantasy, this brief remark calls up a sexually suggestive, even if somewhat ludicrous, image. It is more than mere coincidence that when Dorothy travels to Kent with Nobby, she calls herself Ellen (p. 102); as though inadvertently emphasizing the symbolic importance of this pseudonym, she employs the maid's surname from the time when the Kentish experience ends until she is allowed by Hare to return home on the basis of her apparent exculpation. Also, it should be noted that the phrase by which Orwell designates his heroine, "a clergyman's daughter," is a tongue-in-cheek British term for a woman of dubious sexual virtue. One may infer from this that the heroine, her adult consciousness tainted by the knowledge of sexual evil, cannot find Kent within herself, cannot find any region of undefiled innocence. Consequently, the impulse to love assumes in the imagination the form of a guilt-provoking fantasy.

The "sin of yesterday" that leaves Dorothy emotionally disabled is not to be understood as an actual incestuous experience, nor is the past, the "yesterday" that she hopes to find made spotless, simply her literal past. The past with which Dorothy tries to cope is a subjective reality within her adult, guilt-burdened mind. And the final reconciliation with her father, who seems at the end only a shade less cold than usual, fails to suggest that now, even though far away from London, she is able to embrace life enthusiastically. Despite the fact that Semprill, the externalized projection of the girl's oppressive conscience, is generally discredited and forced to leave town, it is clear that the troublemaker's power is not lessened. Dorothy's touching of her own breasts before setting out for Kent, the discovery of her womanhood (p. 98), implies that state of adult awareness that makes impossible any return to what might be dimly perceived as the guiltless, spontaneous joy of childhood. Consequently, at the end of the novel Dorothy signifies her acceptance of an emotionally ossified existence by constructing a "breastplate" for the school pageant (p. 320).

The link between Dorothy's loss of faith and her rejection of sensual experience may appear less vague if we recall her inability to accept an earthly existence that holds out no promise of immortality. Having reviewed the novel *Tropic of Cancer* several months after the appearance of *A Clergyman's Daughter*, Orwell defended Henry Miller's tendency to deal with the sexual lives of debased and coarsened social types. Justifying this apparent "vilification of human nature," Orwell pointed out that the decline of religious faith had led to a "sloppy idealisation of the physical side of life." Such an attitude was a reaction against the painful awareness that life without religious belief was dismal; for, claimed Orwell, echoing the words of Dorothy Hare, "if there is no life beyond the grave, it is obviously harder to face the fact that birth, copulation, etc. are in certain aspects disgusting. . . . Hence . . . the monstrous soppification of the sexual theme in most of the fiction of the past hundred years. . . . Man is not a Yahoo, but he is rather like a Yahoo and needs to be reminded of it from time to time."[12] Certainly Orwell, guiding us through the Tartarus of Dorothy's tortured psyche, steers clear of any "monstrous soppification."

However, still to be explained is the relationship between the specifically incestuous nature of Dorothy's anxiety and the spiritual decay of modern society. At one point in the novel, Dorothy, having taken a teaching position at a private girls' school in a London suburb, begins to feel that at last she is engaged in an activity that will give some meaning and direction to her life. For running through her adventures after leaving home have been two dark currents that have carried her into the deep waters of isolation and despair—the personal scandal attached to her name and, more generally, the growing awareness that modern civilization, having rejected those ancient beliefs and pieties that once served to bind the elements of a Christian society into a communal wholeness, is now committed to a socially divisive and alienating worship of money.

Despite a number of minor vexations encountered at the school—some springing from the minors themselves, others from the inadequate educational facilities provided by the tightfisted proprietress, Mrs. Creevy—the young woman finds teaching an emotionally rewarding way of life. Critical of the distorted, chauvinistic account of the past contained in the school's approved textbook, Dorothy triggers an enthusiastic response to history among her pupils by having them work on a historical chart, a roll of wallpaper on which the students paste cutouts illustrating various significant events of the past. And the children's eagerness to understand history, the enthusiasm they feel in making history, as it were, instead of merely learning about it in a superficial, mindless way, is matched by Dorothy's readiness to embrace teaching as a lifelong career:

> Almost any job that fully occupied her would have been a relief after the horrible futility of the time of her destitution. But this was more than a mere job; it was—so it seemed to her—a mission, a life-purpose. Trying to awaken the dulled minds of these children, trying to undo the swindle that had been worked upon them in the name of education—that, surely, was something to which she could give herself heart and soul? So for the time being, in the interest of her work, she disregarded the beastliness of living in Mrs. Creevy's house, and quite forgot her strange, anomalous position and the uncertainty of her future. (p. 245)

But Dorothy's career as a teacher is abruptly reversed when, in an attempt to encourage her pupils' spirit of curiosity, she answers their questions about the passage in *Macbeth* where Macduff reveals that he was "untimely ripp'd" from the womb: "About half the children went home and asked their parents the meaning of the word 'womb.' There was a sudden commotion, a flying to and fro of messages, and electric thrill of horror through fifteen decent Nonconformist homes" (p. 249). The upshot of this incident is that in addition to being chastised in front of the irate parents, Dorothy is forced to abandon her innovative teaching methods and follow the mind-deadening pedagogic rituals favored by proprietress and parents alike, and finally she is fired without notice.

Although only one episode in a novel full of rather sensational, even melodramatic, events—the passages dealing with the heroine's stay at Mrs. Creevy's school, and especially those relating to her interest in history and the puritanical suspiciousness aroused by the word *womb*—not only hint at the complexity lying beneath the apparently simple and straightforward plot of *A Clergyman's Daughter* but also direct our attention toward themes and ideas that are important to an understanding of Orwell's vision of reality, particularly as it is expressed in his fiction. Although I shall deal with Orwell's ideas about history in a more detailed fashion in a later chapter, the works we have already examined are indicative of his opinion of contemporary civilization. We might call to mind Flory's attack on Westernization, which he sneeringly refers to as "Utopia" (p. 44). The school episode in *A Clergyman's Daughter* is especially interesting in that it foreshadows the dystopian vision of history presented more fully in *Animal Farm* and *1984*.

Worth noting is the fact that Dorothy's newfound enthusiasm for history, the conviction that her students' collective reconstruction of the past has, along with the teaching of other subjects, given to her own godless existence some meaning and value, is blighted by a misadventure associated with what appears to be some form of sexual indecency (the utterance of the word *womb*). Moreover, insofar as the project upon which the students are working is a re-created history that is supposedly enhancing the lives of the pupils and their teacher, Dorothy and her girls are, in effect, producing a mini-utopia within the school. This being the case, an interesting question arises: What connects the term *womb* to the swift collapse of this pocket utopia and the reassertion of Mrs. Creevy's authoritarian and reactionary control over Dorothy's classroom? What is the link between the outrage over Dorothy's reference to Macduff's parturition and the uneasy relationship between individuals and the historical process?

If, as suggested above, the work of Dorothy and her pupils on the historical chart, that re-creation of history that transforms the class into a new experience, is a utopian gesture, by analogy Dorothy's activities in the Kentish hop fields become, insofar as this rural setting represents a longed-for condition of purity, an interior pageant, personal instead of public, which, at least for a while, heralds the discovery of a pastorally innocent utopia within the depths of her own being. And the satisfaction she feels here of being freed from all thought of past and future suggests that the entry into the region of her birth after her period of wandering represents that final utopian consummation in which the historical process, its work completed, abolishes itself. Of course, Dorothy does not really escape time, nor does she reunite herself with a dreamed-of past, for the element of sexual unease constantly frustrates her quest for peace. As has been shown repeatedly in *A Clergyman's Daughter*, the central character's personal history, the series of events and experiences defining her movement through time and space, is initiated by some form of reprehensible sexuality. Furthermore, historical experience, both personal and social, manifests itself through various kinds of disunity—shame, suspicion, distrust, isolation, exploitation, and emotional alienation. Warburton's attempted seduction leads to Dorothy's amnesia (a mental fragmentation) and separation from home and father; her explusion from an Edenic Kent is traceable to Nobby's violation of the orchard, the theft of forbidden fruit; the collapse of the heroine's snug classroom utopia and her eventual dismissal from Mrs. Creevy's school stem from the parents' outrage at the word *womb*.

The last we see of Dorothy is when she is once more hard at work in the rectory, feverishly preparing costumes for the church pageant: "We *must* make that pageant a success! she thought. . . . The problem of faith and no faith had vanished utterly from her mind. It was beginning to get dark, but, too busy to stop and light the lamp, she worked on, pasting strip after strip of paper into place, with absorbed, with pious concentration, in the penetrating smell of the gluepot" (p. 320). What appears to be an obsessive desire to redeem history, to invest the welter of humanity's struggles in time with a ceremonial orderliness and meaning, is, in fact, an escape from history. Pasted together in an obscure rectory, sponsored by a backwater church, directed by a provincial schoolmaster, this pageant only faintly resembles the real world outside, to a civilization discarding its ancient beliefs and following a secular code of values based on distrust and ruthless competition. Safely insulated within her father's country church, sealed off by the impenetrable armor of thought-constricting toil, Dorothy can blot from consciousness all knowledge of the chaotic great world. What holds her rapt attention is not the historical pageant but the pot of glue, the fascinating emblem of unchanging peace and wholeness, of the womb itself.

Secularized history is open ended, always on the move, a restless protean reality in which innocence turns into evil, security into uncertainty, a fallen, post-Edenic world of time, decay, and dissolution. It is not surprising, therefore, that Dorothy, longing to abolish her temporal identity and to regain an endlessly protective parental embrace, finds comfort in those enclosed places—her father's rectory, Kentish haystacks, the classroom, the cell of a London jail under the command of a "fatherly sergeant" (p. 203), newspaper swathings, which provide a womblike refuge from the divisive gale winds of historical reality, whether public or personal. Indeed, the reaction of one of the pupils to Dorothy's proposal of the historical chart—the child defiantly locks herself in the bathroom (p. 243)—serves as an implicit commentary not only on the teacher's rashly optimistic belief that innocents may safely be exposed to historical experience but also on the assumption that an involvement with history is compatible with the actualization of a truly utopian condition.

As history's imperative to move forward in time becomes more insistent, the Ur-longing for a condition of stasis and containment may become more urgent, assuming the extreme form of an imaginary return to the most primitive state of being conceivable, as is suggested by Dorothy's fixation on the gluepot. And because Dorothy's sense of personal fragmentation so frequently expresses itself in terms of the alienation between men and women—Mrs. Semprill's divisive rumormongering, the ill-natured rivalry between Mrs. Creevy's establishment and a neighboring boys' school (p. 215), Reverend Hare's coldness toward his daughter, her own uneasy relationships with males, and even Macduff's violent and "untimely" separation from his mother's body—the girl's dream of unity and wholeness involves what for her is the most primally intimate male-female union, that between father and daughter. The final scene of the novel, like some ritual designed to transform the dead mother and emotionally distant father into the protectively enclosing parents of her deepest fantasies, represents Dorothy's ultimate reactionary gesture.

However, given the incestuous nature of Dorothy's fantasies, one must conclude that what inner peace she arrives at is bound to be spurious, for the very presence of a nagging sense of sinfulness is in itself a sign that the simple innocence of childhood is irrecoverable. Indeed, we may trace Dorothy's loss of faith to her unconscious incest anxiety, which makes intolerable the thought of a patriarchal God close both to her personally and, by extension, to modern society in general. There can be no real rebirth into some ahistorical condition of purity because Dorothy's sin-burdened, time-bound sensibility is too splintered ever to be made whole. In fact, the attempted flight from her historical and sensual identity is itself a symptom of this fragmentation, since her escape involves a rejection of self, a radical diminution of consciousness, the result being that at the end of the novel Dorothy's state, her will-less subjection to the demands of an indifferent father and benumbed fixation on the womblike container, is little more than a pathetically counterfeit return to the security of the past.

My emphasis on the nature of Dorothy's inner conflicts is based on the belief that Orwell's realistic style—the detailed description of observable phenomena—has at least a partially surrealistic aim: to express as vividly as possible the obscure psychological factors at work within Dorothy's mind. Analyzing the novel in this fashion involves nothing more original than elaborating on an idea first put forth by a very early reviewer: "For all its realism of scene . . . [*A Clergyman's Daughter*] is not in a fundamental sense a 'realistic' novel. The story of the clergyman's daughter . . . is made altogether credible, but the writing that makes it so is of exactly the variety that can sometimes give fantasy concreteness."[13] We might, therefore, regard the two passages describing Dorothy's frantic work on the school pageant—the one just prior to her amnesia and the other at the end of the novel—as actually the separate halves of a single realistically rendered scene, a moment of Dorothy's normal existence interrupted by the bulk of the narrative, her period of wandering, in which are unfolded the successive acts of the interior drama being played out on the stage of her subconscious mind. Viewed from this perspective, the discrepancy between Dorothy's adventures and her emotional condition is less glaring than some critics have claimed. The England through which Dorothy wanders is the territory of her own psyche, and her various experiences represent the dramatization of that private conflict between the utopian longing for primitive innocence and an ineradicable dystopian evil. The triumph of the latter is the underlying reason why Dorothy's work on the church-sponsored pageant of England's past can in no way redeem history by investing it with spiritual value.   .

Although interesting as an example of its author's increasing willingness to exploit the novel's potential for psychological probing, *A Clergyman's Daughter* exhibits the same type of flaw noted in Orwell's earlier works—the tenuous relationship between the main character's inner, sometimes surrealistically expressed anxiety and the disorders associated with the protagonist's social milieu. In part, this problem has to do with the extreme interiorization of the narrative; at times it seems as though the familiar, observable world of external reality loses its substance and becomes little more than the epiphenomenal projection of the central figure's inner conflicts. The character's interactions with society suddenly assume the form of a private psychodrama. This situation would be less disturbing were it not for the fact that, for example, Dorothy's specific emotional stress is of too idiosyncratic a nature to throw light on problems affecting others. Dorothy's "case," her incest anxiety and resultant fear of sensual experience, lacks the resonance that would give it a broadly representative significance. The claustrophobically psychodramatic quality of the heroine's adventures seem not to have any transpersonal dimension. The narrator's remark about Dorothy's sexual neurosis—a problem "too common, nowadays, to occasion any kind of surprise"—does not really bridge the gap. And the most that can be said for Dorothy's frantic self-exhortation to make the historical pageant a success (perhaps an echo of the hope expressed in Orwell's poem that men will find the strength to live "like candle flames in windless air") is that in articulating modern humanity's desperate imperative she expresses, at least for a moment, the collective uneasiness and longing of her era. Had Orwell managed to provide Dorothy with this extra dimension in terms of the narrative as a whole, we could regard her personal troubles, the dramatization of her own interior "pageant," as in some way illustrating her contemporaries' problematic relationship with history. However, the incompatibility between utopian goals and the historical process finds expression almost wholly in terms of the protagonist's personal dilemma: the utopian quest has a private and, therefore, restricted meaning, and the history with which Dorothy has so disturbing a relationship is merely that of her own neurotic existence.

Still, *A Clergyman's Daughter* does give evidence of Orwell's constant struggle to control his art and learn more about his personal complexities. For one thing, Orwell provides the central character with a family, or at least part of one, which is not the case with John Flory. And the fact that so much stress is placed on Dorothy's tense relationship with her father, even though the cause of this tension remains disguised, does suggest that Orwell is ready to approach a bit nearer to the primal family drama. Furthermore, in associating this covertly incestuous situation with the name *Hare*, Orwell may be expressing a vague, not fully conscious commitment to following the spoor of guilt and anxiety back into a distant and idealized childhood, the world of Beatrix Potter.

It could be that in using a female protagonist Orwell is attempting to deal with personally sensitive material in an artistically detached manner. Artistic detachment is probably one of the benefits he expected from Joyce's Circean surrealism, a way to dramatize the elements of the inner self without putting the author's psyche on display.

However, I think that these practices (the use of a heroine and the Joycean technique) are more valuable for what they tell us about Orwell's more or less conscious attitudes than for what specific effect they might have on his later novels. What Orwell gains from Joyce is primarily neither a specific narrative technique nor an increased sensitivity to the potentialities of the English language, but rather the recognition that no area of human thought and behavior is off limits to the novelist and the courage to follow Joyce's path down into the labyrinth of the self. The creation of a female protagonist suggests Orwell's at least partly conscious acceptance of the feminine in himself as the source of his artistic creativity.

Jacintha Buddicom has noted something about Orwell's treatment of Dorothy that a man would most likely overlook. She says: "But if the washed and well-meaning Mr. Warburton . . . filled her with repulsion, then *what* was she doing, rolling about with tramps?"[14] The obvious answer—that Dorothy's reactions are less those of a woman than a man—alerts us to the likelihood of Orwell having projected his own attitudes into his fictional characters. The virginal Dorothy's shying away from the touch of the Warburton who is old enough to be her father may represent Orwell's child self, the self that longs to hold on to its boyhood past and resists its own violation by the adult world. On the other hand, Warburton's portrayal is just ambiguous enough to suggest affirmative qualities. Intelligent, sensitive, and in spite of his past rakishness genuinely interested in marriage, Warburton is really an older Flory who has had the courage to survive. The older man may be a trial self for Orwell, a potential self far healthier than the frightened Dorothy. Her loss of faith sends her rushing back to the sanctuary of her father's rectory; Warburton's travels abroad show that atheism does not reduce his ability to take delight in the world's abundance. I might add that regarding Warburton as a reasonably bullish picture of what Orwell might become with the passage of years is based on more than mere guesswork. "Warburton" is too close to "Edward Burton," a pseudonym used by Blair during his down-and-out wanderings, to be coincidental.[15] And as I shall point out subsequently, this conflict between the assertion of life and escape from it is basic to Orwell's vision of reality.

Chapter V

From Rebel Poet to Common Man

Gordon Comstock, the central character of *Keep the Aspidistra Flying* (1936), rejects the modern worship of money and middle-class life by voluntarily sinking to increasingly lower socioeconomic levels. However, having made his girl friend Rosemary pregnant, he decides to marry her and, giving up his none-too-successful attempts at poetry, gets a respectable job with an advertising firm he had formerly left in disgust. At the end of the novel, Gordon is convinced that by taking his place in middle-class society he is saving himself from a life of meaningless and emotionally unrewarding rebellion.

Despite the apparent simplicity of its plot, *Aspidistra* is in its structure and characterization sufficiently ambiguous (or vague) to have elicited sharply contrasting interpretations. Some critics view the novel as expressing a prudential moral, with Gordon being a sort of modern Alceste who finally comes to his senses. As an impractically idealistic rebel against society, in its domestic as well as commercial aspects, Gordon is, it is claimed, a butt of satire; however, he finally becomes a figure who, because he realistically accepts the world as it is and realizes that he can and must find a positive modus vivendi within society, engages our sympathy and approval.[1]

Other critics, agreeing that the reader is supposed to approve of Gordon's decision to re-enter middle-class society, fault the novel. They feel that Orwell has not dealt seriously with the evils of modern commercialized civilization and that he has slighted the importance of Gordon's rebellion. In this view, Orwell has failed to understand the problem of how Gordon is to preserve his integrity within a world where human values are reduced to a pounds and shillings basis.[2]

Still others deny that Gordon is ever anything but an object of satire. They see the ending of the novel as in effect ironic—Gordon is not regenerated by marriage. Furthermore, so distorted is Gordon's view of life by his private obsession with money that he is never capable of a realistic evaluation of himself or society. For him, there is either total revolt or total surrender.[3]

My feeling is that in judging the relative value of these various critical observations one may as well draw straws and avoid much needless weighing of alternatives. *Aspidistra* is probably Orwell's most confusing, and confused, novel. Practically any statement about it can be documented. One is inclined to agree with John Wain's judgment that although *As-*

pidistra preaches something, Orwell was unable to decide about what he was preaching.[4] However, some of this muddle can be avoided if, instead of taking sides with one or another of these assessments, we edge our way into the work with as few presuppositions as possible concerning the values a person should or should not live by. More interesting than the question of the wisdom or folly of Gordon Comstock's behavior is the manner by which he is defined as a fictional character and his function in relation to the modes of experience dealt with in the novel. The ambiguity of *Aspidistra* may be traceable to the fact that this novel represents a more or less marked transition in Orwell's development as a novelist, that during the course of the narrative the characterization of the central figure undergoes some noteworthy alterations.

In this regard, we might pay heed to Keith Alldritt's comment on the structural disunity of *Aspidistra*. According to Alldritt, Orwell, trying to model himself on Joyce, started *Aspidistra* with the intention of producing his own *Portrait of the Artist as a Young Man* but partway through the novel wisely abandoned this plan:

> The account of Comstock's career as an artist is foisted onto this [theme of the danger of paying service to the money-god] and not endemic to it. The passages that are there to present Gordon as a poet are often characterized by hackneyed meaningless statements and have none of the energy to be found in the descriptions of Comstock's and/or Orwell's horror at the lifelessness and materialism of modern bourgeois civilization. It is as though Orwell starts off to make the portrait of himself as an artist but after the first few chapters, loses interest in this original purpose and realises, as does his surrogate at the end of the novel, that "the whole concept of poetry was meaning-less to him now."[5]

This statement suggests that *Aspidistra*, whatever its flaws, reflects an important shift in Orwell's novels. In *Burmese Days* and *A Clergyman's Daughter*, the central characters are peripheral to their social environment. Although a member of the white community in Burma, Flory, with his delicate sensibility and personal insecurities, is not typical of the colonial ruling class; nor is there any convincing evidence that the plight of Dorothy Hare really represents a crisis affecting contemporary society, or some specific class within it, during the interwar years. Similarly, however poignant may be the condition of Gordon Comstock as he is presented throughout most of *Aspidistra* (the struggling poet trapped in what he considers to be an unpoetically avaricious society), one finds it difficult to view the embittered author of an unsellable book of verse, pathetically entitled *Mice*, as an adequate embodiment of the human condition in the 1930s. The fact that as the novel progresses Orwell allows the poetic identity of Gordon to fade away and be replaced by the more conventional one of lower-middle-class employee, husband, and father-to-be may indicate Orwell's dissatisfaction with a central character who is too much of a special case to serve as a cultural barometer.

A passage presumably meant to exhibit the dishonesty of modern business life and the demoralizing effect it has on those caught up in it indicates in a general way the novel's inadequate treatment of social realities. Orwell's description of Gordon Comstock's work for the New Albion Publicity Company (the title of which is obviously allegorical) does not really make us feel what it is like to be an advertising writer:

> It was that Gordon showed, almost from the start, a remarkable talent for copywriting. He could compose an ad as though he had been born to it. The vivid phrase that sticks and rankles, the neat little para. that packs a world of lies into a hundred words—they came to him almost unsought. He had always had a gift for words, but his was the first time he had used it successfully. Mr. Clew [the chief copywriter] thought him very promising. Gordon watched his own development, first with surprise, then with amusement, and finally with a kind of horror. *This*, then was what he was coming to! Writing lies to tickle money out of fools' pockets! There was a beastly irony, too, in the fact that he, who wanted to be a "writer," should score his sole success in writing ads for deodorants.[6]

The problem in this passage is that although we are told how the advertising game warps the imagination, if not the conscience, we do not see Gordon's sensibility being affected; the reason we do not get a convincing picture of this early form of doublethink is that such a debilitating mode of thought has not really sunk into the character's being. Gordon remains too conscious of the tricks of the trade, too aware of, and, therefore, too emotionally distanced from, the morally deleterious influences of this occupation. Although Orwell conveys the intensity of Gordon's shock and indignation, we gain no insight into the day-to-day process by which the demands of copywriting might subtly corrupt the attitudes and values of the aspiring poet.

What does receive emphasis is Gordon's curiously ambivalent attitude toward money. At times he is more upset by his financial gains than by the lies he must produce as a copywriter:

> Gordon's wages were raised by ten shillings a week. And it was now that Gordon grew frightened. Money was getting him after all. He was sliding down, down, into the money-sty. . . . He saw that now or never was the time to escape. He had to get out of it—out of the money-world, irrevocably, before he was too far involved. (p. 54)

The significance of money is one of the most interesting aspects of *Aspidistra*. Time and again we are reminded how money, or, as is usually the case with Gordon, the lack of it, conditions one's behavior and outlook.

In the course of a country outing, Gordon, brooding over his poverty (the result of his rejection of the commercial world), loses all sexual desire for Rosemary, whereas on a later occasion the mere possession of five pounds emboldens him to such an extent that he attempts virtual rape on the girl. Also, Gordon is certain that because he is poor, people feel free to insult him: "It makes people *hate* you, to know that you've no money. They insult you just for the pleasure of insulting you and knowing that you can't hit back" (p. 91). He is equally convinced that women are to be held only through the power of money (p. 93).

At one point, the narrator informs us that because Gordon is impoverished, he genuinely desires to see civilization destroyed, and also that his vision of London as a scene of decay is merely a projection of his own "inner misery" (p. 84). Later, Gordon himself states that one's view of life is wholly determined by one's financial condition:

> All this talk we make—we're only objectifying our own feelings. It's all dictated by what we've got in our pockets. I go up and down London saying it's a city of the dead, and our civilisation's dying, and I wish war would break out, and God knows what; and all it means is that my wages are two quid a week and I wish they were five. (p. 90)

If we accept the words of both the narrator and the central character, as I think we must, then we are forced to assume that Gordon's re-entry into the business world at the end of the novel—a step that, of course, promises greater financial rewards than does the abandoned poet's career—motivates his fervent claim that "to abjure money is to abjure life" (p. 237), a statement indicating his readiness to embrace a formerly despised middle-class existence.

Terry Eagleton correctly points out that since the central character's judgments on society entirely depend on his economic status, the reader cannot be sure whether the hero really does exist in a money-worshipping society, as he repeatedly asserts, or is simply the victim of an obsession peculiar to himself. The text provides no conclusive evidence to substantiate or contradict the protagonist's statements.[7] The fact that the narrative voice is so often indistinguishable from Gordon's thoughts and utterances, and the fact that Orwell provides us with no basis for evaluating the applicability of Gordon's views to the world around him, forces us to regard the narrative as a record of purely personal responses, as a purely subjective vision of reality. Because Orwell's picture of reality coincides with Gordon's, we are, in effect, locked within a single mind, and all we are in contact with is that mind's private view of life. Consequently, we have no way of judging whether or not Gordon's passage from poet-rebel to wage earner and family man represents a mature acceptance of reality or a moral defeat. We have no objective basis for judging that Gordon's condemnations of modern civilization are any more or less correct than his favorable comments at the end.[8]

This being the case, our attention directs itself toward the psychological ramifications of the money theme. One aspect of this is Gordon's conviction that middle-class domesticity is a trap set by the so-called money god, a means imprisoning the human spirit. Once married, Gordon complains, one is "chained" to a "good job" until one's death. "And what a life!" he continues, "Licit sexual intercourse in the shade of the aspidistra" (p. 104). Although this seems like the age-old male outcry against the boredom of monogamy, there is evidence that Gordon's attitude toward women springs from a more obscure source. It seems that the sexual urge itself is disturbing. "This woman business!" he exclaims. "What a pity we can't cut it right out, or at least be like the animals—minutes of ferocious lust and months of icy chastity." But a man, unlike the beasts of the field, finds himself painfully caught between "his memory and his conscience" (p. 102). Later, preparing to make love to Rosemary during their trip to the countryside, Gordon thinks: "He wanted her to be his, he wanted to *have had* her, but he wished it were over and done with. It was an effort—a thing he had to screw himself up to" (p. 138).

Gordon constantly complains that because he has refused to accept the middle-class money code, he is forced into sexual deprivation. He claims, too, that lack of money takes the joy out of physical relationships; in fact, with only eightpence in his pocket, Gordon states that making love is "physically impossible" (p. 146).

Gordon's deepest shame regarding poverty is linked to the fear of being ridiculed by women to whom he might offer his "Joey," the "miserable little threepenny bit," the "absurd little thing" that he timidly keeps hidden in his pocket (pp. 3–4). Remarking on this passage, Anthony West points out that although the Joey is considered a nuisance, no social stigma is ever attached to it; he concludes that Gordon's excessive reaction reflects not so much the hardship of poverty as the "mood of a man who feels inadequate and despised because he is not rich."[9] There is, however, a more immediate connection between poverty and sexual deprivation than that of West's cause and effect, for penury constantly functions as an expression of sexual inadequacy. Certainly the thought of offering his threepenny bit to a shop girl fills him with a singularly intense dismay that hints at something more than a generalized sense of embarrassment: "The girl at the cash desk would titter" at the coin, he thinks; in a "vivid vision he saw the girl at the cash desk, as she handled his threepenny bit, grin sidelong at the girl behind the cake counter" (p. 71). Later Gordon exclaims: "Without money, you can't be *straightforward* in your dealings with women. For without money . . . you've got to take what women you can get; and then, necessarily, *you've got to break free of them* [italics mine]" (p. 104).[10]

There is reason to believe that Gordon's rejection of the money god, which he associates with the adult world of the wage earner, husband, and father, is, like the descent into tramphood described in *Down and Out*, motivated by a craving to escape the burden of sexual guilt. Even prior to his actual experience of poverty, when he is cut off from women, he becomes, to some extent, aware that to embrace penury entails sexual deprivation. Dissatisfied with his fruitless literary activities, he "vaguely . . . looked forward to some kind of moneyless, anchorite existence" (p. 49). Elsewhere he expresses the conviction that there exist only two alternatives—to worship money or live without women (p. 105).

Besides being associated with his expressed distaste for middle-class life and the more obscure impulse toward sexual deprivation, Gordon's willful sinking into the lower socioeconomic depths after leaving the New Albion Publicity Company is a movement toward what might seem to be the secure, relatively unproblematic world of childhood. It is, therefore, no coincidence that the landladies in whose lodgings Gordon stays during his economic descent are maternal figures, first "Ma Wisbeach" and then "Mother Meakin." In fact, Gordon's period of sexual abstinence serves as a reverse rite of passage from adulthood to youth, the latter condition dependent on the maternal presence. Such a strategy is suggested by the juxtaposition of two ideas—Gordon's conviction that because of his seedy condition no woman will ever look at him again and the immediately following thought that he "must [and this may be read as "can"] go home at once" to Ma Wisbeach (p. 72).

At Ma Wisbeach's boardinghouse, where only single men are allowed, Gordon can live like an anchorite, or more precisely, like a schoolboy. And if the comment that in such an establishment the "key never quite fits the lock" vaguely hints at an atmosphere of sexual futility (pp. 22–23), this observation suggests also that Gordon has not yet found his true home. Life at Ma Wisbeach's is not marked by a sense of innocence and signs of maternal tenderness: there are still disturbing reminders of the flesh. The landlady regards him with an accusing eye, perhaps suspecting him of "smuggling women into the house" (p. 23). In addition to being a place where the ironclad prohibition on sexual activity only increases suspicions about its presence, the boardinghouse is vaguely linked to that childhood state when—as Orwell remarks on years later in the essay "Such, Such Were the Joys"—one's bodily functions are rendered joyless, even guilt provoking. "Making tea" in the bedroom is a heinous offense, and even in the bathroom Comstock has the unsettling feeling that "somebody is listening" (p. 29). And if the old woman causes Gordon to feel disturbed at his own body, there is the slightest of hints that she is also a sexual threat—over his letters she exercises "a sort of droit du seigneur" (p. 33).

The flight from the realm of adult heterosexuality takes Gordon no farther than the homosexual world of preadolescence. The first bookshop in which Gordon works during his descent attracts wispy, effeminate young men, and Gordon himself is constantly trying to get his poetry published in a quarterly that, according to him, caters to the gay set. Flaxman, a scapegrace fellow lodger and a combination of Billy Bunter and Baron Charlus, caps his description of a local barmaid by accosting Gordon: "Flaxman wriggled lasciviously. His tongue appeared between his lips. Then, suddenly pretending that Gordon was the . . . barmaid, he seized him by the waist and gave him a tender squeeze" (p. 26).

Because money is symbolically associated with virility and sexual assertiveness, the possession of cash exposes Gordon to the sexual guilt his various actions seem designed to avoid. With the money received from an American review for a poem, Gordon goes on a drinking spree and ends up in a whorehouse. Here he listens to a homesick youth singing:

> The man that kisses a pretty girl
> And goes and tells his mother,
> Ought to have his lips cut off,
> Ought to _____ [Orwell's omission]

With this suggestion of mutilation hanging in the air, Gordon, about to accompany one of the whores to her room, sees an older client leaving, a "family man," and thinks, "his predecessor. In the same bed, probably" (p. 175). Now Gordon proves to be a helpless child incapable of sex, not the criminal usurper of an older man's bed. Impotent from drink, he is unable to engage in intercourse, and clutching a bottle of wine provided by the whore he sinks into a stupor like a satisfied suckling.

In the brothel scene, we see objectified Gordon's desperate and presumably unconscious desire to escape from his Oedipal guilt and gain a state of innocence. He must not touch the family man's sexual partner, the father's woman; therefore, through drink, which blunts his adult consciousness, Gordon alters his relationship with the woman. Instead of being lecher and temptress, they become infant and solicitous mother.

It is worth noticing that just after the "family man," "the predecessor," departs, and just prior to Gordon's spell of drunken impotency, he catches sight of an aspidistra. Like the boy's sinister ballad, this plant is a warning that to approach a woman is a punishable act. Ma Wisbeach's house is full of aspidistras, the one in Gordon's room bearing a leaf "shaped like Agamemnon's sword" (p. 36), presumably a double allusion to the Greek king's sacrificial slaying of his daughter Iphigenia (thus a symbol of menacing parental authority) and to the murder of Agamemnon, at least partly the consequence of sexual passion. In a sense, we may regard the narrative as a record of Gordon's responses to the aspidistra—from a mixture of fear and hatred to, finally, a curious enthusiasm for the plant (at the end of the novel he demands that an aspidistra be placed in his and Rosemary's flat).[11]

In the chapter following the brothel episode, Orwell gives the impression that his hero has more stages to pass through before arriving at a condition in which the aspidistra is no longer a menace. Although the narrow cubicle of the Black Maria and the cramped cell in which Gordon, arrested for disorderly behavior, is confined after his spree call to mind those images of enclosure that Dorothy Hare associates with peace and security, these spaces do not enable Gordon to escape from his troubling thoughts. Gordon ("the dirty little tyke," as a policeman calls him) is still surrounded by more or less disguised reminders of sexual guilt—jailmates charged with "loitering with intent to enter," stealing money to be spent on whores, and thrusting a knife into a prostitute's stomach (pp. 184–85).

However, Gordon is freed instead of punished when Ravelston, a close friend, pays his fine. Ravelston's purpose in the novel is not immediately apparent. He is a rich socialist whose Marxism is more the product of an abstract sense of guilt than the result of any direct experience with the inequities of capitalism. It is a sign of Orwell's inability to develop fully the sociopolitical material of his fiction that although these two characters talk a great deal about money and the current state of society, the interrelationship of the two men is vague. Therefore, we are justified in saying that Orwell fails to explore the dramatic potentialities of the conflict inherent in a relationship between a representative of the upper class and a man of the "shabby" middle class, two individuals who, sharing the same hostility to society, respond from different motives and sharply contrasting points of view.[12]

The reason the characterization of Ravelston is so unclear in sociopolitical terms is, I think, that his main function is in relation to Gordon's private psychodrama. The sharp distinction drawn between the two—Ravelston is tall, charming, wealthy, and blessed with a willing girl friend, whereas Gordon is short, ill tempered, poor, and sexually deprived—reminds us of the Flory-Verral relationship in *Burmese Days*. However, Ravelston is less an embodiment of sexual aggressiveness that must be suppressed than a kind of paternal figure whom Gordon regards with a childlike mixture of awe and affection:

> Gordon sidled closer to Ravelston as they started down the pavement. He would have taken his arm, only of course one can't do that kind of thing. Beside Ravelston's taller, comelier figure he looked frail, fretful and miserably shabby. He adored Ravelston and was never quite at ease in his presence. (p. 81)

After rescuing Gordon from the hands of the law, Ravelston, representing a forgiving father, takes the "little tyke" home (just as the Reverend Hare allows Dorothy to return home), lends him money, and generally insists on looking after him. It is only after this sign of paternal approval that

Gordon can continue on his journey toward an existence free of the aspidistra, the guilt-burdened conscience. However, Ravelston's solicitude apparently does not entirely calm Gordon's anxieties, for the latter is sure that from now on "the memory of this evil time" will adversely affect their friendship (p. 198).

Leaving Ravelston's place, Gordon moves into the lodging house of Mother Meakin, where he seems to find a subworld (and an inner condition) in which middle-class notions of propriety have no force: "There was no mingy lower middle class decency here, no feeling of being spied upon and disapproved of. So long as you paid your rent you could do almost exactly as you liked; come home drunk and crawl up the stairs, bring women in at all hours, lie in bed all day if you wanted to. Mother Meakin was not the type to interfere." And although even in these disreputable lodgings there is an aspidistra, it is, Orwell comments, "obviously dying" (pp. 207–8).

Gordon's supposed breakthrough into a new mode of existence, into a lower-class world of freedom, is a step closer to childhood. For one thing, despite the atmosphere of sexual freedom that apparently reigns at Mother Meakin's, the features of this life that most appeal to Gordon constitute nothing more than a typical schoolboy's utopian fantasy—lying abed reading thrillers, staying up late, going for weeks without a bath, leaving the bed unmade, and in general feeling a smug satisfaction at surveying his little kingdom of squalor. Gordon seems to have settled into the unreal, innocently carefree life that Orwell describes in the Paris section of *Down and Out*. Thus, Orwell's earlier amused observation regarding the bugs that had paraded across the ceiling of his working-class quarters is used again to indicate Gordon's indifference to middle-class fastidiousness: "One night the bugs came out of one of the cracks and marched across the ceiling two by two. He lay on his bed, his hands under his head, watching them with interest" (p. 208).

As mentioned already, in *Down and Out* Orwell's account of his move to England and period of vagabondage implicitly reveals a sharper awareness of guilt and, at the same time, a need to insulate himself from recollections that might be painful. To some extent, the pattern of events in *Aspidistra* is similar to the earlier narrative, although, as I shall point out, there are also significant differences between the two. Despite Gordon's insistence that at Mother Meakin's he has left his guilt behind him, there are signs that he is still menaced, that his earlier comment about a picture from *La Vie Parisienne* hanging in the whorehouse—"Sometimes the originals don't compare so well" (p. 176)—may still apply. Circumstances draw him back into the world of respectability, to the white-collar job and licit sex under the shade of the aspidistra. Gordon is jolted out of his scruffy schoolboy idyll when, after he makes love to Rosemary, she becomes pregnant, and he, following the dictates of convention, marries her and returns to middle-class life.

The sexual encounter between Gordon and Rosemary is not without a certain Freudian element. While Gordon has, prior to this scene, been acting out the part of a carefree preadolescent, his older sister, Julia, a surrogate mother who cared for him during his childhood, becomes linked to Rosemary ("they had never met, but now Rosemary had got to know Julia somehow"), and the two join in "pursuit" of him (p. 213).

This blurring of roles and identities indicates that the Orwellian protagonists' attitude toward and relationship with women are still conditioned by a childhood fixation. If at one point Rosemary looks at Gordon like a mother gazing fondly at her child (p. 109), elsewhere the link between Rosemary and Julia suggests a brother-sister intimacy. During their country outing, Gordon and Rosemary embrace with the sexless rapture of children; as the two seek privacy in a copse where they plan to make love, we sense that a punishable violation of the childhood past is about to occur: the copse is surrounded by thorns and barbed wire; nearby they see a cottage as "tiny as a child's toy"; as Rosemary, naked, lies at the center of this grove, Gordon suddenly notes her "almost childish" appearance (pp. 138–40).

"It was Mother Meakin," thinks Gordon, "though it did not sound like her knock" (p. 219), as Rosemary, determined to sacrifice her closely guarded virginity in order to save Gordon from sinking lower into slum life, stands before his apartment door. Entering and approaching his bed, she is more the solicitous mother than lover: "She bent her head to show him the three white hairs on her crown. Then she wriggled herself on the bed beside him, put an arm under him, pulled him towards her, covered his face with kisses" (p. 220). Paradoxically, the moment in which Gordon gains a symbolically maternal kiss is also the instant when the period of childlike insouciance ends, and he is forced to re-enter, for better or worse, the world of the middle classes. And just as in *Swann's Way* Marcel realizes that the trick he had played many years before to win his mother's embrace had in fact marked the end of his own happy childhood, so too Rosemary and Gordon's intimacy seems to represent the loss of the condition for which the latter has felt such an urgent need.

At this point, it will be helpful to look at the typical Orwellian central figure in the works of the early thirties. In each case, there exists some circumstance that in one way or another is associated with the individual's being cut off from sensual experience: in *Down and Out*, the shabby clothes that signal Orwell's entry into poverty make women unattainable; John Flory, publicly disgraced for his sexual relationship with his Burmese mistress and horrified by his own "obscene" thought of Elizabeth Lackersteen's wedding night, finds absolute sensual deprivation through death;

and Dorothy Hare's inability to tolerate a man's touch drives her to the protective confines of a country rectory. Moreover, these characters are special cases whose private dilemmas do not convincingly reflect problems that affect society at large, even though the various documentary passages in these works and the repeated references to exploitation, racism, and the like inevitably raise the expectation that the personal states of the central characters will in some way throw light on sociopolitical conditions. As Alex Zwerdling points out, the expressive element in Orwell's early novels, the need to "record urgent, individual emotions," works against the sociological content. The "private and obsessional" material in these works lacks the typicality that should draw our attention to public and political issues. The reader is "too conscious of the neurotic nature of the [central characters] to trust them as commentators on the social scene. They are too thoroughly trapped by their own disabilities to speak with authority, and so we find ourselves looking curiously *at* them rather than through their eyes."[13]

It is a mark of this disunity that Orwell could do nothing more with these troubled individuals—in any event, the fictional ones—than leave them physically as well as emotionally cut off from the other characters who people their fictional world. This is true also throughout most of *Aspidistra*: Gordon Comstock's rebellion against middle-class life is defined in terms of a sexual uneasiness that is too specific and too personal to have any broader significance, and his own rejection of an adult identity suggests a repetition of the conclusion of *A Clergyman's Daughter*.

However, the fact that in *Aspidistra* Orwell altered the pattern of his former novels by having Gordon wed Rosemary and accept, even if somewhat unconvincingly, his middle-class identity suggests an attempt to create a new, more socially representative type. It seems that for the first time Orwell placed at the center of his fictional narrative a character whose situation in life is that of the normal run of humanity—of the common man. If this is the case, then there is a possibility that Orwell was ready to tighten the connection between the central character's private uneasiness and his surroundings, the world of the lower middle class.

Perhaps the most important difference between the earlier works and *Aspidistra* is that the latter is clearly a *Bildungsroman* in that it records the central character's "education" to the ways of the world and his entry into society, which may or may not be a step in the right direction, depending on what one thinks of the civilization whose values he is accepting. The presence in Gordon of sexual, presumably Oedipal, anxiety suggests that Orwell may be dealing with the tension between an individual's sexual drive and the restraints, both internal and external, imposed on it by society. In the two earlier novels, where this conflict is presented only in a confusingly oblique manner, the implications of this tension are not examined closely since the protagonists, caught between private need and a sense of guilt, are simply removed from any social relationships that might allow for a more probing examination into their dilemmas. Orwell brings the careers of these characters to a halt before revealing what connection might exist between their inner turmoil and the sociopolitical institutions existing around them.

For the most part, this is the case with *Aspidistra*. Until the end, the hero is on the run, sealing himself off from the world and being shuttled from one situation to another (the business world, shabby-genteel-boardinghouse life) so rapidly that his experiences and reactions lack any representative value. Only in the final chapter do we detect a new development—the hint of a connection between sexual repression and the individual's assumption of a recognizable social identity.

Gordon's re-entry into a lower-middle-class existence means that now he is in some way affected by the antisensual atmosphere of such a life. When Gordon, preparing for fatherhood, goes to a library to learn about the fetus, the female librarian assumes without question that he is motivated by pornographic curiosity (p. 232). In this kind of world, sexual self-assertion must seem almost criminal. Because the fetus within Rosemary is inescapable proof of Gordon's guilt-provoking sexuality, Orwell must handle Gordon's reactions in a more or less convincing, nonsensational, and socially typical manner. Unlike Flory, Dorothy, and even Orwell the hobo, Gordon cannot be suddenly divested of a sexual role. Now the protagonist does engage in sexual intimacy, and in this scene we can see how the attempt to shield himself from the emotional discomfort that this act produces within him involves the repressive psychological maneuvering apparently demanded by the society whose ranks he is about to rejoin. When Rosemary comes to his room, Gordon, burdened by his lower-middle-class sexual inhibitions, must at least appear to be a helpless victim of circumstance: "He let her do it [seduce him]. He did not want this to happen—it was the very thing that he least wanted." And if the sexual impulse cannot be denied, one can at least refuse to acknowledge deriving any pleasure from it: "So it was done at last, without much pleasure" (pp. 220–21).

To give the central character's private conflict a transpersonal significance and to show that the process of becoming socialized involves some form of sexual repression, Orwell resorts to an allegorical myth to account for the inhibited quality of lower-middle-class life. During the Victorian period, we are told, "Gran'pa Comstock," a man of unfettered vitality, displayed his fierce vigor by making a fortune and producing numerous offspring. But in some way the old man crushed the spirit of his children. Unambitious, impoverished, sickly, infertile—his sons and daughters are withering away, having managed to produce from among themselves only two children, Gordon and his sister. Presumably, the Comstock family allegory mirrors the decline of British society, particularly that of the middle classes. As a result of the old capitalist's oppressive influence on his children (the modern generation), the English society that Gordon at first rejects and in time comes to terms with is populated by a feckless, dispirited citizenry. The national fondness for the aspidistra betokens, Gordon believes, the British people's subjection to the past, to the established order of things. "The aspidistra, flower of England!" Gordon exclaims derisively during one of his rebellious moods. "There will be no revolution in England while there are aspidistras in the windows" (p. 44).

Worth noting is the fact that *Aspidistra* appears less than a year before the start of the Mass-Observation movement in England (early 1937).[14] A collective undertaking on the part of thousands of Britishers, most of whom lacked any special training for the task, Mass-Observation was an attempt to record objectively aspects of contemporary life. The hope was that through the anthropological and sociological examination of people's daily existence (matters ranging from "bathroom behaviour" to "anti-semitism" and including Orwell's "aspidistra cult") there might arise among the masses an awareness of the need for social and political reforms.

Although hardly a call for social activism, *Aspidistra* exhibits features corresponding to the descriptive aims of Mass-Observation. Several months after the publication of *Aspidistra*, Orwell pointed out that second-hand bookshops—particularly the one in Hamstead, London, where he was employed while working on this novel—provided an opportunity to study a "fair cross-section of London's reading public": people not really interested in books, Orientals, "vague-minded women looking for birthday presents for their nephews," "decayed persons smelling of old bread-crusts," male (never female) stamp collectors, true believers in astrology, and even nearly "certifiable lunatics." For Orwell the amateur social psychologist, the most enlightening aspect of the book business is the lending library service, for in this "you see people's real tastes, not their pretended ones."[15]

Orwell's description of *Aspidistra* as a "domestic sort of story with an entirely English theme" suggests an at least partly sociological aim;[16] the passages detailing the contents and clientele of the two bookshops in which Gordon Comstock works, as well as those describing life in various boardinghouses, indicate the author's interest in more or less typical features of the London lower-middle-class landscape.

We may, therefore, regard the "Gran'pa Comstock" story as an explanation of England's twentieth-century decline. This allegory implies that because wealth has become a sign of worth in capitalist England, the economically depressed lower middle class—which, unlike the vital and carefree members of the working class whom Gordon at times envies, accept such a system of value—is afflicted with some kind of emotional and spiritual deterioration, a condition allegorically expressed by the absence of sexual vigor. If we regard the worship of money as an unconscious attempt to compensate for the destructive effects of sexual repressiveness, then, conversely, we can see more clearly the connection between Gordon's periods of poverty and his half-concealed obsession with sexual inadequacy. And the reverence that, as Gordon claims, is paid to the aspidistra by the English and, finally, by Gordon himself, may signify a willingness to come to terms with the capitalist system as it is, to accept the social and libidinal restraints that this system imposes.

There is a certain irony in the fact that *Aspidistra*, a novel that hammers away at the evil of money worship, should have been written simply to make money, as Orwell claimed ten years later—and perhaps poetic justice in his shame at its quality.[17] Whatever may be their imperfections, the former books are often enlivened by colorful descriptions and documentary sections that take hold of the imagination. But such passages are as rare as they are brief in *Aspidistra*. Also, the characterization is frequently flat and implausible. One suspects that Orwell was so intent on relating the *Bildungsroman* form to the allegorical meaning that he neglected to deal adequately with other artistic problems. Ravelston and Rosemary, whose characterizations are vague and insubstantial, primarily exist to facilitate Gordon's conversion from isolated poet to middle-class householder; and Alldritt and Lodge are right in claiming that the treatment of the central character, with its astoundingly sudden shift from splenetic rebel to perfervid apologist for lower-middle-class life and values, is too forced to be convincing as a natural, organic development.[18]

Moreover, there is reason to doubt that Orwell has succeeded in closing the gap between sociopolitical reality and psychology. The connection between the Comstock myth, expressing the decline of the British people under capitalism, and the aspidistra, emblem of the antisensual strain within their mentality, remains quite tenuous because Orwell fails to persuade us that the social world external to Gordon possesses institutionalized means for reinforcing and perpetuating the repressiveness that is, supposedly, at once economic and sexual, and that subtly forces Gordon to accept the inhibited, conformist existence of the common man. There may be a real connection between the prevailing sociopolitical system and a sexually repressed society, as Herbert Marcuse describes in *Eros and Civilization*; but owing to the unreliability of the central character's assessment of that society—and the reader has little else to rely on since the narrator's voice and the thoughts and words of Gordon are so frequently indistinguishable—one cannot be sure that this relationship really exists beyond the latter's imagination. We can see how Gordon's private sexual fears thwart his libidinal self-assertion by making it seem a form of criminal rebelliousness, but so restricted are we to his subjective and apparently idiosyncratic evaluations and behavior that we cannot be certain that sexual anxiety is, in fact, responsible for the joylessness and enervation associated throughout most of the novel with the code of respectability espoused by the English people, particularly by the lower middle class. Toward the end of the novel, Gordon remarks that the people of the lower middle class, among whom he now counts himself, have managed to preserve a standard of decency in the modern world. They have preserved their respectability even while living by the money code; they have "kept the aspidistra flying" (p. 239). Not surprisingly, Gordon demands that the plant be prominently displayed in his and Rosemary's apartment. As an emblem of middle-class decency (including a puritanical distrust of sensual experience), the aspidistra is supposed to be a link between Gordon's newfound respectability and twentieth-century English society.

However, we cannot be sure that in fact the aspidistra has the same significance for others as it has for Gordon. Rosemary, who is repeatedly shown to live by middle-class values, is outraged at the thought of having the plant anywhere in the flat (p. 246).

Even though the last-minute shift in the central figure's identity is only one step in the direction of a more socially representative characterization, the shift itself calls attention to a process that becomes more important in later works. So intense is the need to silence his nagging, shame-oppressed conscience that Gordon tries to sink down into a social subworld "*below* ambition" (p. 203). Appropriately, the last stage in his search for a condition of benumbed and solitary peace is a seedy bookstore where he can drug himself on cheap escapist literature—"the only kind of books that suited him nowadays" (p. 204). But even this existence falls short of expectation. The attempt to retreat into some imaginary boyish Bohemia of innocence and irresponsibility, with days spent engrossed in thrillers and nights whiled away amidst the cozy squalor of Mother Meakin's establishment, fails because he still carries around with him the manuscript of his unfinished poem, "London Pleasures"—a sign that he is still ambitious. The existence of this poetic identity is important for another reason, too, for as long as he is a poet, an individual extremely sensitive to his own moods, he remains inescapably tormented by thoughts of failure and decay. On the other hand, in the final chapter, after he has renounced poetry, Gordon's outlook becomes much brighter. Thoughts of failure as a poet give way to hopes of rising in the advertising business; images of life and survival replace the earlier fixation on personal and social deterioration, and the presence of the aspidistra arouses enthusiasm rather than fear and anger. Although the reader has no sure way of judging whether the one outlook is any more objectively valid than the other, since we are confined to subjective reactions, we may conclude that there exists within the protagonist's mind a link between the suppressive force of the aspidistra and his strangely abrupt leap from tormented poet to euphoric upholder of middle-class respectability.

Standing guard at the gate of memory, barring the conscious self from the cave leading down into the dark precincts of unconscious longings and fears, the aspidistra separates the respectable Gordon from Gordon the neo-Byronic poet whose work in progress, "London Pleasures," sickens him like a man suffering from a past of debauchery. In rejecting his identity as a writer, a rejection signified by the flushing of his unfinished poem down the toilet (p. 240), Gordon symbolically cuts away from consciousness the "dirty" self, the self so painfully aware not only of sexual unhappiness and personal deterioration but also of civilization's degeneracy.

One may infer from this that the transformation from *poète maudit* to good citizen involves a process of mental fragmentation similar to that found in Orwell's earlier works. On the other hand, in *Aspidistra* this process indicates something new. Gordon's insistence on placing an aspidistra not in the bedroom but in the front window of his and Rosemary's apartment, where the "people opposite can see it" (p. 246), implies that now—with private anxiety seemingly masked from consciousness, flushed away like the manuscript—he is ready to assume a public identity, that of the common man.

There is some justification for positing a connection between the appearance of the new Gordon and Orwell's personal growth. In *A Clergyman's Daughter*, we saw that the dilemma of the central character lacked sociological resonance because it was too narrowly defined in terms of a neurotic relationship with her father. In *Aspidistra*, the Comstock allegory is Orwell's attempt to broaden the implications of the Blair family history. The Gran'pa Comstock of the nineteenth century is the fictional version of a nineteenth-century Blair, Thomas Richard Arthur Blair, Orwell's grandfather, who sired only one child less than the eleven of Gran'pa Comstock. In *A Clergyman's Daughter*, the surname Hare serves as a clue revealing the intimate and idiosyncratic nature of the central character's anxiety—its incestuous basis. In *Aspidistra*, however, the name is a sign that Orwell's perspective is expanding from the immediate fictional present back into the previous century, for Hare was the maiden name of Thomas Blair's wife.

The use of his own family to provide a historical context for the events of the narrative means that Orwell is developing the implications of the psychological element in his fiction, not ignoring it. Also his use of themes and techniques characteristic of Dostoevski—the doubling of scenes and characters, the masochistic cravings—underscores Orwell's increasing interest in the irrational.[19] If *Aspidistra* reminds us of Joyce's *Portrait*, it also calls to mind *Notes from the Underground*, with its voice from the mouse hole. Gordon's unappreciated book of poetry is called *Mice*; Cheeseman is the name of the proprietor of the second bookstore where Gordon works; at one stage of his social descent Gordon lives in a room "shaped like a wedge of cheese" (p. 206).

In part 1 of *Notes*, the mouse-man poses as the champion of the irrational against a civilization of blinkered rationality. His capacity to suffer the pain and humiliation he brings upon himself gives him a sense of superiority to ordinary humanity. In part 2, we see the reverse side of the coin—the mouse-man as a petty tyrant, his refusal to give love a mark of his emotional emptiness, his abrasiveness a plea to be noticed. To some extent, Gordon is Dostoevski's mouse-man. On the one hand, Gordon loudly asserts his defiance of modern society and its values; on the other, he longs to be accepted by that society.

The underground world explored by Orwell's character may be even more primitive and disturbing than the mouse hole of Dostoevski's diarist. The Russian reveals the Old Adam that exists beneath the veneer of nineteenth-century humanism. In *Aspidistra*, what exists beneath the public self is a craving for a womblike condition very much like death. Gordon likens his poems to dead fetuses; the picture of a fetus Gordon the expectant father examines in a medical textbook looks lifeless; and Cheeseman's bookshop, the place Gordon feels is nearest the "mud," is a "narrow . . . pipe of a room" (pp. 83, 201, 233).

The comparison between *Notes* and *Aspidistra* is not, however, always to the latter's advantage. In *Notes*, the rhetoric of contradiction is creative: the perverse inconsistencies and the self-canceling assertion of incompatible identities are the source of the mouse-man's dramatic intensity. In revealing the negations that characterize his existence, he affirms it. The rhetoric of Orwell's schizoid protagonist, the vituperation of the rebel and the lyric enthusiasm of the returned prodigal, seems contrived and mutually exclusive. Gordon the poet insists too much on his Dostoevskian origin; Gordon the common man strains too hard to deny it. In *Notes*, the dialectical interrelationship of opposites produces an effect of imaginative concentration and intensity. In *Aspidistra*, the polarity is disjunctive, an either-or dichotomy suggesting Orwell's inability at this stage of his career to reconcile the desire to broaden the representational significance of his fiction with the need to delve deeper into the psychological complexities of modern man. The final scene of the novel, where we see Gordon pressing his head against Rosemary's pregnant body, reflects this disjunction: the gesture may symbolize the birth of a more familiar social type as protagonist, or it may symbolize the reverse—a character still craving the underground.

Chapter VI

Questioning the Past

In September 1938, Orwell began work on *Coming Up for Air*. He wanted to start the book as early as July, when the idea for the novel first occurred to him, but owing to a tubercular lesion discovered in one lung in March of that year he was not able to begin until the fall, after arriving in Morocco to recuperate. A rough draft was completed by January 1939; in March a finished draft was ready; in June 1939 *Coming Up for Air* was published. I mention these dates because one must view Orwell's fourth novel in the light of the political situation existing in the late 1930s. His military service with the POUM militia from January to May of 1937 not only gave him direct experience with warfare but also, and perhaps more importantly, opened his eyes to the ideological complexities and brutalities of modern-power politics. Surely one of the more memorable sections of *Homage to Catalonia* (1938) deals with his painful initiation into the betrayal of left-wing revolutionary aims and the ruthless persecution of one faction by another in Barcelona among men who should have been united in their resistance to Franco. The political violence that Orwell experienced was soon enough overshadowed by more ominous events. In April 1937, Austria, intimidated by Nazi power both within and outside its borders, voted to join the Third Reich; Orwell began *Coming Up for Air* in the same month that Hitler, Daladier, Chamberlain, and Mussolini signed the Munich Agreement, which led to the German invasion of Czechoslovakia and the occupation of the Sudetenland in October; aided by Italian troops and airplanes, the Nationalists took Barcelona in January of 1939 (the month in which the first draft of *Coming Up for Air* was completed); and the completion of the final draft coincided with the German occupation of Lithuanian Memel and Neville Chamberlain's announcement that Britain would aid Poland in any way possible to protect that nation's independence.

On his arrival in Morocco, Orwell, apparently thinking about the Czechoslovakian crisis, expressed his belief that the events of "the next week or two" would determine whether or not war will break out.[1] As I shall point out in more detail in a later chapter, during the late thirties Orwell repeatedly criticized the idea of a popular front against Germany, viewing this movement as a trick (an "anti-fascist racket") to divert the British from their proper goal of effecting a working-class revolution. What worried him more than the external military dangers to Britain was the political threat from within of forces hostile to democracy. He warned that war, or even the preparation for it, would involve a "fascising process leading to an authoritarian regime" in England.[2]

Orwell's pessimistic outlook regarding the security of future freedom can be seen in "Inside the Whale," one of a group of essays he began writing not long after completing *Coming Up for Air* and finished in December 1939. In this essay, Orwell pointed to an important difference between Walt Whitman's all-embracing attitude toward the nineteenth century and that of Henry Miller toward the twentieth. Whitman's was an age of expanding frontiers, of vitality and optimism; whereas, the world Henry Miller embraces is contracting, losing its vitality, and the acceptance of this civilization bespeaks a "passive . . . even 'decadent' " attitude (1. 500).

However, rather than criticizing this passive acceptance, Orwell reacted favorably to Miller's works (for it was foolish to think that men's efforts, whether as individuals or as groups, would be able to preserve the values and institutions of a "liberal-Christian culture") (1. 525). What was ahead was an age of totalitarian dictatorship, a period in which freedom of thought and the autonomous individual would be disappearing. According to Orwell, the political ice age that was settling over Europe would end literature as it had been written in the past. The writer, doomed like the liberal culture that had produced him, could only face—and describe in his works—the harsh reality that nothing could be done to change the course of history:

> Give yourself over to the world-process, stop fighting against it or pretending that you can control it; simply accept it, endure it, record it. That seems to be the formula that any sensitive novelist is now likely to adopt. A novel on more positive, "constructive" lines, and not emotionally spurious, is at present very difficult to imagine. (1. 526)

It may not be unreasonable to suggest a connection between these remarks and Orwell's comment the previous December that the writing of *Coming Up for Air* had revealed to him a "big subject" that he had "never really touched before."[3] Although probably referring to a future novel, Orwell may have tried to explore into this "big subject" in *Coming Up for Air*, especially since he felt so acutely at this period that time was running out for the West. There are reasons for believing that *Coming Up for Air* presents a vision of reality quite similar to that which Orwell detected in the novels of Miller, who, because he depicted the truth about modern man's outlook, "is the only imaginative prose writer [in English] of the slightest value who has appeared . . . for some years past."[4]

Although regretting that Miller's rootless characters are separated from their home environment, being neither workers nor suburban householders, Orwell nevertheless praised Miller for capturing the essence of a type usually ignored in modern literature, the "ordinary man." This creature that Miller has so tellingly depicted is the passive victim of great events, the man who, unable to control his own destiny, "simply lies down and lets things happen to him"(1. 500). What we hear when he speaks is "a voice from the crowd, from the underling, from the third-class carriage, from the ordinary, non-political, non-moral, passive man." (1. 501).

It is likely that in writing *Coming Up for Air* Orwell was thinking seriously about the theme that he considered appropriate to an age on the verge of sweeping changes—the common man, with his sexual uneasiness and his political disillusionment.

To understand the nature of Orwell's aims as a novelist at this stage of his career, we must examine the connection between his increasing gloom about the political future of the West and the need to deal with some new and important subject in his fiction. In addition, we need to discover the relationship between the character types Orwell found so intriguing in Miller's works and George ("Tubby") Bowling, described as a "typical middle-aged bloke with . . . a house in the suburbs, and . . . rather . . . bookish."[5] In this regard, we might look at several relevant essays that Orwell wrote during the thirties.

"Shooting an Elephant" (1936) deals with the cultural deterioration brought about by imperialism. The key figures in the essay are the berserk elephant and Orwell the policeman who, representing imperial power, destroys it. As the narrative unfolds, we see that although the policeman initially considers himself a free agent, he is actually a cog in the machinery of imperial administration. Supposedly master of the situation, he is in fact "an absurd puppet" who, fearing the ridicule of the Burmans who are pressing around him, is forced against his will to shoot the elephant.

However, the narrator's statement about the dilemma of the white man who loses his freedom once he becomes the "conventionalized figure of a sahib" (1. 239) is not the final lesson of the essay, for the structure and narrative strategy of the work point to a deeper, more somber truth. It should be noted that the policeman's realization, appearing two-thirds of the way through the essay, is but one point on an ascending scale of tension, which reaches its peak with the elephant's death. Moreover the speaker's temporal position lends his retrospective account a significance broader than the meaning that is conveyed through the policeman's restricted consciousness, for the narrator in "Shooting an Elephant" has the advantage of historical perspective. He sees now what his earlier self could not perceive—the downward spiral of history, the deadly cultural effect of modern imperialism.

Central to the essay is the elephant's fate. This great creature is more than an ordinary pachyderm: it also embodies an unrestrained primal vitality. Spontaneous and unpredictable, the supposedly tame beast suddenly unleashes its energy in a fearful display of violence. But however destructive of human life and property may be the creature, it does possess the awesome power of life. Next to the elephant, the faceless mass of natives and their puppetlike protector appear lifeless and insubstantial. The behavior of both subjects and master, who are all victims of a devitalizing imperialism, exhibits a mechanical inevitability. Furthermore, what was formerly regarded as a domesticated beast of burden now becomes a ubiquitous spirit, a mystery: "Some of the people said that the elephant had gone in one direction, some said that he had gone in another, some professed not even to have heard of any elephant" (1. 237). By the end of the essay, the animal, shot by the policeman, becomes a tragic figure, a half-mythical being in the throes of some profound calamity:

> In that instant . . . a mysterious, terrible change had come over the elephant. He neither stirred nor fell, but every line of his body had altered. He looked suddenly stricken, shrunken, immensely old, as though the frightful impact of the bullet had paralysed him without knocking him down. At last, after what seemed a long time . . . he sagged flabbily to his knees. His mouth slobbered. An enormous senility seemed to have settled upon him. One could have imagined him thousands of years old. . . . But in falling he seemed for a moment to rise, for as his hind legs collapsed beneath him he seemed to tower upwards like a huge rock toppling, his truck reaching skyward like a tree. He trumpeted, for the first and only time. And then down he came. (1. 241)

The references to the creature's aura of great age and its stubborn resistance to death are significant. In some mysterious way, the animal is a symbol of primitive energy, an almost timeless archetype of vitality. Now, mortally wounded, it succumbs to a newer power, the life-denying force of modern civilization.

It is appropriate that the speaker, situated in the present, is able to invest the elephant's death with a historical import. He can now see not only that the imperial rule in Burma, as elsewhere, stifles human spontaneity but also that times are growing worse. Early in the essay, the speaker recalls that while serving in Burma he did not realize that the British Empire was dying nor that "it is a great deal better than the younger empires that are going to supplant it" (1. 236). Such a political deterioration is foreshadowed by the policeman's actions. At first, he arms himself with an "old . . . Winchester," an ineffective weapon; but preparing to kill the elephant if need be, he selects a weapon that emblemizes a rising empire that is far more skillfully destructive than the old ones: "The rifle was a beautiful German thing with cross-hair sights" (1. 240).

The shooting of the elephant is the slaying of the Old King, but the result is more winter, not renewed spring. If the elephant is the embodiment of a vitality rooted in the past, the creature's death heralds the deterioration of present and future times.

The slaying of the beast indicates, then, that in this essay Orwell is concerned with issues of greater importance than the paradoxes of British colonialism. Cultural decay, the devitalization of man's spirit, is Orwell's theme. In addition to presenting Orwell as the will-less minister of the ridiculous code of imperial rule, the killing also reveals the policeman as the victim of that code. In shooting the elephant, the white man is symbolically killing himself. The description of the elephant's death is the most forceful passage in the essay, and it is the event that evokes Orwell's most intense emotional reaction. The ability to make intellectual generalizations about the ludicrous paradoxes of colonialism deserts him as he confronts the dying beast.

> [The elephant] was breathing very rhythmically with long rattling gasps, his great mound of a side painfully rising and falling. His mouth was wide open—I could see far down into caverns of pale pink throat. . . . He was dying, very slowly and in great agony, but in some world remote from me where not even a bullet could damage him further. I felt that I had got to put an end to that dreadful noise. It seemed dreadful to see the great beast lying there, powerless to move and yet powerless to die, and not even to be able to finish him. I sent back for my small rifle and poured shot after shot . . . down his throat. They seemed to make no impression.

Unable to tolerate the sight of the dying elephant, he leaves the scene (1. 241–42).

One reason for the policeman's flight may be that the dying elephant is a sign of the imperialists' self-destructive future. The narrative suggests a shadowy identity among the policeman, the elephant, and the native it has crushed. In the opening paragraph, Orwell, discussing the Burmans' hostility to their British rulers, states that more than once a native had tripped him on the football field, much to the amusement of the native onlookers. This half-ludicrous indignity, which here represents the imperial rulers' absurd vulnerability, is indicative of a more perilous dilemma. While searching for the rampaging elephant, Orwell finds another man who has taken a fall—a corpse, its mouth fixed in the rictus of death, the body ground down into the mud, and its back stripped of skin by the weight of the elephant's foot.

When the policeman confronts the beast and realizes that he must shoot it, we see more clearly a link being formed between Orwell and the dead coolie. The narrator reminds us that the ground he was standing on "was soft mud into which one would sink at every step"; and the policeman, suddenly aware that the animal could crush him like a "toad under a steam-roller," sees himself "reduced to a grinning corpse like that Indian up the hill." Therefore, as though aping the corpse, he lies "down on the road" to get better aim (1. 240). As the essay moves toward its climax, we see the formation of bonds linking policeman, corpse, and mortally wounded beast. At the moment when the stricken elephant falls, we are made aware of the relationship existing among the three figures: ". . . down he came, his belly towards me, with a crash that seemed to shake the ground even where I lay" (1. 241). This juxtaposition of images—the elephant's collapse into the mud, the reminder that the policeman, too, is lying in the mud, like the dead Indian seen earlier—suggests the terrible condition shared by all three.

Also there is an interesting interchangeability of roles among these three. By mimicking the corpse, as it were, Orwell becomes, like the elephant, both slayer and slain. Furthermore, we have learned that the elephant as slayer has stripped the skin off his victim's back; and, similarly, after Orwell's shots have done their work, the Burmans strip the elephant's body almost to the bones. In effect, the elephant takes on the role of the mutilated native, while Orwell, agent of a destructive imperialism, indirectly acts the part of the elephant. Finally, the destructiveness of the natives is an equal sign that identifies Orwell with the slain elephant. Since the Burmans' thoughtless lust for blood causes the elephant's death, it is appropriate that at the start of the essay Orwell should regard himself as the "obvious target" of the resentful natives (1. 236).

It is worth observing that in expressing somewhat similar ideas in the essay "Marrakech" (1939), written around the time when *Coming Up for Air* was being completed, Orwell, appearing as a tourist and private citizen rather than as a colonial official, is a step closer to the ordinary man whose condition so interested him, although he still represents, at least generally, the white-skinned ruling class. The apparent purpose of this essay, based upon Orwell's experiences in French Morocco, is to reveal the manner in which the Europeans ignored the evils of colonial rule. In "Marrakech," the white population tolerates such a system because they do not—in a sense, they cannot—see the humanity of its victims. The brown-skinned Moroccan worker is practically invisible, as though blending in with the dry soil. Thus, the tourist, attentive only to the landscape, overlooks the native and his terrible poverty.

The essay records a series of encounters that enable Orwell to see the natives as suffering human beings. Morocco at first shyly beckons Orwell through a hungry Arab who asks him for some of the bread he is feeding to the gazelles in a public garden. Then, in the decay-filled ghettos, its call becomes demanding, inescapable, as sickly Jewish ghetto dwellers clamor for his cigarettes. Finally, meeting an old woman—whose body is bent beneath a heavy load of wood—Orwell voluntarily offers something of value—money—only to have the woman whom he describes as "mummified" (1. 391) utter a cry of shocked disbelief. One might add that if self-preservation is nature's first law, then his comment on the woman's stupefaction, that by taking notice of her he is "violating a law of nature," may have more than incidental significance. Watching a line of Negro soldiers, Orwell thinks that every European there with him is wondering how soon these blacks will turn against their white masters.

These events also represent the white man's growing readiness to accept some form of destruction. To make this clearer, we should examine more closely what is said about Morocco and the effects of colonial rule on the European. Perhaps the most striking feature of Orwell's Morocco is that it is a land of death. References to decay, barrenness, and death appear throughout his description of the place. Indeed, the essay begins with a funeral—"as the corpse went past the flies left the restaurant table in a cloud and rushed after it" (1. 387). A line of mourners passes through the marketplace, and later the corpse is thrown into a shallow, unmarked hole scraped out of the dry, sterile earth. The ghetto, where cramped working conditions turn children into physically warped adults, and streams of urine flow incontinently, as it were, down the lanes, is itself a great corpse aswarm with human flies (1. 389). The last scene of the piece has its own funereal atmosphere. Orwell describes a dusty column of native soldiers, their fine bodies squeezed into ill-fitting uniforms and bent under heavy packs, men "dragged from the forest to . . . catch syphilis in garrison towns" (1. 392–93).

We should note that in both essays Orwell, first as the policeman, then as the tourist, represents to a greater or lesser degree a ruling class that is threatened by some future calamity for which it itself is at least partly responsible. Also, in each essay one finds that both of the "central characters" are, or are in danger of being, victimized by circumstances over which they have no control. This dilemma is, of course, basically similar to those in which Orwell's fictional protagonists find themselves. The only important difference is that in the novels (as well as in *Down and Out*) the forces controlling and menacing the central characters are to some extent describable in narrowly psychosexual terms rather than in sociological ones. One of the most difficult problems Orwell was confronted with as a novelist was the artistically convincing fusion of these levels of reality.

Although *Coming Up for Air* has its faults, it marks an advance in Orwell's work. For one thing *Coming Up for Air*, like *Women in Love*, *Remembrance of Things Past*, and *Magic Mountain*, attempts to depict a whole society in a state of crisis, a "disintegrating civilization on the verge of an annihilating war."[6] Also we are aware of a more determined effort to relate the main character's personal anxiety to threatening aspects of his environment. Orwell's hero, or rather antihero, bears a more socially representative identity than do the earlier protagonists—outsiders, would-be rebels, or rootless wanderers whose physical and emotional isolation from the world of everyday humanity tends to call attention to the idiosyncratic nature of their personal dilemmas. George Bowling may not be convincing as Everyman, but he gives the impression of being much less a special case than are the earlier characters. As an underpaid insurance agent, henpecked husband, harassed father, *l'homme moyen sensuel*, disgruntled with contemporary life and nostalgic for a more decent past with which he cannot make contact, he is intended to be an "emblem for the English people."[7]

According to Orwell, the helpless passivity of Henry Miller's characters reflects a fantasy that was widespread during the thirties—the wish to escape from the social and political uncertainties of the age by retreating into a womblike state of indifference and irresponsibility. This, Orwell says, explains the popularity of the story of Jonah and the whale.[8] To some extent George Bowling's impulsive return to his boyhood home of Lower Binfield is motivated by a similar wish. Certainly one memory that draws him homeward is that of a hidden pond that, overlooked for years by fishermen, holds out the promise of a peace and timelessness insulated from the chaos and violence of the thirties: a "pool gets forgotten somehow, nobody fishes in it for years and decades and the fish grow to monstrous sizes."[9] George is ready to become a twentieth-century Jonah.

The journey back to the womb of the past is also the search for a woman. Early in the novel George, understandably worried that his false teeth and increasing girth have made him unattractive, thinks, "no woman . . . will ever look twice at me again, unless she's paid to" (p. 55). It is not by chance that Bowling feels moved to return to his original home only after winning money at the races. Particularly alluring is the thought of finding the secret pool and fishing in it, a hankering that, he believes at one point, money can turn into reality: "Fishing can be rented. . . . I'd . . . pay five pounds for a day's fishing in that pool" (p. 200). As George approaches his birthplace, he compares the undulating fields of wheat to a woman: "It makes you want to lie on it." Moreover this trip, taken without his shrewish wife's knowledge, is not an innocent act; George feels deeply guilty about this clandestine excursion (pp. 203–4).

The return to Lower Binfield teaches George that the old agrarian world is gone. The once peaceful hamlet is now an ugly industrial center, and the name *Bowling*—itself an evocation of a more joyful rustic past—is forgotten. Perhaps most significant is George's encounter with Elsie, who had been his first sexual partner many years in the past. Spotting the woman from a distance, George follows Elsie down the street and into her and her husband's shop, makes a purchase, and leaves, without being recognized. If this scene represents the transitory nature of youthful infatuation, it signifies also George's alienation from his mother and therefore from the past. Elsie is now a "tallish, fattish woman, . . . forty or fifty, in a . . .

shabby black dress" (p. 242). Earlier George remembered his mother as a "largish woman, a bit taller than Father, with . . . a tendency to wear black dresses" (p. 54). Elsie's husband is short, bald, wears a "big . . . moustache" and works his jaw in a "ruminative kind of way" (pp. 245–46). Similarly George's father is remembered as being a "small man," almost bald, with a large moustache, and given to talking "in a ruminative kind of way" (pp. 51–52). Although George again refers to Elsie as "my woman," it is clear that the two people, once intimate, are now estranged. George describes Elsie's rummaging through the various goods as the movements of an aged woman looking for something she has lost, and he recalls experiencing at the same moment a "cold, deadly, desolate feeling." As he pays Elsie for a pipe, we see that money will not bring back the lost mother or his childhood: "Our fingers just touched. No kick, no reaction. The body doesn't remember" (p. 247).

In recalling the events of his boyhood, the pleasant years prior to World War I, George unwittingly reveals the reason he cannot recapture the vitality of the past. The similarity of two memories indicates an underlying connection in his mind between sexuality and an oppressive sense of physical and emotional deterioration. One memory is that of young Bowling staring uneasily at a fish he had just caught as it lay dying on the bank of a pond (pp. 71–73); the other involves his initiation into sex with Elsie, who, like the fish, lies on the bank of the same pond (p. 123). Remembering his earlier relationship with Elsie, George thinks about how he had "done dirty" on her, an ambiguous reference to physical intimacy as well as to his refusal to visit her after the war. Later, searching for the old pool, George implies that adult experience must be rejected if the pond is to be regained. Learning that an insane asylum is now located on the same property, he is sure he will be allowed to roam freely through the area if he claims he is looking for a place to put his insane wife away. But on finding the secret pool, the "kind of place most people don't care to penetrate" (p. 250), George sees that someone has befouled it, "done dirty" on it too. This convinces him that there is no returning to the pastoral simplicity of childhood, no way to "put Jonah back into the whale." There is no more Lower Binfield existing as a "quiet corner" of his mind back into which he can slip (p. 267).

His past identity having been "sawn off at the roots" (p. 186), George becomes despondent. Clearly Orwell wants us to regard George's plight as representative of modern humanity, which, its "vital juice" exhausted, is sinking "into the grave" (p. 198). Thus George leaves Lower Binfield in a mood reflective of the impotence and lifelessness of modern man in general:

> I didn't have much more than three quid left after I'd paid the bill. They know how to cut it out of you at these . . . hotels. . . . I left my

new rod . . . in my bedroom. Let 'em keep it. . . . That kind of thing
doesn't happen any longer, it's just a dream, there'll be no more
fishing this side of the grave. (p. 266)

Looking at the George Hotel, which dates back to his boyhood, Bowling
notes that the old sign, a picture of St. George slaying a dragon, has been
replaced by a more contemporary St. George, a "regular pansy"; his
childhood home, once a seedsman's store, is now a genteel "dolled . . . up"
teashop (pp. 216–21 passim).

In the past, the church graveyard was situated in the center of town as a
reminder of the link between past and present. Now, George implies, the
deadness of contemporary man, his sense of lacking continuity with the
past, makes the graveyard an intolerable reminder of mortality: "Shove it
away—keep it out of sight! Can't bear to be reminded of death" (p. 213).
George himself is obsessed with death. Others may ignore it, but George is
all too aware of the graveyard "full to the brim" (p. 223). He is also obsessed
by the thought of England plunged into war and becoming totalitarian, an
idea that, as Kingsley Amis correctly suggests, is more a malediction than a
warning.[10] The sight of fake-Tudor houses, reminders that the past is really
irretrievable, evokes George's longing for a hand grenade (p. 255). Thus
the loss of his fishing rod, the useless phallus as well as the umbilical cord
severed from the womb of the past, leaves George with nothing except the
pathological certainty of (and perhaps wish for) a destructive future:

> *It's all going to happen.* All the things you've got at the back of your
> mind, the things you're terrified of, the things that you tell yourself
> are just a nightmare. . . . The bombs, . . . the rubber truncheons,
> . . . the machine-guns squirting out of bedroom windows. It's all going
> to happen. . . . It's just something that's got to happen. (p. 267)

The pressure of events and forebodings becoming intolerable, George
finally seeks refuge in a condition of mindless oblivion. His motives for
going to Lower Binfield are no longer of any interest to him, and he is
indifferent to the future. At the end of the novel, we see him sinking into a
comforting obliviousness: "The old life in Lower Binfield, the war and the
after-war, Hitler, Stalin, bombs, machine-guns, . . . rubber truncheons—
it was . . . all fading out" (p. 278).

However, George's final state presents us with a paradox. His final
descent into a sort of mental narcosis is in effect a return to the whale's
belly. What Orwell takes away from his hero he eventually gives back, and
the manner in which this happens reminds us of *A Clergyman's Daughter.*
Like George, Dorothy returns to her birthplace, and both are disappointed
in their attempt to find some consolatory link between what seems to have
been a happy past and an onerous present. Also, just as Dorothy is rumored
to have engaged in scandalous behavior, George's wife, Hilda, accuses him

of sexual hanky-panky. At the end of each novel, the central character retreats into a consciousness-shrunken condition. Furthermore, after their disillusioning journeys both return home certain of their innocent behavior (in response to Hilda's accusation the forlorn George sighs, "If only it had been true!" [p. 277]). But with Dorothy we see that the narrative is partly a surrealistic expression of her struggle to escape the guilt and fear springing from an incest fantasy, and the return to her father's house can take place only after she has renounced the flesh, severed instinct from consciousness. We also note that in concentrating on the inner, psychodramatic nature of Dorothy's adventures, Orwell leaves us puzzled concerning the facts of the situation. Something analogous appears in *Coming Up for Air*, where the author jostles probability enough to slip into a rather startling coincidence.

While in Lower Binfield, George hears over the radio that a certain Hilda Bowling is seriously ill. Suspecting a ruse, he at first does nothing; but later, fearing that she might really be sick, even dying, he rushes home, where he finds her all too healthy—and quite convinced of his philandering. Curiously the report appears not to be a ruse but simply a coincidence: it is some other Hilda Bowling who, as George decides, is dying. Such an intrusion of sheer coincidence is unnecessary to the plot, however, since even before hearing this news George had decided to leave Lower Binfield. But, in another way, this incident does serve a purpose, which becomes clear if we examine H. G. Wells's *The History of Mr. Polly* (1910), a novel that Orwell, since childhood an avid reader of Wells, probably had in mind while writing *Coming Up for Air*.[11]

Unable to tolerate life in the increasingly urbanized and industrialized England at the turn of the century, Mr. Polly deserts both business and wife in his search for a more humanly satisfying existence. Finally, Polly finds a sanctuary from the turbulence of contemporary England at Potwell Inn, a rustic survival from the old agrarian England. Indeed, the intrauterine serenity of the final scene in the novel—with Polly and the affectionate, rotund mistress of the inn sitting peacefully side by side—suggests that Wells's hero has returned to his primal home: "And it was as if [the evening landscape] was all securely within a great warm friendly globe of crystal sky. It was as safe and enclosed and fearless as a child that has still to be born."[12]

Coming Up for Air may be an ironic commentary on *Polly*, a realistic novel transformed into a wish-fulfilling romance. In Orwell's novel, the other Hilda, the dying woman, is becoming inaccessible, just as George's own mother and the womblike pool. At the same time, however, George's Hilda is still alive, still his woman, still watching over him, albeit censoriously. Here Orwell's treatment differs from Wells's. In *Polly*, the central character escapes from the wife who has kept him anchored to an unrewarding style of life and regains a maternal protectress, a mild, domesticated Earth Mother. In *Coming Up for Air*, this dichotomy is collapsed, for at the level of fantasy the cold, suspicious wife is also the ageless mother.

Hilda's suspicions regarding George's supposed sexual misbehavior are aroused by a Mrs. Wheeler, Hilda's friend and constant companion. Although she has appeared only once before, very briefly, in the novel, we now learn that she "knows all about . . . George" because she once had a husband "*just* like" him (p. 277). There is, moreover, another Wheeler in the novel, "Mother Wheeler." That this earlier Mother Wheeler is symbolically linked to George's memories of the dying fish and sex with Elsie is indicated by the fact that the odor of peppermint in the candy store is present also in the two other recollected scenes. (It may be significant that Elsie, the former girl friend whose identity merges with that of George's mother, runs a sweetshop in contemporary Lower Binfield.) Finally, if Mrs. Wheeler, who is certain of George's guilt, is Hilda's close friend, it should come as no surprise that George recalls his mother as having been an avid reader of a magazine entitled *Hilda's Home Companion* (p. 60).

It seems, therefore, that in George's mind the original mother has become fragmented, taking the forms of Mother Wheeler and the ever-watchful Hilda. More than this, she becomes the carp-filled pond, the gateway into a mythical Eden of the imagination that is not, George hopes, subject to time and decay.[13] The mother is also the dried-up, trash-polluted hole that betokens the sexual guilt that has robbed the pool of its vitalizing power within the protagonist's soul, and, to extend the significance of the image of the womb, the dark and comforting cavity of mindless passivity into which he descends at the end of the novel.

Why, we might ask, should George, whose trip to Lower Binfield convinces him that the past cannot be recaptured, actually regain the mother? And what is the connection between this reunion and the eradication of his political consciousness? A further examination of Wells's novel may provide answers.

Women play an important part in Polly's development. With his three affectionate female cousins he enjoys an innocent promiscuity; even with the least demonstrative one, Miriam, his future wife, there are hints of a bolder sensuality. Her hair in "disorder," she betrays an erotically tinged fascination with Polly's bicycle, marveling at the trouble involved in keeping it clean and expressing a special curiosity about the contents of "that little bag thing" on it. And as though accepting a sexual invitation, Polly, enthusiastically summoned to the young women's home, confidently pushes his bicycle into the "narrow, empty passage" of their hallway (pp. 110–11).

However, a later visit is much less promising. Retreating from the advances of the most ardent cousin, Polly rushes out to protect his bicycle from the teeth of a nonexistent dog; and as though bent on subduing something "up somewhere," he pinches the tire. Now Polly directs his attentions solely toward Miriam, whom he perceives for the first time as having a "lean and insufficient body" (p. 147).

This changed attitude stems from Polly's meeting with the schoolgirl Christabel as he is bicycling down a country lane between visits to his cousins. This "maiden" who, perched atop a wall enclosing the school grounds, repeatedly stresses her need to stay in "bounds," arouses "daring thoughts" within him (pp. 123, 129). His clumsy attempt to scale her wall, to go beyond bounds, results in cuts, abrasions, and humiliation. Significantly Polly tells his cousins' mother that his wounds resulted from a bicycle accident (p. 138).

Later his aunt's colloquial greeting of "Law!" takes on a phonetic appropriateness, for now merely touching one of the cousins makes the chastened gallant feel guilty (pp. 138–40). As though signifying the end of Polly's sensual experience, Wells's Miriam (primly alarmed at the habitually unbuttoned state of her mother's blouse) resolutely closes the "gaping orifice" at the moment Polly announces his intention to marry the girl (p. 159).[14] Miriam's action suggests too that Polly, in assuming the role of husband, is exiling himself from the mother, the past.

Earlier Polly spontaneously associates the curiously homelike appeal of a Gothic cathedral with "portly capons," his term for medieval churchmen (p. 59). The process by which he regains the maternal past involves his own transformation into a portly capon. In rejecting the stresses of a sensually, frustrating middle-class domesticity, a petty bourgeois life of emotional constraint, Polly abandons his sexual identity. One of his most important duties at the inn is the defense of the premises, particularly the orchard, from "predators"—mainly Jim, a local troublemaker, who, one-eyed and serpentine, stands for the phallicism threatening the Garden's purity. Especially vulnerable is the owner's nine-year-old niece whom Jim, intent on "giving her ideas," is turning into a "little beast" (pp. 280–89 passim). In ridding Potwell Inn of the covertly lecherous Jim, Polly is actually casting off that part of himself that threatens to undermine his position there: at the first sight of Polly the proprietress takes him for the ruffian; in having deserted Miriam and in having accepted insurance money for a fire he himself started in his shop during a bungled suicide attempt, Polly is, like Jim, a truant and a thief (pp. 271, 284).

Polly's mock-epic battles with Jim involve not simply the latter's ouster from the inn but also the alienation of Polly's stressful phallic self. The first encounter, a tug-of-war over a broom, ends with Polly's release of the implement, sending it and Jim into the river. Jim's second defeat involves the loss of his weapon, an eel, which, wrested from his grip, becomes a "mere looping relic on the sward." In his final retreat from the inn, Jim runs off with Polly's rifle, a "foul and dirty" instrument that our hero has kept carefully hidden in the bedroom away from the eyes of the inn's mistress (pp. 302–16 passim).

The central character's regeneration—his ultimate renunciation of the phallic identity associated with the adult world of competition, struggle, disharmony, and frustration—is symbolized by the drowned Jim, who, dressed in Polly's clothes, is mistaken for the latter. Thus in ousting Jim, the brutish and libidinal part of himself, Polly achieves a childlike innocence. Earlier, vaguely wishing to escape the irreconcilable tensions produced in him by Christabel (sensual longing versus romantic idealization), Polly wishes that his were a girl's name (p. 127). At Potwell Inn, his wish comes true. "Polly" becomes a girl's name (that of the innkeeper's little niece). In protecting the innocence of his prepubescent namesake, Wells's hero is in effect allowing his anima—the femininely passive child-self untainted and uncoarsened by the adult world of struggle and frustration and guilt—to rise to the surface.

The ironic treatment of Wells's mixture of comic realism and romance was Orwell's way of asserting the difference between himself and his Edwardian predecessors. Several years after the appearance of *Coming Up for Air*, Orwell claimed that because Wells was a prewar writer he was totally unaware of social and political developments beyond England's shores. Like such contemporaries as Bennett, Shaw, and Barrie, Wells was "untouched by any European influence." If this insularity sustained the Edwardians' faith in the notion of progress, it has also made their view of life anachronistic: "It is very rare," Orwell claimed, "to find in a writer of that time anything we should now regard as a sense of history."[15] The implication is that he himself, a man of the uneasy thirties, does have a sense of history.

Polly's flight into a desexualized pastoral Eden, with its innocent maiden and maternally benevolent employer, implies a degree of optimism regarding the individual's ability to change his life for the better. On the other hand, for Orwell's protagonist there are no rural sanctuaries offering a refuge from the oppressiveness of modern life. In *Polly*, destruction leads to a comic resolution: when the fire Polly starts in his shop spreads to neighboring buildings, he saves an old lady's life and becomes a local hero, a plot reversal that, in freeing Polly from his helplessness, prepares him to overcome the obstacles between him and the blissful world of Potwell Inn, Old England. But in *Coming Up for Air*, destruction is not regenerative. The partial destruction of Lower Binfield from an accidental bombing by a British airplane foreshadows the mass destruction that George and his contemporaries await as an unavoidable apocalypse: the explosion is "like the Day of Judgment" (p. 262).

In contrast to Polly, George cannot recover a secure and peaceful past because he is menaced from within as well as from without. The ersatz frankfurter that at one point seems to explode in his mouth—he calls these sausages bombs (p. 28)—links him to one of the bombed buildings in Lower Binfield:

> Its wall, the one that joined the greengrocer's shop, was ripped off as neatly as if someone had done it with a knife. But what was extraordinary was that in the upstairs rooms nothing had been touched. It was just like looking into a doll's house. . . . But the lower rooms had caught the force of the explosion. There was a frightful smashed-up mess of bricks, plaster, chair-legs, bits of varnished dresser, rags of tablecloth, piles of broken plates and chunks of scullery sink. A jar of marmalade had rolled across the floor, leaving a long streak of marmalade behind, and running side by side with it there was a ribbon of blood. (pp. 264–65)

This structure, its wall torn away to reveal the interior, represents a disturbing truth about George and, by extension, contemporary society in the same way that the multi-storied Ekdal home in Ibsen's *The Wild Duck* exposes the contradictory forces at work within both the individuals and the society of late-nineteenth-century Europe. People, George included, may try to delude themselves into thinking that their civilization will survive, that the menace from abroad cannot radically alter traditional ways of life. But the wreckage below indicates that the unconscious mind, the soul, is already stricken.

What Orwell is questioning is the Edwardian myth of the autonomous self, the individual largely unconditioned by social and personal determinants and therefore free to unfold and fulfill himself. In other words, what Orwell is criticizing is the assumption that man's essential humanity, his progressive development as a human being, exists apart from history, apart from social, economic, and political factors.

Moreover in *Coming Up for Air* Orwell closely scrutinizes any type of literature—Wellsian comic realism, the modernist psychological novel, and even his own earlier works—in which such factors are not granted their due importance. If the narrator's references to decidedly nonvirile males (who seem to have inherited the English earth) call attention to the alarming distance between modern civilization and a more vital past, his passing remarks on the decadent effeminacy of art in present-day Lower Binfield—the unmanly St. George, the "dolled up" hotel, the "arty-looking sign" in front of the tea shop—suggest that in the thirties, when the insularity of British society is about to be massively violated by outside forces, the artistic ideal is still that of a narcissistic emphasis on the personal and private. Contemporary art reveals a Proustian obsession with the flaws and perversities of the isolated psyche. That this reclusive homosexual's

exploration into the past and into the imagination of his fictional persona—
the Marcel of *Remembrance*—is an artistic anachronism in the thirties is
suggested by George's revulsion at the mass-produced sausage he has once
bitten into: "And then suddenly—pop! The thing burst in my mouth like a
rotten pear. A . . . horrible soft stuff was oozing all over my tongue" (p. 27).
Unlike the madeleine cake that opens the way back into Marcel's interiorized past, the exploding sausage betokens the alienation of Orwell's
narrator from a regenerative past, just as does the likelihood that before
long enemy bombs will obliterate the building that, once the Bowling seed
store, is now a shop serving "HOME-MADE CAKES" (p. 221).

In Orwell's earlier novels, we have seen that often there is only a tenuous
connection between society and the central characters' private anxieties
and longings. So obsessive are their problems that the attempt to escape
from them becomes in effect a flight from time itself, a rejection of one's
historical identity. Although George Bowling sinks down into a domestic
womb where the problems of the world are reduced to the comic postcard
dimensions of a shrewish wife's jealous anger,[16] there is some evidence that
here Orwell is more conscious of the need to break free from the psychological insularity of his earlier fiction. One sign of this is the reappearance of
Nobby, in *A Clergyman's Daughter* the good father of the heroine's private
fantasy. Now Nobby appears as one of George Bowling's comrades-in-arms
during World War I. However, instead of inhabiting the dreamworld of the
central character's Kentish birthplace, Nobby is set in the un-idyllic landscape of war-ravaged France (pp. 95–99). The first Nobby plays his part
within the closet drama of his companion's unconscious emotional life; the
second Nobby moves across the vast stage of modern history.

Even more significant is Orwell's attempt to de-individualize Bowling,
to plane away idiosyncratic elements in order to evoke a more broadly
allegorical resonance. Even more than with the Gran'pa Comstock allegory
in *Aspidistra* Orwell tries to convince us that the protagonist's personal
troubles are both a symptom and sign of a cultural malaise. Thus Bowling's
sexual uneasiness and alienation from the maternally restorative female is
indicative of the plight of an industrial society uprooted from the agrarian
past and consequently unable to control its latent destructiveness.

Orwell's use of a first-person narrator is an attempt to bridge the gap
between the central character and the world around him. As long as the
narrator's symbolic and allegorical function is clearly established, there
need be no discontinuity between the public self, the self existing within a
realistically described society, and the private self; since both selves are
being re-created in the narrator's memory, both external and internal
modes of experience are united in a shared subjectivity. Because the
subjective view of reality is no longer confusingly divided between fictional

character and authorial narrator, as in earlier novels, it should be easier for Orwell to skirt the problem of reconciling psychological and sociological levels of meaning.

However, in trying to invest the activities and feelings of this "ordinary bloke" with a more general significance, Orwell puts before us a patchwork character.[17] It strains plausibility that "Tubby" Bowling—a lower-middle-class insurance agent with little formal education, by his own admission vulgar and insensitive (p. 23)—has read, among others, Conrad, D. H. Lawrence, Wilde, George Moore, and even Ibsen, and that he should be a close friend of an Oxford-educated classical scholar whom he presciently lectures on the contemporary political situation (pp. 185–86). One cannot help feeling uneasy when Bowling begins making solemn generalizations about modern man's devitalized condition. This voice from the third-class carriage is a little too self-consciously that of the maimed Fisher King taking the reader on a lecture tour through the waste land of the 1930s.

Actually there are two central characters sharing the same surname: Tubby Bowling the ordinary bloke of limited mentality, frustrated, passive, and ripe for a mindless acceptance of destruction, and George Bowling the sociopolitical cognoscente who is quick, perhaps too quick, to make weighty pronouncements about the plight of twentieth-century humanity. The latter, the all-knowing sage and seer, is in fact an Orwellian mask. Realizing that one of George's main functions is to make rhetorical generalizations on the basis of the troubles of his less enlightened alter ego—Tubby the common man—we may begin to suspect that the experiences of Orwell's central character do not generate quite the allegorical resonance needed for a "big subject." The glibness with which the narrator as wise man insists on this resonance raises doubts in our minds.

Orwell himself was not entirely convinced that in *Coming Up for Air* he successfully merged public and private levels of reality. A decade after the novel's publication, he admitted that the narrator's personality is that of his own. Orwell's explanation regarding this is interesting for what it indicates about the relationship between the writer and his personal feelings and experiences. "One difficulty I have never solved," he stated, "is that one has masses of experience which one passionately wants to write about, e.g. the part about fishing . . . and no way of using them up except by disguising them as a novel."[18] The fact that fishing is closely connected to the protagonist's personal fears and longings and symbolic of the instinctual, life-affirming energy no longer present in contemporary society makes us assume that in *Coming Up for Air* Orwell is engaged in a strenuous, even if not entirely successful, effort to transform personally obsessive material into a more general vision of reality.

Moreover the irony in *Polly* is evidence that Orwell was willing to confront, perhaps also challenge, his past. Because *Coming Up for Air* is an implicit criticism of Wells—who "fascinated" the young Blair and was a "very early influence" on him[19]—we may regard this novel as the author's reappraisal of ideas and attitudes carried over from the days of his youth, from his Edwardian past.

The two Bowlings may be viewed as different and conflicting aspects of their creator. Bowling the narrator is a skeptical and realistic Orwell who, alert to the political and cultural crises of the twentieth century, feels duty bound to explode the Edwardian myth of the individual unconditioned by irrational, unpredictable forces in society or in himself and therefore master of his private and public destiny. Another Orwell—one insulated from history by an obsessive concern with narrowly personal dilemmas, drawn more to the underground world of nightmare and wish-fulfilling fantasy, by turns passive and escapist—is represented by Tubby Bowling, who, despite the appearance of being disarmingly ordinary, is the latest in that line of Orwellian protagonists who are victimized by self-defeating illusions of personal inviolability and, as literary creations, are defined in so singular and idiosyncratic a fashion as to undermine their usefulness in terms of broader thematic purposes. Although at the conclusion of *Coming Up for Air* the two Bowlings (and the two Orwells) remain divided, we sense that now, as the age of Hitler and Stalin encroach upon the world of Wells and Proust, Orwell is becoming more aware of the urgent need to examine critically his own literary aims, practices, and allegiances.

Chapter VII

Politics and the Imagination

Although Orwell assumes various roles in his writings—social critic, moralist, patriot, iconoclast, psychologist, man of letters—his works tend to share a bipolar vision of reality. Often this bipolar structure takes the form of more or less sharply antithetical terms, such as decay versus vitality, ignorance opposed to awareness, or innocence set against guilt. These terms mark the limits that define the "movement" within a work or group of works. For instance, in both Orwell's novels and nonfiction we may observe an individual moving from a state of innocence to a state of guilt or between some form of vitality and deterioration. The movement may terminate when one pole, one alternative, exerts a decisive pull.

This is, of course, a rather simplified model of what is frequently a more complex situation: although these pairs of antitheses are not always of equal importance in a particular work, it would be difficult to find an instance when the appearance of one pair does not suggest the presence of other contrastive states. Thus the decay-survival antithesis may be implicitly relevant to those writings in which either the guilt-innocence or concealment-exposure duality, or both, are prominent elements.

Underlying these polarities is the opposition between integrity and violation, an opposition basic to Orwell's vision of reality. Implying wholeness, integrity takes such forms as the continuity between past and present; an awareness of one's relationship to society; an ability to make moral distinctions and act on them; the interpenetration of thought and feeling; and a sense of one's living connection with nature. The violation of this wholeness endangers the intellectual, emotional, and moral integrity of the individual and even society in general. As we have seen, once a violation occurs, Orwell's protagonists become trapped in an intolerably polarized reality. Their attempts to regain their original wholeness are often futile and, in some cases, disastrous. The effort to negate the disruptive effects of violation by ignoring them simply emphasizes the fragmentation within these characters.

Violation, *polarities*, and *fragmentation* are not just thematic elements confined to Orwell's novels; these terms can be equally relevant to his essays and reportage. One example is the decency versus evil polarity that structured his vision of society, a polarity manifesting itself in several ways. First, it appears as a contrast between a relatively humane past and an immoral present. Second, within the present (which for Orwell usually meant the second quarter of the twentieth century, the age of totalitarianism) the evils of political participation stand opposed to the relative innocence of apolitical modes of existence. Also the manner in which Orwell expresses this bipolar vision sometimes indicates his own desire to segregate the condition of innocence from that of guilt, to keep the former inviolate. Moreover, we should note that although Orwell does not ignore the observable effects of men's actions, he is usually more interested in states of mind, the inner self as it is affected by this polarity as well as by any other.

In comparing past to present, Orwell regards the former as a time when men were relatively free of the awareness of evil. The dominant characteristic of the boys' magazines *Gem* and *Magnet*, which date back to pre-World War I days, is an innocence of either actual or potential immorality. The problem of sex never arises, and the snob appeal of these magazines, with their emphasis on wealth, is "completely shameless."[1] The attitudes embodied in this literature reflect our forebears' guiltless enjoyment of material prosperity.

Apparently forgetting the social criticisms of, among many others during the nineteenth century, Dickens, Henry Mayhew, and Engels, Orwell claims that up until World War I money was worshipped with an untroubled conscience. In fact, a "glittering car, a title or a horde of servants was mixed up in people's minds with the idea of actual moral virtue."[2] On the basis of this view of the past, Orwell can defend Kipling against modern detractors who attack his easy acceptance of imperialism. Orwell says that the contemporary mind, oppressed by an awareness of economic injustice, cannot pass a fair judgment on a man possessing a nineteenth-century mentality. Kipling was unaware of the economic exploitation underlying imperialistic expansionism; to him imperialism was not a money-making concern but rather a "sort of forcible evangelising."[3] Orwell's Kipling may be unenlightened, but he, like the colonial administrators who shared his outlook, is not a conscious mouthpiece for capitalist exploitation.

The past is also characterized by a code of ethics that, Orwell assumed, finds expression in the popular literature of the age. A standard situation in the old-fashioned boys' magazines is that of a youth who, accused of a misdeed actually committed by another boy, adheres to the sportsman's code by refusing to reveal the truth.[4] Raffles, E. W. Hornung's famous burglar, also embodies an older set of values. Raffles lives by the code of a gentleman, and whatever remorse he may feel over his thefts springs from an awareness of having brought shame upon his school tie, of having exiled himself from upper-class society.[5] Raffles accepts society's values (he will neither steal from a host nor commit murder), and in the end he redeems himself by a patriot's death.

In view of the importance Orwell attaches to one's childhood vision of life (a subject I shall deal with in Chapter VIII), it is appropriate that his picture of the uncorrupted innocence of nineteenth-century North Americans is derived from such works as *Helen's Babies* and *Little Women*. The characters in these books, presumably like the people who lived in the last century, "have something that is perhaps best described as integrity, or good morale, founded on unthinking piety."[6]

Once in a while the decency of the past can even mitigate the evils of modern life. The refusal of the Spanish police, engaged in one of the political witch hunts that marked the moral corruption of the republic during the Civil War, to turn his wife out of bed while searching the Orwells' apartment is evidence that even with the triumph of Franco the nobility of the Spaniards, a nobility that does "not really belong to the twentieth century," will at least make Spanish fascism bearable.[7]

Frequently Orwell's thinking tended toward a dichotomy along class lines, with the lower classes set apart by their goodness from their social superiors. In *The Road to Wigan Pier*, Orwell finds a pure spirit of equality among tramps. Free of prejudice, this social stratum is, according to him, "a small squalid democracy—perhaps the nearest thing to a democracy . . . in England" (p. 187). In "The Lion and the Unicorn" (1941), he points out that justice and liberty are still articles of faith among the common people of England, in contrast to the general cynicism of the age.[8] Moreover their feelings and attitudes have remained basically Christian in an unChristian era (2. 59).

Especially important are Orwell's views regarding the common man's relative freedom from the modern evil of power worship. Somewhat simplistically taking popular literature as a direct reflection of the masses' attitudes and values, Orwell claims that despite the success of violence-filled novels, one still expects from "low-brow fiction" a clear distinction between moral and immoral behavior.[9] Boys' weekly magazines exhibit this same disinclination to hold up crime and immorality for the admiration of their readers (mainly lower-middle-class and working-class youths).[10]

The comic art popular among the English common people reflects a political outlook uncontaminated by the hatreds of a fiercely ideological age. Orwell observes that after the rise of Hitler, jokes directed at Jews disappeared from comic postcards, and even the anti-Hitler sentiments of these cards lacked any real vindictiveness.[11] The political attitudes of the characters in the boys' weeklies provide Orwell with what he considers a valuable clue to the patriotism of the common people. Untainted by admiration of power-politics or ideological brutality, these fictional schoolboys, like their real-life devotees, exhibit a patriotism as deeply rooted as it is unconcerned with the political turbulence beyond England's shores.[12]

Whether or not it is an exaggeration to say, as does T. R. Fyvel, that Orwell's most strongly held belief was that the Great War had shut modern man off from a world of innocence and security, it is clear that Orwell regarded the post-Edwardian age as socially and culturally decadent.[13] He saw the latter as a period when the money worship of the upper classes had led to a callous indifference to the plight of those lower down the social scale.

In *Down and Out*, he bitterly attacks capitalist society, especially the debasement suffered by English tramps, the most economically depressed group in the nation. Forced into tramphood by the instability of the capitalist system, the vagrant is a constant victim of injustice. In *Wigan Pier*, Orwell expresses deep moral revulsion at the way the cash nexus is coarsening human relationships. To the Brookers, owners of a seedy lodging house in Wigan, the miserable old-age pensioners who room there are simply burdens. The landlords feel nothing but loathing for one boarder, who is dying of cancer, because he is a financial liability, and they are "quite openly pining for him to die" so that they can claim his insurance benefits (pp. 13–14).

Although granting in *Wigan Pier* that socialism can produce an egalitarian society, Orwell complains that bourgeois socialists hold a vicious set of values. Unlike the "warm-hearted . . . typical working-class Socialist," who, in Orwell's somewhat sentimentalized view, wants simply to abolish poverty, the typical middle-class socialist is an "inhuman" individual quite ready to "throw our present civilisation down the sink" (p. 214).

During the early and middle 1930s, Orwell constantly thought in terms of class structure. However, as the international situation became more threatening, his polarizing tendency shifted away from this rather Manichaean dualism between the lower and upper classes and assumed a form indicating an increasing concern over political authoritarianism. In line with this newer interest Orwell increasingly emphasized the theme of violation. He felt that any educated man living in the 1930s was, unlike men of the past, almost inevitably drawn into politics. But instead of satisfying the imperatives of one's social conscience, political commitment introduced one to a world of madness and even greater guilt: "In our age there is no such thing as 'keeping out of politics.' All issues are political issues, and politics itself is a mass of lies, evasions, folly, hatred and schizophrenia."[14]

One of the more significant aspects of this and similar warnings is their special relevance to a social type to which Orwell himself belonged, the writer-intellectual. The contemporary writer's knowledge of social evils and the personal guilt to which such knowledge gives rise compel him to become so involved with current problems that a purely aesthetic outlook becomes impossible, and a sense of shame attaches itself to any ideas that are not progressive, democratic, and revolutionary.[15] The resulting compulsion to "falsify his subjective feelings" is a sign that the writer is no longer autonomous. Ideally he is exercising his freedom when he caricatures and distorts external reality to convey his own ideas, but it is a mark of bondage when, because of political pressures, he begins to deny his personal convictions, to misrepresent the "scenery of his own mind."[16]

This mental scenery, akin to the old Protestant inner light, is subtly contaminated by an atmosphere of political orthodoxy that filters deep into the mind. The critic motivated by parti pris may judge a work even before reading it, "and yet, with a dishonesty that sometimes is not even quarter-conscious, the pretence is kept up that genuinely literary standards are being applied."[17] The novelist is in a particularly dangerous position. Almost a Protestant art form, the novel can be produced, Orwell maintained, only by free and autonomous individuals, not by "orthodoxy-sniffers" or men "conscience-stricken about their own unorthodoxy."[18] But political discipline demands group loyalties, which in turn lead not only to artistic falsification but also to a desiccation of the writer's power of invention.[19]

In calling attention to the way ideology violates the imagination and intellect, Orwell is in effect examining his own dilemma as artist and thinker, just as he earlier examined his morally equivocal role as imperial policeman in "A Hanging" and "Shooting an Elephant." There is, however, an interesting difference between the Burma essays and those dealing with the politically committed intellectual. In the former, Orwell the narrator and his earlier self are separated by a span of years; there is a distance between the essayist, situated in the 1930s, and his morally intolerable position as imperial policeman during the twenties. But in the later essays, Orwell is writing about immanent dangers, about forces threatening him and his fellow writers at that moment. Because these are immediate and personal dilemmas, his works of the late thirties and forties indicate an urgent need to grapple with these problems now, not later. Moreover the stakes are higher for Orwell the writer-intellectual than for Orwell the imperial policeman: the policeman can, as Blair eventually did, at least partly free himself from his intolerable situation by quitting the service and exposing the evils and follies of colonialism as an Orwell unburdened by uniform and rank. But, one may ask, can the writer abandon his profession and suppress his imagination? Can the intellectual cease thinking and stifle his need to examine and criticize the world around him? The potential dilemma of the modern writer is more complex and subtle, the struggle to maintain his integrity more fierce, because the violation he risks by an ideological commitment may affect the deepest levels of his mind, like the bomb that demolished the bottom level of the house in Lower Binfield.

Begun about a month after Orwell left Spain because of a serious bullet wound in the neck, *Homage to Catalonia* (1938) is valuable not simply as an eyewitness account of the Aragon front from January to May 1937 but also as an expression of the writer's entry into the labyrinth of modern politics and his maneuverings to avoid moral contamination.[20]

In Orwell's retrospective view, the combat zone along the Aragon front, where ideological differences are absent and an egalitarian atmosphere prevails among the ranks, is a near-classless society (p. 27). Far behind the lines, journalists are busy writing lies about rival anti-Fascist factions, whereas in the trenches, surrounded by men of every shade of left-wing belief, Orwell, a member of the Trotskyist POUM, is never once called a traitor (p. 65).

In terms of Orwell's bipolar design, the front is morally redeeming. Here "nearly all of the vicious hatreds of the political parties evaporated" (p. 202).[21] To some extent, the fighting front is a moral sanctuary: cut off from the outside world, Orwell has only a "dim conception" of Barcelona's backsliding into evil, the reappearance of class divisions and the various political factions more hostile to one another than to Franco (pp. 66, 103, 110–11).

The Orwell who appears in the pages of *Homage to Catalonia* is a political innocent who almost by chance finds his way into the trenches of the progovernment forces and later is exposed to the ideological malevolence that is undermining the moral and political integrity of the anti-Franco forces. Orwell's reaction to this treachery and violence is that of the honest soldier trying to remain inviolate from the evils around him. In recounting his naive (and dangerous) plan, while visiting his wife in Barcelona, to take a holiday on the beach, even though he belonged to a Trotskyist faction being hunted down by opponents, Orwell is suggesting that at that time his mind was so untouched by the prevailing ideological hysteria that he was unable even to think in terms of partisan hatreds (p. 117).

In Orwell's account, the polarization of good and evil, decency and treachery, expresses itself even in terms of spatial relationships. Mingling among the workers who are blocking the Barcelona streets with sandbags in preparation for internecine fighting, Orwell the soldier longs to get a weapon. But later, looking down on this activity from atop a tall building, he sees the utter folly of the workers' thirst for combat (pp. 127–30 passim).

Although the narrator occasionally looks with irony on his earlier attempts to remain naively innocent of politics, the structure of the narrative itself, in which the chapters dealing with ideological conflicts (chapters 5, 9–11, 13, and 14) are more or less segregated from descriptions of front-line life (chapters 1–4, 6–8), implies a need to keep his relatively innocent war experiences free from the moral taint of political treachery. A similar strategy underlies his shifting attitude in the book toward England. Early in *Homage*, he contrasts the simple idealism of the Spaniards with the cynicism to be found in the "hard-boiled, sneering civilization of the English-speaking races" (p. 6); but near the end, looking back on the reign of terror that, as he sees it, has nullified revolutionary idealism, he thinks of

England as almost a realm of innocence: "It is not easy to [describe the conditions in Spain] because . . . the thing essential to such an atmosphere does not exist in England. In England political intolerance is not yet taken for granted" (p. 198).

Although Orwell the writer-turned-soldier loses innocence to the extent that he is forced into a disillusioning awareness of ideological brutality, he still preserves his personal humane feelings. He is an observer of evil doings, in some degree a victim, but not a participant. He remains an onlooker, one who is, after all, only passing through the country of political malevolence.

Yet there is in *Homage* a tonal and stylistic shift indicating a movement from relative innocence to a less welcome condition. Six of the first seven chapters deal with the Aragon front, and in these chapters Orwell's narrative voice ranges from dryly humorous descriptions of his initial culture shock to boyish enthusiasm at roughing it to sheer outrage at his possible death to pity for the soldiers carrying him back to an ambulance. Of the last seven chapters, six deal with the betrayals and purges going on in Barcelona, and in this section the tonal range shrinks considerably. The anecdotes convey Orwell's emotional fatigue, confusion, and bitterness. Those passages defending the Trotskyists—passages studded with the initials of the various factions, with newspaper quotations, and the enumerated points of Orwell's arguments ("i . . . ii . . . iii . . .")—are about as gripping as a legal brief and confirm his claim that political partisanship and vivid prose do not mix. The way in which the account of sordid ideological cunning and viciousness gradually encroach upon the more humanly appealing material concerning the decency and heroism at the front reminds one of Orwell's forebodings about the political ice age settling over Europe.

If the political infighting taking place in Barcelona affected Orwell's style, the urgent need to alert the West against the evils of Stalinist Russia resulted in at least one significant slip of the pen. At one point in *Animal Farm* (1945), Orwell gives us a curious piece of misinformation. Ben the donkey and the mare Clover are standing before a barn on the wall of which is written the terrible truth about the revolution: ALL ANIMALS ARE EQUAL BUT SOME ARE MORE EQUAL THAN OTHERS. Because Clover's eyesight is failing, "for once," the narrator states, Ben consents "to break his rule" against reading.[22] But this is not true. Once before he has broken his "rule"—when reading aloud the sign on the side of the van that reveals the approaching death of the horse Boxer at the slaughterhouse (p. 101).

This discrepancy is as puzzling as it is interesting. Given the fable's brevity and simplicity of plot, one wonders how so obvious an inconsistency could have survived a revision, especially since at the time of writing

Animal Farm Orwell was so alarmed at the way journalists and political leaders were distorting the truth. Also we are reminded of discrepancies in earlier works that reveal covert aims and attitudes. To grasp the implications of this misstatement, we must examine Orwell's views on the political crises of the age.

In his writings as well as in his life, Orwell has a knack for turning weakness into strength. In *Wigan Pier*, the recognition of guilt in having participated in the "spiritually ugly . . . bullying" of imperial service has made him especially alert to his contemporaries' inclination toward power worship, and the ex-policeman's disgust at "every form of man's dominion over man" (p. 180) has sharpened his concern for the oppressed and exploited. So intense does his feeling for the goodness of the lower classes become that in *Wigan Pier* he asserts that the social and spiritual regeneration of England depends on the middle and upper classes abandoning their class values and leveling themselves downward (pp. 193–94).

In 1941, Orwell was convinced that England was becoming a classless society. Technological advances had facilitated the mass production of inexpensive housing, clothes, food, and entertainment, with the result that there would no longer be any significant difference in the tastes and habits of the English. But to his dismay the leveling had been upward. Bourgeois society was absorbing the workers, rather than the reverse, and was planing away their class characteristics: "The old style 'proletarian'— collarless, unshaven and with muscles warped by heavy labour—still exists, but he is constantly decreasing in numbers. . . ." The product of capitalism rather than the socialist movement, this new society of skilled technicians and professionals represents the same break with the past that Orwell feared was the goal of bourgeois socialists: "It is a . . . restless, cultureless life, centring round tinned food, *Picture Post*, the radio and the internal combustion engine." It was a disturbingly modern society, a "civilisation in which children grow up . . . in complete ignorance of the Bible."[23]

Orwell's alarm resulted from his suspicion that this newer civilization was violating England's past rather than uniting it nationally. Orwell's increasing disenchantment with socialism as a practical means for social regeneration may be attributable to his conviction that this unfortunate upward leveling was continuing even with the advent of the postwar Labour government.

Orwell's reaction to contemporary political events both at home and abroad was one of pessimism, if not despair. Early in World War II, he claimed to have known since 1931 that a disastrous future was approaching.[24] After Germany's defeat he foresaw no likely alternative to either increasingly destructive wars or the rise of vast and enduring slave empires.[25] To blame was a revolutionary activity, which was more harmful than good: "We are living in a nightmare," Orwell wrote during the forties, "precisely *because* we have tried to set up an earthly paradise."[26] The Russian revolution was inherently fated to degenerate into tyranny, with or without Stalin, for the idealism of all successful revolutions was "fatally mixed up" with the selfish longing to wield power.[27] Attempts to reorganize society by force had only directed the course of history along a downward spiral, so that "once [a revolutionary] struggle is well over, there is always the conservative who is more progressive than the radicals who have triumphed."[28] In the end, revolutionary idealism faded away, and what remained was a "cult of power" openly celebrating brutality as an end in itself.[29] Contrasting the "innate decency" of the working class to the immoral opportunism of its leaders, Orwell was "almost driven" to conclude that "men are only decent when they are powerless."[30]

The conflict in Orwell between the need to protect England from foreign invasion and the danger of national self-violation expresses itself in his political writings of the forties by a back-and-forth movement between the conviction that the defense of England demands a quick, forcible regeneration of society and a fear of seeing revolution actually break out. England will defeat Hitler, he claimed, only if it fights "against the sins of its own past."[31] But as he points out in "The Lion and the Unicorn," these sins are still unpurged. Capitalism has shown itself to be criminally indifferent to the nation's wartime needs: domestic luxuries abound while shortages of arms and supplies have brought the nation to the edge of military collapse. And this potentially disastrous "tug-of-war between private profit and public necessity" continues. England is still the world's most class-ridden nation—Orwell wrote during the early days of the war—a land of privilege and snobbery governed by the "old and silly" (2. 67). The adverse effects of this situation are immediate and dangerous: ". . . the lady in the Rolls-Royce car is more damaging to morale than a fleet of Goering's bombing planes" (2. 90).

The solution was obvious. In 1940, announcing vehemently that only a revolution could save England, Orwell envisioned the day when the London gutters would "run with blood" and "red militias" would billet "in the Ritz."[32] Less than a year later, he proclaimed in "The Lion and the Unicorn" that for socialism to succeed there must be a change in both the structure of English society and its leadership—"New blood, new men . . . a revolution" (2. 83). His language was uncompromising: socialists must "drive" pro-Fascists out of the government and "wipe out" injustices (2. 94).

Yet at the same time Orwell shies away from revolution in "The Lion and the Unicorn." If in one passage he sounds like a Trotsky demanding quick, violent action, in another he is an early Shaw calling for peaceful reform. England becomes for him less a Darwinian jungle than a rather stuffy

Victorian family in which rich relatives lord it over poor ones and the lives of the young rest in the hands of "irresponsible uncles and bed-ridden aunts." Still, the English ruling class is not so much wicked as unteachable, and one does not slaughter dull-witted uncles and gouty aunts. A less fiery Orwell claims that revolution does not mean crimson banners and shooting in the streets (2. 68–86 passim). And two years after the writing of "The Lion and the Unicorn" Orwell's call for social change has lost all its urgency. He still wants the common man to gain a better life "sooner and not later"—by which, however, he means "sometime within the next hundred years."[33]

This shift from revolutionary fervor to a soberly evolutionary attitude stemmed from Orwell's growing belief in the social and moral destructiveness of revolutionary activism. Moreover the threat of moral contamination from the power worship inherent in a revolutionary program points toward another important shift in Orwell's writings—another manifestation of his bipolar view of reality. On the one hand, in "The Lion and the Unicorn" he explicitly claims that a socialist England can and will win the struggle against Hitler (2. 95), but on the other he casts doubt upon socialism's practical utility by suggesting that England might be defeated even after a socialist revolution. Military victory or defeat now become secondary issues; the important thing is to keep alive the "*idea*" of true socialism (2. 108). This transfer of emphasis, in line with Orwell's feeling that modern revolutions have been inherently tyrannical, points to an idea that gains in importance in Orwell's political writings, the cleavage between the inner moral ideal and the immoral external world of political history.

For Orwell there is a great split between the outer world of political experience, of history, and the inner world of the spirit. Thus the "vision of a world of free and equal human beings, living together in a state of brotherhood . . . never materialises, but the belief in it never seems to die out."[34] It is not in the fallen world of historical reality but rather within the hearts of men that the purifying ideas of justice and equality can exist unharmed. Insulated from political reality, innocence is preserved; exposed to such an environment, idealism can be perverted by power hunger. Subjectively, the New Jerusalem can remain uncorrupted; build it of brick and mortar and it becomes the Kremlin. This is the reason why Orwell finally shies away from the idea of the common people as agents of revolutionary violence.

It is important to note that political activism poses an even greater threat to the integrity of the intellectual, for he is especially susceptible to the enticements of power worship and the betrayals it demands. In 1941, Orwell charged that the British intelligentsia, motivated by its Russophilism to engage in pacifism and irresponsible carping at Britain, had so harmed the nation's morale that Hitler had been encouraged to attack.

Orwell calls this the "intellectual sabotage from the Left."[35] Having discussed James Burnham's predictions regarding the inevitable decline of democratic societies, Orwell claimed that Burnham was expressing the secret wish of the English intelligentsia, the longing to subvert democracy and establish a hierarchical society in which the intellectual "can at last get his hands on the whip."[36]

As a number of critics have noted, the basic assumption of *Animal Farm* is that revolutions are bound to fail, merely replacing one group of oppressors with another.[37] The ideals of equality and justice cannot be actualized because the existence of the liberated farm demands a continuous interaction with the surrounding world of humanity, which, in terms of the allegory, stands for oppression and exploitation. Paradoxically, the need to maintain an economically and politically viable society, a need that can be met only by reinstituting a hierarchical order and by trafficking with human beings, inevitably leads to the subversion of the beasts' utopian aims.

The action of *Animal Farm* takes place between two poles: at one extreme is the condition of animality, representing loyalty, decency, and a mode of existence untouched by the evil associated with the wielding of political power. At the other end is the immoral behavior of the animals' human masters, whose ways Old Major warns them against adopting. The tale records the unavoidable deterioration of the farm as the utopian dream transforms itself into the ugly reality of another tyranny.

However, we should remember that if this political fable has a tragic quality, it also has a comic dimension. This becomes clearer if we bear in mind that the basic design of the work is the innocence-guilt polarity. The problem implied by this tension has to do with morality rather than political practicality: the central concern is the preservation of innocence, not the success or failure of revolutionary activity. The essential action is a movement either toward or away from one pole or the other. The comic aspect of *Animal Farm* derives from the fact that for some of the animals the movement toward immoral humanity is no sooner begun than it is reversed, and their innocence is left intact.

A key factor in this pattern is that of intellectual superiority. "Generally recognised as being the cleverest of the animals," the pigs "naturally" become the teachers and organizers in the farm community (p. 13). Because the pigs are the only animals able to substitute long-range planning for mere impulse, they are destined to lead the revolution, a role that unavoidably exposes them to moral corruption. The outward signs of their lost innocence start to appear during the second revolutionary stage (after the forcible ouster of Farmer Jones) when, as a result of their expanded awareness, they develop a historical consciousness. It is the descendants of Old Major who transform, and in effect pervert, his simple teachings into a "complete system of thought" (p. 14). As leaders the pigs must articulate goals and implement them by means of specific programs entailing institutionalized duties and restraints. In so doing, they are led to embrace the world of men with its brutality and double-dealing. The pigs, whose increased self-consciousness quickly turns to selfishness, are the first to betray communal solidarity by their cunning theft of milk intended for all the animals. And Napoleon's slaughter of animals that are guilty of petty offenses represents the appearance in their midst of cruelty, heretofore a uniquely human quality. Thus the development of political cunning, the end result of the pigs' innate intellectual capacity, involves an exodus from the innocence and stasis of the old farm and a wandering in the spiritual wilderness of political activism, in the unregenerate world of history.

Remembering Orwell's disinclination to attribute revolutionary power hunger to the lower classes, we need not be surprised that for the humbler beasts the failure of the revolution is closely linked to the fact that their garden has not been lost. Before they can be defiled by the taint of humanity, the humbler beasts are saved by a series of fragmentations. The physical movement of the pigs toward the farmhouse, where they take up residence, outwardly expresses the unbridgeable moral gulf that Orwell needs to place between rulers and ruled. And not only must the guilty be segregated from the innocent but also guilt-provoking knowledge must be fragmented from consciousness. The humanoid animals must be shown wholly cut off from the other beasts, and the minds of the latter must remain inviolate from even the awareness of evil. Because their violent overthrow of Farmer Jones springs from impulse and not from ideological formulations—"with one accord, though nothing of the kind had been planned beforehand, [the animals] flung themselves upon their tormentors"—their innocence is not imperiled by power hunger and the moral ambiguities associated with the assumption of a politico-historical identity. The humbler beasts are not guilty, indeed, cannot be guilty, of the premeditation of the political ideologist: ". . . .almost before they knew what was happening, the Rebellion had been successfully carried through" (pp. 16–17).

Sheer mental incapacity preserves the animals' minds and spirits from the consciousness of evil. Because their memories are short, the humbler animals are not sure whether or not they earlier had passed a resolution against trade. Consequently Napoleon's proposal to begin commercial relations with the outside world gives them only a vague discomfort. For the same reason, the animals need feel no uneasiness about the breakdown of their social experiment after the pigs selfishly alter the wording of the commandment against sleeping in Jones's bed (pp. 57–58); and the rulers' slight rewording of the prohibition against killing sets the minds of the naive beasts at rest over the execution of supposedly disloyal comrades (p. 76).

Since revolution implies change, the revolutionary identity is rejected when change is denied. While Napoleon physically reorganizes the old farm and Snowball puffs an electrification program to produce a technologically sophisticated utopia, something entirely new in animal experience, their ignorant subjects feel that life is no better now than before (p. 77). The humbler beasts prefer the song "Beasts of England," which expresses their longing for a utopia vaguely situated in the future, to the recently adopted hymn celebrating the existence of a new order in the present. It is a sign of the animals' relatively untainted consciousness that they finally forget Snowball's vision of luxury, and even the rebellion itself becomes "only a dim tradition" (p. 107).

If the general action of *Animal Farm* is so structured as to express Orwell's need to see the common people uncorrupted by revolutionary ambitiousness, the career of Boxer exemplifies the ruinous effects of upward leveling. Boxer is an emblem of the old-style working class, and throughout most of the fable he is one of the least human members of the community. By nature he is a beast of burden, and it is his basically worker-animal role of tireless drudge that earns him the admiration of his comrades. In fact, it is just this predilection for mindless toil that, in making him ignorant of the leaders' wickedness, renders his spirit immune (at least in the beginning) from the revolutionary urges triggering the pigs' latent viciousness: "His two slogans, 'I will work harder' and 'Napoleon is always right,' seemed to him a sufficient answer to all problems" (p. 53).

At first Boxer's innocence and goodness are not affected by the rebellion. Jones's stable boy, whom Boxer fears he has slain during the fighting, suddenly comes to life (p. 37); and later the horse, as though disclaiming any impious desire to benefit personally from the installation of an electricity-generating windmill, wishes only that it may be "well under way" before his retirement (p. 92).

In time, however, we see signs of an ominous change in Boxer. During the fray that is almost fatal for the stable boy, the ordinarily gentle Boxer, as though mimicking his human oppressors, becomes bipedal, a gesture releasing a savagery alien to his normal behavior: ". . . the most terrifying spectacle of all was Boxer, rearing up on his hind legs and striking out with his great iron-shod hoofs" (p. 36). Significantly Boxer's eventual doom is described in terms of an inner pollution, symbolized by the ingestion of medicine taken from Jones's bathroom and administered by the pigs. With this potion, this "human" element, inside him, Boxer shows the first signs of consciously giving up his identity as a worker and moving toward an upper-class (porcine-humanoid) status: he begins to look forward to retirement when he will have the "leisure to study and improve his mind" by learning the alphabet (p. 100). It is consistent with Orwell's apprehensions that Boxer, thinking that his entry into the world of humanity will bring him renewed vitality (he is supposedly being taken to a veterinary surgeon), is actually being shipped off to a horse slaughterer.

If Boxer's fate indicates his creator's alarm at those forces eating away the class identity of the common people, the final state of the pigs expresses Orwell's certainty that political ambition has a morally destructive effect on the leadership. The two ace of spades that the porcine and human card players simultaneously throw down at the end of the fable symbolize both the pigs' ethical decay and, given the deadly significance of the ace of spades, the passing away of their working-class identities.

In the world of *Animal Farm*, revolution becomes a matter of good lost and evil got. Because it involves a development in the direction of "humanity," of evil, revolutionary activity is the greatest threat to the animals' spirit. But as I have already indicated, the farm is a split world: one region in which the knowledge of evil and change cannot thrive and another in which baseness and mutability cannot be denied. In the end, the humble and ignorant beasts are still victims. Yet as the story of Boxer reveals, this is the necessary condition for the preservation of their innocence, their group identity. If they are still oppressed, they are also still untainted, still the communal embodiment of the socialist ideals of brotherhood and equality.

Animal Farm is, in effect, a fairy tale, a mixture of fantasy and harshness, of mysterious dangers happily overcome by some characters and terrible punishments falling on the heads of others. The subject animals exist in a comic world, their goodness and simplicity magically protected from the witch's brew of politics and revolution. But their leaders are captives in a world of fearful transformations—where the Circe of awareness turns pigs into men.

There is another transformation that bears on Ben's second reading aloud. During the narrative appear signs that Boxer and Ben are doubles, and as such they dramatically express the conflict in the mind of their creator, Orwell the writer-intellectual trapped in an age of political madness. Like Orwell, suffering from a lung ailment, Boxer is the enthusiastic true believer who becomes involved heart and soul in the revolution, working year after year to turn the old farm into a brave new utopia. If Boxer is sheer energy and commitment, Ben, the friend and constant companion with whom Boxer hopes to share his retirement, is the horse's prudential self, his knowing half.[38] It is a mark of his freedom from dangerous ambition that in contrast to Boxer, who marvels at the windmill, Ben remains unenthusiastic (p. 59). Because he rejects progress, he feels confident of being immune to the fearful changes occurring on the farm: "Donkeys live a long time," he asserts. "None of you has ever seen a dead donkey" (pp. 25–26).

Yet there is something disturbingly ambiguous about Ben, who occupies an indefinite position between the porcine state of cunning, immorality, and historical awareness, and the ahistorical animal world of impulse, ignorance, and innocence. His class identity is uncomfortably vague. Lacking the selfishly humanoid wiliness of the pigs, he is not a leader; however, his mental capacity—he can "read as well as any pig" (p. 28)—keeps him from being wholly within the realm of the humbler animals. We might regard him as a representation of the disillusioned intellectual of the 1940s who, unlike his less perceptive compatriots, is cursed with the dispiriting awareness of the inevitable degeneration of revolutionary idealism into power worship. Figuratively as well as literally he can read the handwriting on the wall.

To repeat my earlier observation, twice, not once (as Orwell erroneously states), Ben has read, has broken his rule. That is, more than once, and more than the narrator cares to admit, Ben has revealed an affinity with the porcine condition of intelligence, and, therefore, evil. To add to the ominous significance of this second transgression, the exercise of this humanoid skill involves the pronunciation of words that themselves represent the breaking of a rule, the subversion of the seven commandments established to keep the animals free from the corrupting effects of humanization.

Ben's fate is rather curious. Soon after reading aloud a second time, the donkey simply drops out of the narrative, even though he is one of the more important and more fully developed characters. One explanation for this abrupt and puzzling disappearance is that Orwell—too intimately acquainted with the intellectual's inner complexity to leave Ben in the thoughtlessly innocent realm of the humbler animals, yet morally repelled by the other alternative—allows the donkey to vanish into a limbo apart from either polarity. This turn of events underscores Orwell's view regarding the moral vulnerability of the intellectual unprotected by the mental limitations that make the lower animals, the common folk, resistant to inner contamination. The intellectual cannot combine escape with self-preservation. It is through a blind, instinctive assertion of their original collective identity that the animals remain inviolate. The intellectual's only refuge entails a self-negating loss of identity.

Because Ben's dilemma is so close to that of Orwell, the latter has failed to treat this character with the same artistic objectivity as he has done with the others. This need not, however, be the last word on the matter, for Ben's vanishing act calls attention to some interesting technical and thematic developments in *Animal Farm*. For one thing, since Ben is defined in terms of an inner tension between the desire to participate in the innocence of the humbler beasts and an effort to suppress the humanoid-porcine qualities that prevent this, he is a more complex and, therefore, more realistic character than the others, even Boxer, who unself-consciously play out their two-dimensional allegorical roles of goodness and villainy, naive enthusiasm and single-minded cunning.

In "Inside the Whale," Orwell predicts that the "autonomous individual is going to be stamped out of existence" with the advent of totalitarianism (1. 525), a warning reiterated several years later in "Literature and Totalitarianism" (2. 135). A few months after the publication of *Animal Farm*, he explained why under a tyranny the idea of personal autonomy was illusory. To be autonomous one had to be "free *inside*," but in a totalitarian society even one's thoughts were controlled by the state. In fact, with the loss of free expression the mind itself becomes torpid, for it is "almost impossible to think without talking."[39]

Ben is the autonomous individual caught in a double bind. The refusal to voice an opinion about the animals' utopian experiment is supposed to insure his moral survival as well as his physical safety, yet his reluctance to speak out makes him in effect a silent partner to the pigs' conspiracy and gradually erodes his autonomy. His disappearance from the narrative suggests that he has been "stamped out of existence."

There may be an emblematic connection between the disappearance of this relatively complex character and Zwerdling's observation that during the forties Orwell was consciously attempting to abandon the conventions of the realistic novel, which, because of its documentary specificity and thematic obliqueness, was not flexible enough to satisfy Orwell's artistic needs or to deliver a direct message within the context of an enlarged historical perspective. By employing the fable, Orwell could invest *Animal Farm* with "permanent mythic life" and set forth the basic pattern of social revolution.[40]

The transparency of the fable, its ability to convey meaning directly and with a minimum of authorial intrusion, makes the withdrawal of Ben appropriate, since he lacks the allegorical simplicity of the other figures. In *Coming Up for Air*, Tubby Bowling, the passive common man, fades away into a state of potentially self-destructive apathy; whereas the other Bowling, Bowling the author's mouthpiece, has, as the observer and recorder of his alter ego's decline into quietism, the last word. This, however, is not the case in *Animal Farm*, where Ben, as much the judgmental Orwellian persona in his silences as in his speech, is not allowed to outlast the narrative. This circumstance hints at Orwell's willingness to draw back from the events, to let the story (the final half dozen pages, at least) tell itself. The impression we are left with is that in the world of the forties there are no safe heights from atop which an author or his persona can calmly survey the violence below and formulate grand generalizations.

The withdrawal of the authorial commentator from the dramatized narrative action may also indicate a change in Orwell's relationship to the modernist tradition. The Orwell of the thirties often was making a forced march to join ranks with the moderns. Partly to achieve his childhood goal of literary fame, partly to expand his intellectual and imaginative horizons, Orwell chose as models those writers generally considered most sensitive to the moral and psychological ambiguities of contemporary man. From *Burmese Days* to *Coming Up for Air*, the Orwellian voice is noticeably derivative, and at times we feel that Orwell's admiration for such writers as Eliot and Joyce has outstripped his ability to adapt their imaginative worlds to his own creative aims. For reasons I shall examine in the following chapter, during the forties Orwell turned his attention to other literary models better suited to the atmosphere of the age, with its technologically sophisticated barbarism, its tyrants able to mesmerize whole populations, and its rejection of the idea of individual freedom.

Finally, it is worth noting that in exposing the savagery concealed behind the official ideology of revolutionary activism, Orwell has chosen a relatively primitive literary form, the animal tale. Whether or not Jacintha Buddicom is correct in claiming that the original source of *Animal Farm* is Beatrix Potter's *The Tale of Pigling Bland* (which the young Blair read to her),[41] the decision to examine social conflict "from the animals' point of view"[42] suggests Orwell's willingness to experiment with a view of reality normally associated with a child's perspective and attitudes, his and ours. Although such an approach is obviously useful in creating ironic and satiric effects, we should be aware of the dangerous game Orwell the fabulist is engaged in when he blurs the distinction between man and animal to reveal the viciousness of the former. For the adult, the animal is something to be used as physical or literary beast of burden, as a source of amusement, as prey, or as object of scientific examination. But for the child—and this includes the child within the adult—the animal is a marvel, a source of wonder, perhaps even a magical being. In exploiting this creature for adult ends (for example, sociopolitical commentary), the writer has risked violating the sacred grove of his own childhood world. What remains of the child's primal response to life may wither away if yoked to the adult's moralistic or political obsessions. To understand why Orwell felt he had to take this risk, we must examine the relationship between his ideas on the political irrationality of the twentieth century and the writer's childhood vision of reality.

Chapter VIII

The Age of Unreason

During the 1930s, Orwell devoted much of his energy to exposing the abuses of a money-worshipping society. In such works as *Down and Out* and *Wigan Pier*, he carried forward the social and economic criticism of nineteenth-century and Edwardian reformers, calling attention to the class inequities and exploitation characteristic of a capitalist-industrial civilization. During the forties, however, Orwell's interest shifted as he displayed increasing alarm at the emergence of neo-barbarism into contemporary life.

In 1936, Orwell underwent an upsetting personal experience as he was passing through Paris on the way to Spain. Having decided to drop in on a friend, he hailed a taxicab; but because the ride was short, the elderly driver, feeling cheated, became angry. An argument started, and after a harsh exchange of words the two men parted unreconciled. As a result, Orwell concluded that the old man must have regarded him as simply one more idle and patronizing tourist, and he told himself that his motives in going to Spain were similar to those that produced the taxicab driver's hostility: both men were caught up in the revolutionary fervor of the times.

However, this retrospective attempt to see himself and the old man as basically political allies is not wholly successful, for the most vivid passages of this piece in "As I Please" (1944) center on the sudden outbreak of hatred—the Frenchman's irrational suspicions and Orwell's own frightening capacity for violence, and not on the narrator's remarks concerning the attitudes that the two of them might share. Enraged at earning the equivalent of only threepence, the old man accuses Orwell of deliberately imposing on him. Explanations fail, the argument grows more intense. Orwell states candidly: "In the end I lost my temper and, my command of French coming back to me in my rage, I shouted at him, 'You think you're too old for me to smash your face in. Don't be too sure!' He backed up against the taxi, snarling and full of fight, in spite of his sixty years." Orwell not only maliciously pays the fare with a bill so large that the driver cannot make change but also refuses to tip the man. Afterward, sad and disgusted at the whole incident, Orwell can but helplessly wonder, "Why do people have to behave like that?"[1]

With its eruption of hatred and the anguished awareness of the participants' readiness to engage in violence, this vignette is a microcosmic counterpart to the West as a whole during the second quarter of the twentieth century. Those interests and needs that should have brought men together, such as common political attitudes, were not strong enough to withstand the culturally destructive effects of man's propensity for suspicion and brutality.

Orwell's near-bloody encounter with the taxicab driver was symptomatic of an outbreak of atavistic emotions and behavior endangering Western civilization as a whole. In 1942, Orwell expressed the fear that even the struggle against Hitler would itself brutalize the English. "In a year's time you'll see headlines in the *Daily Express*," he remarked to someone during the German blitz, " 'Successful Raid on Berlin Orphanage. Babies Set on Fire.' "[2] Although the press did not become quite so brutal, Orwell noted with disgust that British newspapers contained presumably approving photographs of humiliated, disfigured French collaborators and hanged Germans.[3] Even more disturbing was what Orwell saw as the trend in modern Europe away from the less inhumane drop method of hanging, which is supposed to kill instantly, back to the older method of strangulation. Moreover the idea of executing criminals was no longer regarded as reactionary: "it is a mark of enlightenment not merely to approve of executions but to raise an outcry because there are not more of them."[4]

In the essay "The Sporting Spirit" (1945), he uses such phrases as "viscious passions," "orgies of hatred," "savage combative instincts," and "sadistic pleasure" in describing the nature of modern international sporting events and the feelings they arouse among spectators (4. 40–44). This glorification of brutality heralded the advent of an age of irrationality. In Orwell's view, the modern world was losing its grip on reality, and political strongmen were fulfilling the dream of Dostoevski's underground man in creating an intellectual atmosphere in which "two and two will make five when the Leader says so."[5] Closely allied to the political barbarism of the time was what Orwell claimed was a peculiarly modern form of greed fueling contemporary imperialism, sheer power hunger.[6] Although Orwell did not define this term in a systematic manner, he did suggest that power hunger was a longing to exert total mastery over life, a longing that found its extremest political expression in totalitarian states, in which no moral qualms existed to inhibit the falsification of records, the torture and murder of prisoners, and mass bombings. Also the mystique attached to power had very little to do with concrete goals, for Orwell suggested that it was an end in itself—"the cult of power tends to be mixed up with a love of cruelty and wickedness *for their own sakes*."[7] In any event, power hunger was a moral and intellectual disease especially virulent in the twentieth century.

While discussing the basic irrationality of anti-Semitism in "Notes on Nationalism" (1945), Orwell points out that the prejudice against Jews is only one form of a more widespread "disease . . . called nationalism."[8] He states that nationalism is a mode of thought that dispenses with concrete sensory experience. It operates by abstraction, classifying human beings in terms of general categories that are then used to determine the moral worth of these individuals. Taking the form either of loyalty to one abstraction or hatred of another, nationalism is much more than a prejudice regarding a specific nation or ethnic group. Hate and loyalty can just as easily be directed at political groups within a country, at religious or economic classes (3. 362–63). The dynamics of nationalism are especially relevant to Orwell's views on the mental deterioration of modern men. Although nationalism is bound up with the desire for power, the nationalist wants power not for himself but for a cause—be it nation, church, or political ideology—into which he sinks his own individuality. And this combination of power hunger and self-submergence is irrational: "The nationalist does not go on the principle of simply ganging up with the strongest side. On the contrary, having picked his side, he persuades himself that it *is* the strongest, and is able to stick to his belief even when the facts are overwhelmingly against him. Nationalism is power-hunger tempered by self-deception" (3. 363). In effect, the nationalist severs nearly all ties with the world of concrete, observable reality: "Some nationalists are not far from schizophrenia, living quite happily amid dreams of power and conquest which have no connection with the physical world" (3. 372).

Such is the nationalist's instability that an ideology or group that he has slavishly worshipped for many years may suddenly become hateful, and then another object of worship will immediately take its place (3. 368). Forsaking rational calculation, self-interest, and even physical reality, the nationalist is involuntarily bound to an impulse that autonomously follows its own course. This impulse forces the individual to worship or hate one thing after another. Only the subjection of the individual, the submergence of his ego, remains a constant element. Nationalism, is, then, a distillation of the primitive, irrational drives that, in Orwell's judgment, are menacing liberal democratic society. It is certainty without proof—the purest form of superstition; service without reason—the purest form of subjection.

Orwell's confrontation with the irrationality of the present moved him to examine and define his ideas about the past. Although granting that material progress had occurred—the nineteenth-century London slums no longer existed—Orwell was convinced that it left dead civilizations in its wake.[9] Having examined the past centuries, he saw history as moving downward. Whatever might have been the goal of the Puritan Revolution, it failed to bring real liberty and equality; and the succeeding age of capitalism—with the horrors of the Industrial Revolution, colonial oppression, and the destruction of cultures—was probably not superior to feudal society.[10] Despite the progressivist optimism of nineteenth-century and Edwardian liberals, modern history was not only heading downward but was also spiraling far backward toward unexpectedly primitive conditions. In the 1930s and 1940s, reactionary emotions suddenly reappeared: slave empires were springing up in Europe, a situation thought impossible only a few decades earlier; the ideals of army, fatherland, and glory were becoming far more potent in France that were internationalism and humanitarianism; and admiration for Russia was conjuring up all the old, supposedly banished superstitions—patriotism, military greatness, and imperialism.[11] In fact, the technological advances once regarded as the basis of a liberal, democratic, and progressive society were being used in the twentieth century to destroy the values of such a society:

> Modern Germany is far more scientific than England, and far more barbarous. Much of what [H. G.] Wells has imagined and worked for is physically there in Nazi Germany. The order, the planning, the State encouragement of science, the steel, the concrete, the aeroplanes, are all there, but all in the service of ideas appropriate to the Stone Age.[12]

The paradox that had invalidated the Edwardian vision was that now, at the very time when material progress had set up the conditions for peace and liberation, the crude desires to suppress freedom and engage in warfare had burst forth.[13]

Contemporary outbreaks of irrationality, the increasing willingness to embrace absurdity, were signs of a slackening of the ties between the present and a saner past. In the essay "Decline of the English Murder" (1946), we see contrasted the essential meaninglessness of a recent example of murderous violence, the Cleft Chin murder case, with past slayings in which there were more or less understandable motives at work. These older murders—Orwell concentrates on the period from around 1850 to 1925—were not gratuitous acts of violence; rather they were products of a "stable society where the all-prevailing hypocrisy did at least ensure that crimes as serious as murder should have strong emotions behind them" (4. 101). Orwell's typical old-fashioned murderer is a respectable middle-class citizen, perhaps a Conservative party official or socially prestigious Nonconformist, who has engaged in some kind of disreputable activity and, to preserve his good name, commits murder, although only after a struggle with his conscience. Whatever the details of the traditional murder, the crime springs from clear, humanly intelligible motives—sex, money, or the maintenance of social status. Above all, the unfolding of the case and its eventual solution exhibit an orderly and significant pattern: "In most of the cases the crime only came to light slowly, as the result of careful investigation . . . and in nearly every case there was some dramatic coincidence, in which the finger of Providence could be clearly seen" (4. 99).

The modern crime, such as that of the Cleft Chin outrages, is quite different, he claims. Karl Hutten, an army deserter and self-styled Chicago gangster, and his would-be gun moll act out their fantasies by running over one girl, robbing and attempting to drown another, and finally murdering a taxicab driver. What engaged Orwell's attention was that these grave crimes had been motivated by whim, a fleeting desire to play a role, a sudden craving for a little spending money. In short, they were meaningless.

The abandonment of the past had left the idea of history drained of meaning. History had stopped in the sense that power hunger had led to the disbelief in the "existence of objective truth" and the conviction that truth was what the totalitarian leader wanted it to be.[14] According to Orwell, during the war there had appeared an official Soviet publication containing tables of dates from which was excluded any mention of the Russo-German Pact of 1939,[15] and a London newspaper had falsified the date of Maurice Thorez's departure from France to Moscow apparently to conceal the fact that the French Communist Party leader had deserted from the French army after the war had broken out rather than before.[16] Two aspects of this falsification of history were particularly disturbing to Orwell. Lying about the past and the present was integral to totalitarianism and not a temporary expedient during some transitional period in its development. Totalitarian rulers thought of history as "something to be created rather than learned." They had to rearrange history to conceal from the faithful any evidence of their mistakes and misjudgments. For what was at stake was the infallibility of leaders who were, in effect, the ruling caste in a theocracy. Thus, it was in the nature of totalitarianism to demand the "continuous alteration of the past."[17]

Interpretations of history were becoming wholly dependent on the capriciousness of party zealotry. Belief or disbelief in atrocity stories was based solely on one's political attitudes; and stranger still, political expediency could turn fact into falsehood overnight.[18] In Spain, propagandists on both sides, eschewing petty falsehoods, invented history on a grand scale, creating fictional battles and allowing real ones to go unrecorded.[19]

But Orwell was alarmed by more than the distortion and suppression of facts by prejudiced writers, for he felt that histories had always been biased and inaccurate. What was particularly disturbing was the peculiarly modern rejection of historical truth as an independently existing body of fact. In the past, he asserted, most people believed that historical facts did exist, but now in the 1930s and 1940s "it is just this common basis of agreement, with its implication that human beings are all one species of animal, that totalitarianism destroys."[20] The dilemma was this: since traditional Christianity, with its transcendent significance, was no longer acceptable, and since the basic need for some kind of religion remained, we had to create a new one, the central creed of which was the immortality of a human community extending itself from the past to the present and into the future; however, the irrationality of contemporary politics, insofar as it denied the idea of historical truth, destroyed the necessary basis for a belief in the human community as a continuously existing entity.

If the willful distortion of history and even the disbelief in the existence of historical truth indicated a loss of contact with a decent and intelligible past, there were forces at work severing man's ties with his immediate environment. In the article "Pleasure Spots" (1946), Orwell examines someone's description of a pleasure resort of the future. With their artificial regulation of temperature, ubiquitous attendants, and continuous, thought-deadening music, such places are, says Orwell, nothing more than the fulfillment of an unconscious desire to return to the womb. And the widespread interest in them is a sign that man's power hunger, his recently developed ability to blast aside mountains and alter the earth's climate, has diminished his "religious awe" at nature. The pious response to the natural world is tied in with man's sense of "littleness and weakness against the power of the universe," a condition promoting within us a reverential "sense of mystery" concerning nature. It is the gradual loss of this religious awe that produces in some people a spontaneous disgust with the increasing complexity of our mechanized existence. "For," Orwell asserts, "man only stays human by preserving large patches of simplicity in his life (4. 78–81).

There was another form of alienation that, as I have indicated elsewhere, Orwell regarded as an immediate threat to the artist: too close an involvement with the lies and delusions of politics might weaken the writer's link with his own nature, his private mental landscape. Loyalty to a group might at times be necessary, Orwell admitted, but it had a blighting effect on that personal and individual view of reality that a writer needed to embody in his works. Group loyalty endangered one's creative impulse, "the result is not only falsification, but often the actual drying-up of the inventive faculties."[21] Even in the case of a person who was free from any specific ideological commitment and bias, there was, Orwell suggested, a possibility that life in a totalitarian age might force upon one an awareness of political issues that, by its presence, would undermine the individual's personal responses to the world around him.

This dilemma is vividly expressed in the short essay "Some Thoughts on the Common Toad" (1946), which can be viewed as a monologue exposing the alienation from nature taking place within the speaker. At one point, Orwell clearly sets forth the implications of this conflict between one's innocent enjoyment of nature and the dispiriting influence of modern politics:

> I think that by retaining one's childhood love of such things as trees, fishes, butterflies and . . . toads, one makes a peaceful and decent future a little more probable, and that by preaching the doctrine that

nothing is to be admired except steel and concrete, one merely makes it a little surer that human beings will have no outlet for their surplus energy except in hatred and leader worship. (4. 144)

Man impoverishes his own existence when he turns his back on the green world, the living organic world of nature.

The essay begins with the speaker's celebration of spring's return, its first sign being the appearance of the common toad. Orwell pictures the creature's gradual awakening, its emergence from the mud where it has lain dormant since the previous fall, and its eager scurrying to the nearest pool of water. It is immediately clear that the speaker's knowledge of toads is not a bookish one—he has gone to the trouble of digging up toads who have remained underground far into the summer—and the detailed description of the newly arisen amphibian's golden eyes indicates his appreciation of nature's less obvious beauties. At this stage of the "monologue," the speaker's mood is playfully lighthearted. Whimsically he characterizes the hungry toad as looking like an especially pious Anglican at the end of Lent; and as though stressing the closeness that can exist between man and nature, he pauses in his discussion of toads' mating habits long enough to describe the amusingly tenacious way the excited male clings to one's finger (4. 141–42).

Turning from rural nature to the signs of spring in London, Orwell introduces a new element into the essay, man's destructiveness, with his reference to shrubs growing on "blitzed" sites. An irrepressible gloom is breaking into the speaker's spring song even as it celebrates the green world's return to the city. Spring "comes seeping in everywhere, like one of those new poison gases which pass through all filters." Orwell's reference to the miraculous return of spring after what has seemed like years of endless winter indicates that at this point his thoughts are losing their simple connection with nature: the passing remark on the rigors of the English climate during the forties is also an allusion to the war that nearly destroyed the nation (4. 142–43).

Now the speaker is aware that enthusiasm over nature might be linked to guilt. Is it "politically reprehensible" to rejoice in nature while millions suffer from capitalist exploitation? The question is not wholly rhetorical, for in the past his favorable references to nature have provoked abusive letters accusing him of being reactionary. Feeling compelled to defend himself, Orwell replies hotly that these critics possess the newer sensibility, which places a higher value on the frenetic multiplication of wants than on the enjoyment of existing sources of pleasure, and which worships the machine while refusing to recognize the validity of urban man's attraction to the country.

The speaker regains his composure long enough to rebut the charge of dilettantism and state his own credo regarding the value of retaining one's childhood love of nature. But this confident mood does not last. The defiant tone of his concluding statement hints at an almost paranoid anxiety:

> At any rate, spring is here . . . and they can't stop you enjoying it. . . .
> How many a time have I stood watching the toads mating . . . and
> thought of all the important persons who would stop me enjoying this
> if they could. But luckily they can't. . . . The atom bombs are piling up
> in the factories, the police are prowling through the cities, the lies are
> streaming from the loudspeakers, but the earth is still going round the
> sun, and neither the dictators nor the bureaucrats, deeply as they
> disapprove of the process, are able to prevent it. (4. 144–45)

Untroubled delight in nature has turned into anxiety over the multifarious dangers of the Cold War age. The Orwell who, earlier in the essay, sees spring reflected in the "pleasant shade of blue" of a policeman's tunic becomes at the end a man whose mind is oppressed by a vision of police "prowling" through the streets.

Taken as a whole, Orwell's essays during the late thirties and forties are indicative of his expanding interest from the plight of tramps, coal miners, and the lower middle class to a concern for the fate of Western civilization in general. At the same time, we note a shift away from exclusively political matters. Within this enlarged perspective he develops a more pronounced interest in the moral—even spiritual and religious—dimension of human existence. Regarding this, we might do well to look at Orwell's somewhat ambiguous attitude toward Christianity, as is indicated in an article written for *Time and Tide* in 1940. Modern man, says Orwell, is like a wasp he had once cut in two. Paying no heed to its condition, the wasp continued to eat the jam on Orwell's plate, the food simply trickling out from behind as fast as it was ingested. Similarly, for a time during this century men failed to realize that the human soul was missing. This removal was necessary, however, for by the nineteenth century the notion of an immortal soul had become a lie to keep the underprivileged classes docile. The fact that for years—decades—religion was at the service of reaction forced thinking men to rebel, and literature became an effective weapon in the assault on the Christian world view. These writers—Orwell's list ranges from Voltaire to Joyce—succeeded all too well in undermining Western man's belief in personal immortality and other dogmas, and the results were appalling: lunatics becoming national leaders, constant warfare, illegal executions and slave societies. The wound left by the soul's removal had gone "septic" (2. 15–16).

In this article, Orwell holds out some hope that the loss of religious faith need not lead us ever deeper into a "cesspool full of barbed wire." He feels that there is a viable alternative to the turmoil of the present, for men can develop a sense of community even without belief in God or personal immortality. The fact that human beings are ready to sacrifice their lives for an abstraction and find consolation in being part of a larger entity that they consider immortal convinces Orwell that with a "very slight increase of consciousness" this loyalty to a limited community or ideal could be shifted to the idea of humanity itself (2. 17).

But Orwell's mood changed. Some four years later, he returned to the same problem, the social and political troubles that arose from disbelief in immortality. Now, however, there was a difference. Whereas earlier Orwell talked about humanity and brotherhood, in 1944 he stressed the need for an unyielding code of morality, a "sense of absolute right and wrong" even without the supportive belief in personal immortality.[22] There was no discussion about new, more humanly valuable allegiances. Orwell was more impressed by the difficulties of providing a replacement for personal immortality. Instead of providing us with a positive proposal in his writings, Orwell gives a criticism of socialism's failure to provide men with a reason for living—and again he brings up the matter of our need for a moral code not based upon belief in an afterlife.[23]

Orwell's growing awareness that men's need to believe had taken disturbing forms was probably the motivating factor for this later, less optimistic view. Even before the war, in January of 1939, Orwell suspected that modern power hunger, the worship of the unscrupulous and brutal leader, had become a "universal religion."[24] The deeply felt need for hardship and discipline and struggle accounted for the success of modern dictators. The hedonistic enticements held out by Western democracies, the physical comforts and economic security, were not enough; the progressive vision of the good society had failed to recognize people's longing for a cause that demanded self-sacrifice.[25] Instead of expressing itself in terms of an all-encompassing human solidarity, a brotherhood of all men, the religious impulse toward self-sacrifice had resulted in the many and socially divisive outbreaks of nationalism. Rather than regenerating man, these group loyalties, especially those that took the form of political movements, were producing moral deterioration, a brutalization of the sensibility, and a kind of mass insanity. Because of their contempt for the past and their encouragement of enmity between classes, political parties, and nations, the secular ideologies that had replaced traditional Christianity were responsible for the weakening of the common man's commitment to the ideal of a community of mankind extending from the past into the future—a belief that could have reconciled him to the fact of his mortality.

One way that Orwell reacted to the spectacle of a civilization caught up in a chorea of folly, treachery, and violence was to become increasingly interested in those more or less private aspects of life that thread their way from the past into the present. Surely Orwell's respect for ordinary reminders of permanence and continuity lay behind his defense of the traditional English system of measurement.[26] It seems clear that for Orwell the eleven steps of his recipe for the "perfect cup of tea" constituted a ritual celebration of one of the people's most cherished domestic customs.[27]

It appears that in comparison with the absurdities of modern politics, the everyday activities of common life are precious springs of sanity. Even so trivial an occupation as preparing the family budget from one week to the next keeps one in touch with reality, whereas the belief that political ideas need not be measured against "solid reality" leads one into a "non-Euclidean world" of contradictions and confusion.[28]

In addition to putting one in closer touch with reality, private activities can be morally regenerative. Throughout the essay "A Good Word for the Vicar of Bray" (1946), Orwell repeatedly, and seriously, asserts that an individual can purge himself of guilt, especially guilt associated with anti-social behavior, by planting trees and shrubs for the enjoyment of future generations. And as if to show that he is not mesmerized by the social problems of the day, Orwell adds that the money with which he has purchased Woolworth roses has been better spent than if it had been used to buy a Fabian Research pamphlet (4. 151).

These scattered observations do not, of course, indicate a radical disengagement from the public turmoil of the age; even until the end Orwell's writings reveal a constant interest in current political events. Still, as is indicated by works like *Coming Up for Air*, *Homage to Catalonia*, and *Animal Farm*, there is reason to believe that alongside Orwell's political involvements are appearing other, more personal concerns. Here and there, we detect not only a need for purification, a need to keep some portion of himself undefiled, but also an implicit connection between such a condition and the renunciation of current forms of political activism.

In this regard, it is instructive to examine Orwell's views on two interrelated topics—Mahatma Gandhi and pacifism. Most of Orwell's earlier references to both are far from commendatory. In 1941, Orwell attacked the pacifist principles espoused by Alex Comfort by pointing out first that to regard the social abuses in England as being just as bad as those in Nazi Germany revealed a lack of a sense of proportion, and second that whatever might be the long-term effects of passive resistance, the short-run effects were simply helpful to Germany.[29] Less than a year later, Orwell stated categorically that from an objective point of view pacifism was pro-Fascist, for the dissemination of pacifist propaganda endangered those countries that permitted free speech and thereby aided totalitarianism. In addition to pointing out the adverse effects of nonviolence, Orwell exhibited an interest in the psychological processes by which those who began with "an alleged horror of violence end[ed] up with a marked tendency to be fascinated by the success and power of Nazism." Understandably in a man committed to the struggle against Nazism (and in reaction against his own earlier feeling that war with Germany would be a sham struggle engineered by capitalist forces at home), Orwell emphasized the political shortcomings of pacifism and explicitly stated that he was not concerned with "pacifism as a 'moral phenomenon.' "[30] One year later, Orwell published a scathing poem attacking the political irresponsibility of the pacifists ("Your hands are clean, and so were Pontius Pilate's"—one line reads) who, while their compatriots performed the dirty work of waging war, combined self-righteousness with a readiness to denounce only those groups who would not retaliate. For the pacifist, this "half-way saint and cautious hero," Orwell had only contempt.[31]

Although not quite so overtly hostile to Gandhi, Orwell's views on the Indian during the war were less than favorable. In the early forties, Orwell emphasized the political usefulness of Gandhi to the British imperialists, who found nonviolence easier to cope with than resistance. Gandhi's personal honesty was a trait that Orwell recognized but did not stress.[32] As for the spiritual appeal of Gandhi, Eastern mysticism as an alternative to Western values, Orwell had only harsh words:

> As soon as you have "rejected" industrialism, and hence Socialism, you are in that strange no man's land where the Fascist and the pacifist join forces. There is indeed a sort of apocalyptic truth in the statement of the German radio that the teachings of Hitler and Gandhi are the same.[33]

And the next year, 1944, in discussing the tendency of nationalistic movements to form themselves around "some superhuman Fuehrer," Orwell listed Gandhi with, among others, Hitler, Stalin, and Franco.[34] Although Orwell never overtly attacked Gandhi on a personal level, after the Indian's assassination he cryptically referred to "dark suspicions" about him.[35]

However, toward the end of his life Orwell's attitude toward Gandhi shifted in a direction indicating an interest in personal regeneration, a leaning away from the world of the commissar toward that of the yogi. In "Reflections on Gandhi" (1949), one of his last essays, Orwell—who, it should be remembered, was born in Bengal—is remarkably gentle to the pacifist leader. He carefully shows that Gandhi was neither neurotic, spiteful, cowardly nor vulgarly ambitious. He was a saint but not an impractical visionary. According to Orwell, within the Indian there was a shrewd intelligence that would have made him a successful lawyer, administrator, or businessman—the implication being that Gandhi's career was based on a voluntary choice, a freely willed rejection of material self-advancement, and not the result of being an embittered misfit (4, 464–65). He is not Conrad's Donkin.

Orwell does not blindly praise Gandhi. He finds the man's ascetic striving toward sainthood a mode of existence that is irreconcilable with a humanistic commitment to life, with its pain and frustration and risk of moral corruption, and he suggests that the Indian's campaign of nonviolent resistance to imperial control succeeded only because the British, unlike modern totalitarians, were unwilling to silence him. However, despite these reservations, Orwell cannot reject the man's philosophy out of hand. "It seems doubtful," Orwell remarks, "whether civilisation can stand another major war, and it is at least thinkable that the way out lies through non-violence"; and a few lines later he admits that he does "not feel sure that as a political thinker [Gandhi] was wrong in the main" (4. 469). But it is Gandhi's virtue, not so much his political canniness, which now evokes Orwell's interest—and his most appreciative remarks. The last words of the essay are a tribute to that quality of Gandhi that has come to be so urgent a matter for Orwell, the ability to avoid being corrupted by politics: ". . . regarded simply as a politician, and compared with the other leading political figures of our time, how clean a smell he has managed to leave behind!" (4. 470).

One of the most interesting aspects of Orwell's novels is, as we have seen, the tension between, on the one hand, a personal condition of innocence and vitality and, on the other, a disruptive awareness of evil and guilt. We have seen, too, how various characters have become fugitives from those modes of experience that have threatened their peace of mind, taking flight from forbidden knowledge. In some cases, the escape from experience has involved a repressive control over one's mental and emotional life, a diminution of consciousness (Dorothy Hare, Gordon Comstock, George Bowling, and the backward farm animals); in other instances, the flight is more extreme, taking the form of death (John Flory) or an abrupt disappearance from the narrative (the donkey Ben).

For several reasons, Orwell's probings into the villainy and dementia of the present exposes him to forbidden knowledge. The fact of a Europe suddenly transformed into a totalitarian slave empire forces its way into the mind and blights that humanistic faith in man's inviolable decency rooted in Orwell's Edwardian past. At the same time, the journey into the world of sociopolitical madness may become an exploration into the darker regions of the explorer himself, an unwelcome and even frightening encounter with his own irrationality.

One suspects that Orwell's increasing emphasis on the inner self and private modes of experience springs from two seemingly different impulses: the longing to escape, at least for a while, the violence of the world outside, and the need to mark out an impregnable area of personal goodness, to establish a base camp of emotional and moral health from which to begin the trek into the modern country of the blind. However, as a reader of Wells might expect, the traveler risks losing his own sight. Paradoxically, the imperative toward personal righteousness, the determination to arm oneself against the dangers of such an exploration, may undermine that humanistic commitment to life that has in the first place motivated him to expose the totalitarian menace at home and abroad. In an essay written toward the end of Orwell's life, "Lear, Tolstoy and the Fool," we can detect the uneasy tension between an involvement with life and what takes the form of a puritanical rejection of the world.

In this essay, Orwell examines Tolstoy's criticism of Shakespeare in the Russian's pamphlet *Shakespeare and the Drama*. According to Tolstoy, Shakespeare failed to treat matters of moral importance seriously. Therefore, he was a frivolous and superficial writer unworthy of the adulation he had received through the centuries. Orwell is not interested in rebutting Tolstoy's judgments on Shakespeare. Rather he wants to expose the attitudes and motives underlying the moralist's hostility. Investigating Tolstoy's criticism of *King Lear*, the play receiving the most attention and abuse in the pamphlet, Orwell concludes that the Russian's grievances spring less from high-minded moral outrage at the play's presumed triviality than from the pamphleteer's personal frustrations. Basically, Tolstoy hated *Lear* because it reminded him of his own failure to find peace of mind through renunciation. Hoping to find happiness by obeying God's will, Tolstoy renounced his estate, title, and copyrights. But like Lear, he gained nothing but persecution and anguish. Consequently, says Orwell, Tolstoy reacted against the tragedy's implicit message that renunciation does not bring happiness.

On the basis of this explanation, Orwell points out the antithetical views of life for which Shakespeare and Tolstoy stand. Shakespeare is a humanist, a man who loves life with all its variety, all its pain and pleasure; whereas Tolstoy is a saint, one who rejects life on earth in hopes of otherworldly happiness. But, Orwell claims, Tolstoy is not content merely to reject the humanist outlook. He wants everyone else to imitate him, and to this end he attempts to denigrate Shakespeare by fair means and foul. With some asperity Orwell brings to light Tolstoy's real intent in writing his pamphlet:

> He is not demanding that the police shall impound every copy of Shakespeare's works. But he will do dirt on Shakespeare, if he can. He will try to get inside the mind of every lover of Shakespeare and kill his enjoyment by every trick he can think of, including . . . arguments which are self-contradictory or even doubtfully honest. (4. 302)

Orwell concludes his essay by pointing out with apparent satisfaction that Tolstoy's attack has had absolutely no effect on Shakespeare's prestige.

It is interesting to note that in the quotation above, Orwell's focus is on the insidious influence of fanaticism on the human mind. So obsessed is Tolstoy with justifying his ascetic view of life that his judgment is undermined, his evaluations distorted. In fact, Orwell tells us, the Russian's moralistic prejudices caused him actually to misread *Lear*: Tolstoy has "misunderstood one phrase and slightly changed the meaning of another,

making nonsense of a remark which is reasonable enough in its context"
(4. 291). However, even though the general tone of "Lear, Tolstoy and the
Fool" appears at first glance to be one of hostility to the Russian's life-
denying tendencies and their effects, there is reason to believe that the
speaker is secretly sympathetic to Tolstoy; for Orwell's attitude toward
Shakespeare's humanism—and his understanding of *Lear*—is, like
Tolstoy's, clouded by distrust.

Discussing Tolstoy's dislike of *Lear*, Orwell interprets the Russian's
impatience with the Fool as indicating a deeply rooted hostility to Shakespeare's humanistic values, his commitment to this world. The Fool, says
Orwell, embodies this commitment, confirming man's ability to endure his
earthly existence. The Fool's jokes, riddles, and mocking thrusts at Lear's
"high-minded folly" are elements of sanity in the play, "a reminder that
somewhere or other, in spite of the injustices, cruelties, intrigues, decep-
tions and misunderstandings that are being enacted here, life is going on
much as usual." Tolstoy's real argument, continues Orwell, is with the
Fool, for the nineteenth-century ascetic wants to "narrow the range of
human consciousness" and reduce as much as possible "our points of
attachment to the physical world and the day-to-day struggle" (4. 293–94).
In short, Tolstoy's anger at Shakespeare represents a conflict between
humanism and its antithesis, the "religious" attitude toward life (4. 295).

What should not be overlooked, however, is the fact that Orwell is
actually much harsher toward the Fool, who is the spokesman for the
humanist commitment to life, than is Tolstoy. At one point in the essay,
Orwell asks the reader to recall the plot of *Lear* and then gives his own
recollection of it. After summarizing the heath scene (act 3), he turns in
memory to the end of the play where Lear, "still cursing, still understanding nothing, is holding [Cordelia] in his arms while the Fool dangles on a
gallows somewhere in the background" (4. 293). This is, of course, incorrect. Still alive and jesting, the Fool drops out of the play in act 3, scene 6,
and never reappears. In the last scene of the play, Lear comes onstage,
carrying the corpse of Cordelia, whom he has just discovered hanged.
Throughout the remainder of this scene, Lear does little else than mourn
for his daughter. His final words are:

> And my poor fool is hang'd! No, no, no life!
> Why should a dog, a horse, a rat, have life,
> And thou no breath at all? Thou'lt come no more,
> Never, never, never, never, never!—
> Pray you, undo this button: thank you, sir.
> Do you see this? Look on her,—look,—her lips,—
> Look there!—look there! (5. 3. 306–12)

Lear's "my poor fool," a term of endearment, cannot refer to the Fool, who
is neither present nor mentioned anywhere else in this scene. Taken in

isolation, line 306 might cause some confusion; however, the passionate grief for his dead daughter that Lear expresses throughout his final appearance, especially his obvious reference to the girl in the above-quoted passage, leaves no reasonable doubt that the hanged "fool" is Cordelia.[36]

By relying on his own memory instead of re-examining the text, the speaker, falling into the same misrepresentation that he attributes to Tolstoy, exposes the tenuousness of his own commitment to the humanistic attitude toward life. The speaker inadvertently reveals an opposition to humanism, to the celebration of man's will to endure all that life in this world offers, that is greater even than Tolstoy's. Tolstoy only rejects the Fool, but the speaker in Orwell's essay kills him.

Orwell's feelings about literature at times indicate that the desire to withdraw from the turmoil of the present is as strong as his determination to become involved in it. In the mid-forties, Orwell, daily exposed to propaganda and false atrocity stories, began to emphasize his interest in the literature of a saner, more decent age. He found in the 1810 issues of the *Quarterly Review* a fair-minded attitude toward Napoleonic France, the enemy, that stood in sharp contrast to the uncompromising anti-German prejudice of contemporary newspapers.[37] Certainly, one important reason for the appeal of such early journals was their temporal remoteness from Orwell's times: "The great fascination of these old magazines is the completeness with which they 'date.' "[38] In browsing through these musty volumes, Orwell was probably attempting to cleanse himself of the ugly political realities that were always forcing their way into the mind.

Although in discussing Orwell's works from *Down and Out* to *Coming Up for Air* I have pointed out the influence of various literary figures, above all writers more or less directly associated with the modernist tradition, I have delayed a detailed examination of Orwell's ideas about writing because the essays in which his literary biases and interests are most clearly set forth do not begin to appear until the late thirties, and only in the works of the last decade of his life do we find enough material to serve as the basis for generalizations regarding his views on literary values and the creative process. An investigation of Orwell's statements about the test of superior literature will reveal more fully the nature and aims of his own writings. As we have seen, Orwell has expressed continual alarm at the social and political transformations taking place in the world around him. It is, therefore, not surprising that he shows a marked admiration for literature that has resisted time and oblivion. He states that "for any work of art there is only one test worth bothering about—survival," a criterion upon which he has based his praise of Joyce, Eliot, D. H. Lawrence, and others who produced significant works between 1910 and 1930.[39] Another writer, but from an earlier period, who meets this test is Dickens. Dickensian scenes and phrases stick in the memory, unexpectedly breaking into consciousness throughout one's lifetime, and his characters make an ineffaceable impression upon the mind.[40] Orwell found particularly appealing those works that transport us into a special kind of reality. Thus, in reading *Ulysses* one feels that there is an intimate connection between Joyce's mind and one's own, "that there exists some world outside time and space in which you and he are together."[41]

One factor responsible for literary survival is that the superior artist concerns himself with problems and experiences common to mankind as a whole. *A Tale of Two Cities* is valuable partly because in it Dickens deals with matters relevant to man's basic capacity for good and evil. Dickens's moral view is much broader than that offered by Marxist criticism, which, Orwell claimed, concentrates on human conflicts appearing only at specific and predetermined points in history.[42] And even in the twentieth century, when poetry is not highly regarded, according to Orwell, Kipling's verse remains popular because it deals in a memorable way with "some emotion which very nearly every human being can share."[43]

Other remarks in the essay "Rudyard Kipling" are noteworthy because they show how Orwell's view of literature gradually assumed more and more importance in his critical works—literature, especially prose fiction, as the expression of an inner vision. Orwell points out that when reading Kipling one is often taken in even by "spurious" sentiments, that his most popular verses convey ideas that "may not be true"; however, these often platitudinous and sentimental thoughts are of the type that frequently influence our own outlook on life (2. 195–96). Such expressions of subjective truth are vividly presented in the novels of Dickens. What one remembers from *A Tale of Two Cities* is the Reign of Terror, the description of which has a "terrible intensity." Orwell pictures Dickens brooding over the frenzied revolutionaries with a "curious imaginative intensity"; even though historically false, this "sinister vision" has been accepted by later generations of readers. This kind of inner vision can wield great power over a reader's mind. According to Orwell, everyone remembers the frightful scenes of revolution because "they have the quality of nightmare, and it is Dickens' own nightmare."[44] His characters are fantastic and unbelievable in terms of the real world of everyday reality, yet they remain rooted in our minds, existing within a "never-never land, a kind of eternity" (1. 455).

In regard to Orwell's emphasis on literature as an intensely subjective vision of reality, it is helpful to recall his warning that a writer must not let external pressures, especially political ones, violate the sanctity of his inner life. Discussing the dangers of totalitarianism, he warns that without imaginative spontaneity the writer cannot create. The imagination is like those "wild animals" that "will not breed in captivity."[45] And even though admitting that there is intellectual progress from one period to the next,

Orwell stresses that any writer really intent on writing well should avoid trying to alter his mentality, his inner world, in order to seem up-to-date. It is wiser, Orwell advises the middle-class writer who wishes to think like a proletarian, to preserve "one's early acquired vision" of life.[46]

It is this preadult view of reality, whatever the writer's social class, which gives to a work that intensity and vividness characteristic of great literature. Certainly much that Orwell found so captivating in Dickens resulted from his ability to re-create the child's picture of reality. Even while reading Dickens's description of, for example, the Murdstones from an adult perspective that makes them appear as semi-comic grotesques, a reader can, owing to the novelist's ability to share and re-create a child's viewpoint, feel that David Copperfield's tormentors are also sinister and threatening.[47] In line with this is Orwell's observations on the relationship between Swift's life-denying attitude and those childhood feelings we have all experienced: "A child, when it is past the infantile stage but still looking at the world with fresh eyes, is moved by horror almost as often as by wonder—horror of snot and spittle, of the dogs' excrement on the pavement, the dying toad full of maggots, the sweaty smell of grown-ups, the hideousness of old men, with their bald heads and bulbous noses."[48]

Before examining the further implications of these statements, we should note that the modern writers whom Orwell praises in "Inside the Whale"—the "Joyce-Eliot group" flourishing during the twenties—felt no compulsion to deal with narrowly political matters. Their works, Orwell claims, direct our attention "to Rome, to Byzantium, to Montparnasse, to Mexico, to the Etruscans, to the subconscious, to the solar plexus—to everywhere except the places where things are actually happening." The "cosmic despair" and "sense of decadence" indulged in by these writers, their "yearning after lost faith and impossible civilisations," were possible because they lived in an unusually "comfortable epoch," an age in which modern totalitarianism was not yet a real threat (1. 507–9 passim). And in the same essay Orwell makes clear his belief that with the appearance of the totalitarian menace the bourgeois civilization that has produced and sustained the modern writer is disappearing, and literature as it has been known is going into eclipse (1. 525). He repeated this warning in the early forties, pointing out that the belief that had consoled writers like Joyce and Lawrence during World War I, the assurance that soon society would regain its sanity, was no longer tenable.[49]

These remarks suggest that Orwell, intent on capturing the demonic spirit of the age in his own works, is preparing to move beyond the moderns. The implication is that now the writer may have to draw upon his own irrational depths if his work is to reflect the cultural barbarism down into which history has suddenly spiraled. Such an assumption underlies Orwell's tendency to deny any necessary connection between artistic genius and a sane and realistic view of external reality. For all their grotesqueness, Poe's stories (whom Orwell regards as almost insane) still ring true. His fictional world has a "maniacal logic" capable of evoking an imaginative response from readers: "When, for instance, the drunkard seizes the black cat and cuts its eye out with his penknife, one knows exactly *why* he did it, even to the point of feeling that one could have done the same oneself."[50]

In a later essay, "Politics vs. Literature: An Examination of *Gulliver's Travels*" (1946), Orwell puts forward the thesis that Swift endures not despite his reactionary and even life-denying qualities but precisely because of them. He sees Swift as a Tory anarchist, a man as contemptuous of governments as he is suspicious of libertarian ideals. Above all, Orwell's Swift is a neurotic. Physically impotent, torn between a "sincere loathing" for and a "morbid fascination" with sex, and pathologically horrified by human excrement, Swift cannot believe that there is any value to life on earth. As a result, *Gulliver's Travels* is a savage denigration of humanity. The Houyhnhnms' life of reason—with its emotional flatness, lack of stimulating conversation, limitations on birth, and anti-sexuality—is really the expression of a death wish. The aim of the Houyhnhnms is to be "as like a corpse as is possible while retaining physical life" (4. 218).

Swift's mind may have been diseased, writes Orwell, but there is something within all of us that responds to his pathological vision. Beside our normal love of life there exists somewhere within us a "horror of existence," a mixture of pleasure and disgust in our attitude toward the body. Swift possessed a "terrible intensity of vision" that enabled him to pick out a "single hidden truth" and magnify and distort it into an effective work of art. From this Orwell concludes that one's vision of life, if it is intensely held, can produce great literature even if it should be just barely sane (4. 222–23).

Given Orwell's concern with the irrational and the importance he attached to the preservation of one's childhood mental landscape, it is probably no coincidence that those subjective, even grotesque, visions of reality that so fascinated him come from the pens of writers—Dickens, Poe, Swift—usually first read during childhood, or at least during the childhood of Orwell and his contemporaries. The nightmarish intensity of these works is, therefore, deeply buried in the imagination, ready to be tapped as a source of creativity by the writer intent on exposing the world's madness.

As we have seen, the novels of the thirties obliquely express psychological dilemmas commonly associated with adolescence or earlier stages of life, and the realistic narrative supposedly dealing with sociopolitical types of experience becomes a psychodramatic re-enactment of the central character's Oedipal conflicts. By the midforties, however, Orwell was ready to face his childhood and use it as the basis of a broadened view of reality.

An important example of Orwell's more conscious and systematic exploration into childhood is the essay "Such, Such Were the Joys" (1946), one aim of which is to unearth the child's "distorted. . . vision of the world," his "irrational terrors and lunatic misunderstandings" (4. 366–67). In Orwell's retrospective view, enrollment in St. Cyprian's stands for Blair's entry into an alien world in which the grotesque is normal. Blair is convinced that local townspeople are spies employed by the school to report on the off-campus activities of the boys (4.342–43). Falsely assuming that a female visitor to the school, informed of his bed-wetting, will be assigned the task of whipping him, the boy has a "terrifying vision of her arriving for the occasion in full riding kit and armed with a hunting whip" (4. 332). The feeling arises that the young and their elders are different species of humanity: the Swiftian image of adults as physically repulsive, as "joyless grotesques" with no reason for staying alive past thirty, leads to the child's conviction that aging is an "almost obscene calamity, which . . . will never happen to itself" (4. 367).

Here Orwell is more than the cartographer of the child's mental landscape; he is also mapping out that authoritarian terrain dealt with later in *1984*. In "Such, Such Were the Joys," reality appears divided: Blair's remote childhood within the confines of the family home is an area of experience distinct from his life at St. Cyprian's, and the latter divided into menacing adult figures of authority and students.

The preschool period remains in the mind only as a dim, fragmentary memory mainly of pleasant experiences. Becoming aware of sex at about the age of five or six, he engages in "vaguely erotic" games with little girls, games that give him a "definitely pleasant thrill." "About the same time," the speaker notes, "I fell deeply in love, a far more worshipping kind of love than I have ever felt for anyone since, with a girl named Elsie" (4. 352). Elsewhere the speaker recalls the love he had had at this time for his mother, the only adult able to arouse this emotion in him (4. 366).

Orwell recalls that his home was a place of love, not fear (4. 349). The reverse is the case at St. Cyprian's: fear rules and love yields to anxiety. If, however, entry into St. Cyprian's means the loss of one's original home and family, as is suggested by references to his parents' inability to mitigate the harshness of Sambo, the headmaster, a closer look at the essay hints at a shadowy connection between home and school. At one point, Orwell sees himself as having been "flung" into St. Cyprian's (4. 334), and later in the essay he likens this experience to "suddenly [being] taken out his warm nest [his home] and flung" into an evil world (4. 349). Rather than a natural, even if painful, separation, movement forward into school life becomes a violent parental rejection, as though the punishment for some misdeed. This impression is given by the suggestion that the remembered preschool existence is a scene of conflict between Eros (the boy's sexual play and his intense love for the mother) and suppression, the latter represented by the "gruff-voiced" father's habitual command "Don't" (4. 360).

Orwell's re-creation of the atmosphere at St. Cyprian's, where the flesh is mortified and exposure to the physically disgusting is the rule, indicates that school exists to curb and chastise the libidinal self. Here it is normal for a boy to be a wretched "snotty-nosed creature, his face almost permanently dirty, his hands chapped, his nails bitten, his handkerchief a sodden horror, his bottom . . . blue with bruises." So skimpy are the boys' meals that they eagerly steal leftover scraps from the masters' plates (4. 346). The schoolboy is constantly assailed by revolting reminders of his and his companions' flesh—sweaty socks, dirty towels, faecal smells, resounding chamber pots, and the sight of human excrement (4. 348).

More than a place of punishment, life at St. Cyprian's may be a symbolic enactment of some earlier offense only vaguely suggested by the memories of the preschool years. Certainly the expression of libidinal urges brings down the wrath of the authorities. The discovery of the boys' sexual activity, presumably group masturbation, results in a frenzied outbreak of interrogations, confessions, floggings, and repentances. Justly or not, each boy feels implicated—"guilt seemed to hang in the air like a pall of smoke." And even though wrongly accused of the deed, young Blair feels that he, too, is guilty.

Contributing to the tension is the circumstance that at St. Cyprian's, as presumably in the past, the system provokes what it punishes. Thus Flip, the headmaster's wife and mother-surrogate to the boys, embodies the most disturbing ambiguous fantasy of womanhood—the female as both siren and scourge. On the one hand, she is a brutal and callous tyrant, a woman as willing to administer a caning as she is to fill a boy with self-contempt. On the other hand, she is the object of the boys' vaguely erotic longings. Some days the youths cower before her accusing eyes, but at other times she becomes "a flirtatious queen surrounded by courtier-lovers," a woman capable of turning detestation into servile attraction—"at [her] first smile one's hatred turned into a sort of cringing love." Part harpy, she is also part seductress in the midst of vulnerable youth—"before Flip one seemed as helpless as a snake before the snake-charmer" (4. 350–51).

In Orwell's view, existence at St. Cyprian's involves a continual self-violation: the atmosphere of guilt seeps into one so that the youngster becomes his own betrayer. Having discovered Blair's urine-stained sheets, a school matron commands, "REPORT YOURSELF," and overhearing the boy's boast that Sambo's beating has not been painful, Flip cries, "RE-PORT YOURSELF AGAIN!" (4. 332–33). Within such an atmosphere of self-accusal, one's very body, once a source of joy, turns Judas. Young Blair accepts unquestioningly Flip's unnerving assertion that black rings around the eyes are a sure sign of sexual depravity (4. 354).

One reason for Orwell's attraction to the intense and even bizarre qualities in the works of Dickens, Poe, and Swift is that in distorting reality they reveal truths not communicable through a more realistic style or mentally stable outlook. Similarly, the child's distorted reality and "lunatic misunderstandings" dealt with in "Such, Such Were the Joys" have a validity that the adult may not recognize. At one point, Blair, mulling over the crime of which the boys are guilty in the eyes of the masters, assumes that their depravity is in some way connected with the tendency of the penis to become erect (1. 353). Superficially misleading, this apparent misconception is "true" in terms of Orwell's vision of reality, for one suspects that insofar as St. Cyprian's is a sort of penal colony, its basic imperative is the suppression of the libidinal self. It is important to note that Blair's anguished awareness of the world's harshness and his own wickedness appears immediately after Orwell's description of the boy's double beating, a punishment ultimately traceable to his bed-wetting. In fact, enuresis is the first element mentioned in the essay: "Soon after I arrived at St. Cyprian's . . . I began wetting my bed. I was now aged eight, so that this was a reversion to a habit which I must have grown out of at least four years earlier" (4. 330–31).

One implication of this is that in some way the boy is in effect asserting the need to regain the lost world of childhood by means of the penis; or perhaps, since the penis acts on its own outside conscious volition, what (from the viewpoint of a child ignorant of the urethra) might seem that member's incontinence stands for the body's blind striving to regain its primitive condition of instinctual freedom. Ironically, the second period of bed-wetting, this symbolic return to the past, may be vaguely linked to Blair's expulsion from childhood and his oppressive sense of being exiled in an alien and unloving world. Indeed, this anarchic behavior of the body may be the nodal point from which stem the boy's other discontents, just as the reference to enuresis is the starting point for the essayist's exploration into his past.

At St. Cyprian's, the teaching of history actually discourages any curiosity about the past. The masters' determination to retain the annually awarded Harrow History prize results in history lessons involving nothing more than the rote memorization of factual answers to questions likely to be asked during competition. As a result, the students become conspirators in their own educational victimization. Reading between the lines, one suspects that this mindless drilling—Orwell describes' them as "orgies" in which the boys, wildly vying for the favor of headmistress Flip, jump up shouting out the correct answers (4. 337)—is an opiate designed to create a false sense of euphoria and optimism. This meaningless aggregation of unrelated data is official history, history as the masters wish it defined to conceal the unofficial reality that behind the facade of institutional respectability is taking place a grim, at times even barbaric, struggle to suppress the body's instinctual urgings. Like the frenzied political pep rallies in *Animal Farm*, the hysterical excitement of the classroom fosters the comforting illusion that history, rather than a tragic sacrifice of primal vitality on the altar of social regimentation, is a triumphal march toward collective happiness.

The dilemma of Orwell the writer is analogous to that of Blair the schoolboy: authoritarian pressures from outside are violating the integrity of adult and youth alike. The writing of "Such, Such Were the Joys" is Orwell's attempt to revitalize his own creative powers; the autobiographical journey into the internalized past is a search for the headwaters of his imagination. In another essay written at about the same time, "How the Poor Die" (1946), Orwell vividly demonstrates the effect of the childhood past—irrational, intense, and in this case irrepressible—on the adult's reaction to a particular situation.

The essayist recalls a night in 1929 when, ill with pneumonia and feverish, he had entered "Hôpital X" in a working-class district in Paris. His memories of this place are unpleasant. The public ward where he is sent for treatment is alarmingly dirty, and the sterilization of instruments is rare. Both doctors and medical students show a callous lack of concern with the sick as human beings, and the nurses perform their duties with an inefficiency never allowed in an English hospital.

But despite descriptions of how the poor are denied good medical treatment, the main thrust of the essay is not directed at sociomedical problems. Orwell admits that the hospital was atypical. Indeed, most of the patients can resign themselves to the poor conditions, while some—such as the penniless malingerers who make themselves useful to stay in the ward during the winter—find the life almost comfortable. Something much more subtle and intriguing claims the attention of Orwell the patient—the survival here of a nineteenth-century "atmosphere" (4. 230–31).

This idea of atmosphere is central to the essay. And it is important to note that this atmosphere is not simply something contained in the hospital. Rather it is a function of two factors: the directly observable instances of suffering and, more important, Orwell the patient's psychological predisposition to experience these things in terms of his own childhood vision of hospitalization. What he sees and hears and smells here call up within Orwell powerful emotional responses whose roots lie far back in his childhood.

On first entering the hospital ward, Orwell becomes conscious of "a strange feeling of familiarity," the origin of which he cannot discover at that moment (4. 224). At the end of the essay, Orwell discovers the source of this feeling in his experiences with an old sick nurse who had taken care of him twenty years previously, during his childhood:

It happened that as a child I had had [Tennyson's poem "In the Children's Hospital"] read aloud to me by a sick-nurse whose own working life might have stretched back to the time when Tennyson wrote the poem. The horrors and sufferings of the old-style hospitals were a vivid memory to her. We had shuddered over the poem together. (4. 233)

The bulk of the essay shows just how Tennyson's gruesome poem, combined with the nurse's own nineteenth-century attitude toward hospitals, conditions Orwell the patient's response to his present surroundings; for unlike the majority of the patients, who can resign themselves to the hospital, or the malingerers, who find there a welcome refuge from the cold, Orwell reacts as though confined within a chamber of horrors.

The narrator points out that during the nineteenth century people customarily regarded the hospital as a dungeon, a place of torment and death—in short, an "antechamber to the tomb." The same attitude is shared by Orwell the patient. The behavior of the staff may arouse his criticism, but what evokes at once his deepest revulsion and most vivid passages of prose are the instances of mortal decay and death. One patient screams in pain from the mere weight of his bedclothes, another continually coughs up "blood-stained mucus," and the dead body of a third is allowed to lie in the ward for hours. Orwell's reaction to the sight of this corpse is one of deepest fear:

As I gazed at the tiny, screwed-up face it struck me that this disgusting piece of refuse, waiting to be carted away and dumped on a slab in the dissecting room, was an example of "natural" death. . . . There you are, then, I thought, that's what is waiting for you, twenty, thirty, forty years hence. . . . One wants to live, of course, indeed one only stays alive by virtue of the fear of death, but I think now, as I thought then, that it's better to die violently and not too old. People talk about the horrors of war, but what weapon has man invented that even approaches in cruelty some of the commoner diseases? "Natural" death, almost by definition, means something slow, smelly and painful. (4. 228)

Orwell's terror of the "mental atmosphere" he senses in the hospital is a reaction deriving from his childhood, essentially nineteenth-century vision of this "antechamber to the tomb."

As suggested above, this old-fashioned, even primitive, attitude toward hospitals is not confined to Orwell the patient. The speaker, the present-tense Orwell, has the same anxiety, although he is more capable of rationalizing it:

I would be far from complaining about the treatment I have received in any English hospital, but I do know that it is a sound instinct that warns people to keep out of hospitals if possible, and especially out of the public wards. . . . However great the kindness and the efficiency, in every hospital death there will be some cruel, squalid detail . . . arising out of the haste, the crowding, the impersonality of a place where every day people are dying among strangers. (4. 232)

The speaker recognizes, too, the unconscious nature of this attitude. Although this dread of hospitals has recently "disappeared," it still exists as a "dark patch not far beneath the surface of our minds" (ibid.). Like the memory of Orwell's childhood experience of his nurse's shudderings forgotten by him for twenty years, it can suddenly come alive and take control over one's responses. In "How the Poor Die," we see, then, how a childhood experience awakens within the adult Orwell an acute sense of terror regarding hospitals and, by sharpening his emotional responses to Hospital X, keeps him from sinking into the passive torpidity characteristic of the other patients. Charged with the intensity of childhood anxiety, the later confrontation with death survives the passage of almost two decades to expand itself into a general statement about man's unconscious fears.

Orwell's ideas about the literary significance of a writer's personal vision of life might be summed up as follows: a good novel, for instance, must embody an attitude toward life that the common reader has experienced and to which he will be able to respond, presumably either consciously or unconsciously. Orwell indicates that this vision need not be compatible with the utilitarian logic of probability that we follow in our everyday transactions with the external world. In fact, in his later critical writings (of which the essay on Swift is a good example), the emphasis is placed on those visions that appeal to deeper, less rational areas of the personality, which involve attitudes rooted within our unconscious minds. If this is a correct paraphrase of Orwell's views, then it becomes easier to understand his interest in preserving the childhood view of reality, for the most deeply ingrained vision of life possessed by an individual takes form in his earliest days. It is the core of his character, the most durable, and probably the most influential, element in his entire psychological makeup. Consequently, the artist's personal past is the main source of his imaginative vitality, the force without which creativity must wither away.

It may seem inconsistent to stress both Orwell's need to shield himself from the moral and intellectual insanity he observed in contemporary life and his interest in preserving an often irrational, even morbid, vision of reality. This is, however, less confusing if we assume a direct relationship between Orwell's fascination with the literature of the grotesque and his development as a novelist. If Orwell the moralist condemned the world's madness (the psychotic nationalism, the transformation of historical truth into ideological myth, the emergence of barbarism), Orwell the imaginative writer found this irrationality liberating. In praising the savage and hallucinatory qualities of Swift, Dickens, and Poe (a list that he later extended), Orwell was implicitly acknowledging a truth about his own fiction—that his creative energy manifested itself most powerfully in near-surrealistic expressions of disgust, terror, power hunger, sadism, and violence. Although Orwell regarded the childhood vision of reality as the imagination's vital center, close inspection revealed it to be less the inviolable secret garden of the romantics than a Freudian jungle—or the Lake Isle of Innisfree transformed into the island of Doctor Moreau.

Orwell implies as much in the two essays just discussed. Undercutting young Blair's attempt to segregate subjective feelings from the demands imposed on him by a hostile and accusing outer world is the admission that the inner self is full of hate (4. 360); so strong is the older Blair's childhood terror of hospitals that it compels him to flee from the Hospital X into the winter night even before his treatment is completed, a potentially suicidal act (4. 229).

However, Orwell's willingness to confront the disturbing ambiguities of his own personality, coupled with his interest in those writers whose fantastic creations have withstood the test of time, suggests that, in the 1940s, he was better prepared to transform a subjective vision of reality into collective experience.

Chapter IX

The Golden Country

One metaphor Orwell uses to characterize contemporary society is that of a gravely ill "patient," the victim of a "mental disease" that must be "diagnosed" before he can be cured.[1] Orwell the writer is, therefore, also Orwell the diagnostician constantly probing into himself and into society. The essay on comic postcards, "The Art of Donald McGill" (1941), suggests that no aspect of life is too minor to deserve scrutiny in Orwell's search for signs of social health or deterioration.

According to Orwell, our first impression on looking at comic postcards is of their juvenile quality:

> They have an utter lowness of mental atmosphere which comes out not only in the nature of the jokes but, even more, in the grotesque, staring, blatant quality of the drawings. The designs, like those of a child, are full of heavy lines and empty spaces, and all the figures in them, every gesture and attitude, are deliberately ugly, the faces grinning and vacuous, the women monstrously parodied, with bottoms like Hottentots. Your second impression, however, is of indefinable familiarity. What do these things remind you of? What are they so like? In the first place, of course, they remind you of the barely different postcards which you probably gazed at in your childhood.

In this essay, we can detect Orwell's interest in the broader significance of childhood experiences. These cards, with their crude simplicity, also embody experiences that have persisted through the ages. What we see in these drawings "is something as traditional as Greek tragedy, a sort of sub-world of smacked bottoms and scrawny mothers-in-law which is a part of western European consciousness" (2. 156).

Especially important in cultural terms is the fact that most of these comic postcards are sexually obscene but not immoral, by which Orwell means that the references to illegitimacy, adultery, and the like are amusing only because they exist within a larger social context where a wedding is considered an exciting event and the rightness of domestic fidelity is still recognized. What these cards express is a widely shared fantasy existing below the surface of our accepted codes of morality; they give voice to the Sancho Panza self who dreams of physical comfort, idleness, and sexual gratification.

Besides conveying Orwell's interest in the more or less archetypal quality of these postcards, "The Art of Donald McGill" reveals his concern over the relationship of civilization to man's sensual needs. Noting that within the last four hundred years, the body-soul dualism has received increasing emphasis, Orwell warns that the celebration of the body, of the anarchic joy in physical gratification, may be declining. Social order has led to the suppression of the Sancho Panza self: "There is a constant world-wide conspiracy to pretend that he is not there, or at least that he doesn't matter" (2. 163).

The development of the essay itself parallels this centuries-long process of suppression. If the essayist's first assertion, that these bawdy cards "are on sale everywhere" (2. 155), implies a belief in the omnipresence of mankind's dream of sensual fulfillment, his concluding statement reflects an alarmed awareness that the Sancho Panza world is shrinking:

> In the past the mood of the comic postcard could enter into the central stream of literature, and jokes barely different from McGill's could casually be uttered between the murders in Shakespeare's tragedies. That is no longer possible, and a whole category of humor . . . has dwindled down to these ill-drawn postcards, leading a barely legal existence in cheap stationers' windows. (2. 165)

However, by the midforties Orwell turned his attention to the irrational, even perverse, collective fantasies of contemporary society. In "Benefit of Clergy: Some Notes on Salvador Dali" (1944), Orwell examines a far different kind of artist, one whose popularity is on the rise and whose works reveal something about his admirers as well as about himself.

Although not doubting that Dali shrewdly flaunted his outrageous behavior in order to gain a reputation for originality, Orwell feels sure that other, more arcane motives are at work in the eccentric Spaniard. Dali's autobiography, with its catalogue of sadistic deeds, is, Orwell claims, less important as a record of facts than as the expression of fantasies stemming from deep-seated desires. In Dali's *Life* wish becomes fact. However, it is not enough simply to pin onto Dali's bizarre surrealism the Marxist tag of middle-class decadence. Orwell insists that we must go further, must probe into the area of sexual pathology to understand not only Dali himself but also the reasons for his current widespread appeal. We must ask "*why* the *rentiers* and the aristocrats should buy his pictures instead of . . . making love like their grandfathers" (3. 164).

As I have pointed out, Orwell's criticism of the Edwardians was directed at what he regarded as their inability to understand the contemporary world. The sane and rational mind of H. G. Wells, or any other progressive intellectual of his time, we are told, cannot grasp the brute fact that the violent eruption of irrational forces in the West has made a mockery of liberal hopes: "Tamerlane and Genghis Khan seem credible figures now, and Machiavelli seems a serious thinker, as they didn't in 1910."[2] The difference between 1910 and the 1940s is that the latter period is a political stone age. Particularly alarming is the circumstance that it is from the depths of the Western soul itself that the rough beast of neo-barbarism has emerged and begun slouching its way toward the centers of modern civilization to be born.

As Orwell's remarks on Dali's popularity and the brutality of modern life suggest, two important symptoms of cultural illness are pathological sexuality and power hunger. In James Hadley Chase's gangster novels, especially *No Orchids for Miss Blandish*, the two are linked. Reminding us of repeated scenes of perversely erotic violence, Orwell points out that Chase is not dealing in ordinary pornography: Chase's stress is on cruelty, not sensual pleasure. The sex is sado-masochistic, and the motivating force behind the displays of perverse brutality is the "pursuit of power."[3]

Chase is singled out because he is a British writer who, presumably never having lived in the United States, has allowed the imported American fantasy world of gangsterism, as presented in books and films, to control his imagination. Moreover the British reading public, which once sought escape in such relatively harmless "old-style" tales as the *Raffles* stories or the *Sherlock Holmes* mysteries, is now fascinated by the newer literature of sado-masochistic violence. American "realism"—with its assumption that greed and moral debasement are normal, that power and righteousness are identical, and that there is something laudable in the triumph of the strong over the weak—is mentally and morally violating the sensibility of the common people. The mass appeal of Chase's novels implies the disappearance of any restraints on what the English are willing to accept: "Emancipation is complete, Freud and Machiavelli have reached the outer suburbs" (3. 224).

Although "Raffles and Miss Blandish" is not a detailed and carefully documented study of contemporary literary taste and its relationship to social and political attitudes, the fact that Orwell assumed some "interconnection between" sado-masochism and totalitarian power hunger (3. 222) is a clue to the direction of his thinking during the later forties. Also this essay reminds us of Orwell's ability to turn dross into gold, the "golden country" of his last novel. If Orwell the diagnostician found Chase's sado-masochistic novels symptomatic of a cultural malaise and Orwell the moralist viewed the popularity of such works as a sign of spiritual degeneration, Orwell the creative writer saw in the widespread acceptance of Chase's brutal fantasies a green light for the expression of his own vision of hatred and violence in *1984*. In line with this, Orwell expanded his list of writers who were gifted with the ability to expose the savage tendencies existing below the surface of our civilized consciousness. To Swift, Poe, and Dickens he added Jack London and Eugene Zamyatin.

According to Orwell, the "Fascist strain" in the former gave him a "feel" for the brutal anti-hedonism of the ruling class depicted in *The Iron Heel*, a circumstance that makes this novel more credible than Wells's *The Sleeper*

Wakes.[4] For much the same reason Huxley's *Brave New World* comes off second best when compared to Zamyatin's *We*, in which we are more aware that "ancient human instincts" are still operative. Noting the deliberate parallel in the novel between society in the present and ancient slave states, Orwell concludes that Huxley lacks the Russian's intuitive comprehension of the primitive element in totalitarianism.[5]

The essay "Arthur Koestler" (1944) provides several other interesting clues as to what, in Orwell's opinion, the political novel should deal with. Discussing Koestler's first novel, *The Gladiators*, Orwell points out that Spartacus, leader of the ancient slave revolt and central character of the book, is meant to be "an allegorical figure, a primitive version of the proletarian dictator," and a "modern man dressed up" (3. 237). Orwell does not object to such a treatment of historical figures, but he is critical of Koestler's failure to deal adequately with his allegory. The novel is weakened by Koestler's vagueness regarding the protagonist. Although in some places the book sets forth the idea that the use of force and cunning perverts the original idealistic aim of the revolt, Spartacus does not embody this theme. He is not shown to be either a visionary or a man hungry for power. His motives never made clear, he remains a confusing figure pushed along by forces that neither he nor the reader can understand. In Orwell's view, the fact that the slave leader's motives are shadowy and do not produce a single-minded commitment to political activism disqualifies him from being a satisfactory allegorical representation of modern revolutionary leadership. In short, *The Gladiators* fails because Koestler allows historical truth to interfere with allegorical truth. His explanation of the slave revolt's collapse, as well as his characterization of Spartacus, may possess historical validity, but it does not throw light on the essential factors responsible for the unbridgeable gulf between power and righteousness in modern revolutionary movements (3. 238).

Orwell's criticism of *The Gladiators* has some bearing on his own aims in *1984*. One may infer from Orwell's remarks that the political novelist must not allow historical facts to divert his attention away from the more important task of probing below the surface of events to unearth the hidden motives at the root of political activity. Even more important than describing what happens on the stage of history is the novelist's responsibility to understand and convey what occurs in the minds of men involved in political struggles. The criticism of Koestler's failure to invest Spartacus with an excessive craving for power directs our attention to one of the most important motives to be dealt with in *1984*.

At one point in *1984* (1949), Winston Smith and his girl friend Julia are in their hideaway, she sleeping and he carefully studying Emmanuel Goldstein's *The Theory and Practice of Oligarchical Collectivism*, which describes the development of England into the center of the totalitarian

empire Oceania. Just as Winston arrives at Goldstein's all-important revelation of the basic and original motive behind the Party's rise to power, he
looks at Julia, the upper part of whose body is exposed, and then, shutting
the book in midsentence, he climbs into bed beside her and pulls the cover
over them both.[6]

This failure to read on, to finish the sentence that will expose the central
truth about Oceania, is quite remarkable, considering that Winston has
been engaged in what appears to be a desperate attempt to break the
Party's grip on society. However, even if this secret is never presented in
the abstract terms of the political scientist, the dramatic events of the
narrative are a revelation. But before examining these events to discover
the completed meaning of Goldstein's sentence, we need to look at another
essay that indicates Orwell's interests in the forties—"New Words," which
was never published during Orwell's lifetime and, according to the editors
of *The Collected Essays, Journalism and Letters*, may have been written
in 1940. In this short piece, Orwell complains that the English language is
unsuited to describing psychological realities. For example, we cannot
accurately describe a dream because there are no words that convey the
special atmosphere of a dream. What makes this lack all the more serious is
that most of our motives—our preferences and aversions, our moral and
aesthetic feelings—spring from preverbal areas of the mind (2. 3–4).

Orwell goes on to claim that the language of imaginative writing is a
subtle "flank-attack" on this problem of communication, the words of the
poet and novelist connoting something beyond their dictionary meanings.
Still, unless a writer is especially gifted, words are more likely to falsify
inner feelings than accurately express them. How, then, wonders Orwell,
can we find a really adequate vocabulary to make the inner self accessible,
to "give thought an objective existence" (2. 10). His tentative solution is,
first, to concentrate on delineating those unverbalized feelings common to
people in general and, second, to enrich our vocabulary by exploiting what
he believes is the natural correlation between certain sounds and meanings, for example, the sounds "plum" and "plun," which, according to
Orwell, we associate with "bottomless oceans" (2. 11). Although he does
not directly connect film techniques with verbal experimentation, he
strongly implies that by using words and syllables in this manner we should
be able to reproduce much the same type of dream effects as are conveyed
by images on a screen. He claims that "there is very little in the mind that
could not *somehow* be represented by the strange distorting powers of the
film" (2. 10).

Although none of Orwell's following essays deal explicitly with the need
to develop a literary means for expressing fantasies, there is reason to
believe that the topic continued to interest him. Several years afterward, in
"Raffles and Miss Blandish," he refers to *No Orchids for Miss Blandish* as a

"day-dream appropriate to a totalitarian age" (3. 223); and as I shall point out later in *1984* he employs pictorial and phonic devices to reveal the secret fears and longings at the heart of Oceanian society.

Underlying many interpretations of *1984* is the assumption that it is, as one writer states, an examination of the "social reality" and "public events" of modern times, and that within this work totalitarianism is presented as a problem understandable only in political terms.[7] Consequently adverse judgments on the novel are often directed at those features that are sociopolitically implausible. Critics have found fault with the docility of Orwell's proles and the relative freedom of their personal lives from government interference.[8] The claim is made that the concept of power hunger, offered as the explanation of the Party's brutality, is too vague to be meaningful,[9] and that the relationship between the rulers' aims and their suppression of sex is not really clear.[10] And because it is frequently supposed that the style of *1984* is, or is meant to be, naturalistic, depicting the surface texture of external reality,[11] those aspects of the work that are unrealistic—the two-dimensionality of the proles, the melodramatic quality of Big Brother, O'Brien, and the Party's torture devices—receive disapproval.[12]

Although one cannot deny that to some extent *1984* deals with narrowly political matters in a realistic, even naturalistic, manner, past assessments of this novel may be seen in a new light if we focus on its psychological significance. To gain a deeper understanding of *1984*, we must recognize not only that Orwell is concerned with a form of reality as much subjective as publicly political but also that his realism of detail is generating a surrealistic atmosphere.[13] Whether or not the fictive world of *1984* is a depiction of events that do or might exist in the more or less familiar realm of social and physical reality, it is, in any event, a figurative representation of an inner condition. If various elements contribute to the illusion of an external world of recognizable sociopolitical events and conditions, these same elements help define obscure motives and states of mind.[14]

An example of this duality is to be found in Goldstein and his Brotherhood, the ruling Party's archenemies. Goldstein is the "primal traitor, the earliest defiler of the Party's purity. All subsequent crimes against the Party . . . [spring] directly out of his teaching." He has a "Jewish face . . . and a small goatee beard"; his attacks on the Party are "perverse." Goldstein may be in command of a "vast shadowy army," the Brotherhood. "It was impossible . . . to be sure that the Brotherhood was not simply a myth. . . . There was no evidence, only fleeting glimpses that might mean anything or nothing: . . . faint scribbles on lavatory walls" (pp. 13–19 passim).

Insofar as Goldstein is a real or imaginary outcast, the putative author of a historical treatise on the revolution, he is, politically speaking, a sort of

Trotsky.[15] However, these quotations—in suggesting a veiled reference to Freud and, by extension, to psychoanalytic ideas—indicate another dimension to the narrative. The reference to Goldstein as the "primal traitor" calls to mind the Freudian concept of the primal crime—a prehistoric rebellion involving patricide and the usurpation of the slain father-chieftain's sexual rights over his wives and daughters by the envious tribal sons (the brothers), which, Freud hypothesized, lay at the beginning of civilization. Subsequently there was formed in the mutinous sons a conscience, a device for controlling the outward-directed thrust of destructive aggressiveness by turning it inward to function as a check on the anarchic sexual instinct. According to Freud, because it represents a restraint on sexual drives and a deflection of aggressive urges, the conscience (or superego) is responsible for the appearance of civilization and essential to its continued existence. And just as the tribal sons were able to embark on the path of civilization once prohibitions (taboos) against unbridled sexual gratification and murderous impulses were formed within them, so too each individual becomes civilized by acquiring an internal, even unconscious, set of taboos.[16]

Irving Howe calls Oceania a "model of the totalitarian state in its 'pure' or 'essential' form," that is, Orwell is presenting an *"extreme instance"* of the condition toward which totalitarianism drives.[17] I am inclined to modify this view to the extent of regarding Oceania not as a freakish aberration from the historical norm but rather as that condition toward which the civilizing process tends by its very nature. Oceania stands for that ultimate repressive stage of social organization marked by the dominance of the aggressive instinct over life-affirming Eros, an imbalance that, Freud suggested, could cause widespread misery.[18] Social and aggressive characteristics exist together in O'Brien, a high Party officer, who combines "civilized" and "urbane" manners with "brutal" features and a single-minded commitment to the Party's aim of eliminating the sexual instinct (pp. 12, 270–71).

The idea that sensuality and society are irreconcilably opposed is reflected in Winston's dream of a young woman who, by throwing aside her clothes, seems to "annihilate a whole culture" (p. 32), a judgment he later repeats as Julia strips off her Party overalls. The naked woman is the primal temptress, an emblem of that carnality that—a standing challenge to civilization's restraints—the Party is determined to suppress.

But whatever may be the theoretical dangers of uncontrolled sexuality, the deadening quality of life as it is actually experienced by Winston and others results from the perversion of libidinal impulses. For as Julia bitterly remarks, Oceania is full of hate, sadism, and violence because "sex [has] gone sour" (p. 134). And despite the enmity existing among the three world empires of Oceania, Eurasia, and Eastasia, the "Death Worship" of the last is "barely distinguishable" from the philosophies of the other two (pp. 197–98).

Winston himself is controlled by a destructive force. His first reaction to Julia is one of lust and violence: he has visions of flogging her to death with a rubber truncheon (a favorite weapon of the Party), shooting arrows into her naked body, and raping her while cutting her throat at the moment of climax. Although attributing his initial hatred of the woman to the Anti-Sex League banner she wears, he is in fact reacting as much to her sensual attractiveness, which is, paradoxically, accentuated by the tightly fitting sash (pp. 11, 17–18). A similar contradiction determines the course of their whole relationship. Despite the appearance of asserting the claims of Eros against the Party's life-denying ideology, the lovers themselves are subject to some obscure drive toward destruction. Renting a room as a trysting place, they are "intentionally stepping nearer to their graves" (p. 141). Both take a strange pleasure in thinking of themselves as "corrupt to the bones"; and as though making an implicit comment on the consequences of their relationship, Julia, describing to Winston the route to a woodland meeting place, draws a map in the dust (pp. 127, 137).

The oppressive society within which Winston plays out his futile rebellion (a personal revolt that may be more apparent than real) is also a surrealistic expression of his own inner condition. Orwell is not simply showing how a totalitarian government makes use of psychology to control the minds of its members. The situation is more complex: the whole narrative—the settings, characters, institutions, and events—is an objectification of Winston's inner self. Like Orwell's earlier novels, *1984* is to a great extent a psychodrama within a single mind, although in this case the relationship between private and public levels of experience is more convincing. There is no contradiction between the surrealistic quality of the narrative and O'Brien's assertion that reality exists only in the mind of the Party (p. 252), for the Party is itself part of Winston's own psyche. The Party's suppressive machinery of social control is the outward expression of the relentless civilizing conscience that brands certain thoughts as criminal whether or not they result in actions: "in the eyes of the Party there was no distinction between the thought and the deed" (p. 246). Winston's inner life and the institutions of Oceanian life—of all three empires, for that matter—are complementary aspects of a single solipsistic entity.

The threatening and repressive conscience appears in several forms. It is the Thought Police, who, Winston is certain, "alone" will read his secret diary. It is also the ubiquitous telescreen that, as an inner censor, shrilly interrupts his dangerous dream of the girl whose nakedness menaces civilization. Because civilized man's system of prohibitions is internalized, he cannot escape it: "You had to live . . . in the assumption that every sound you made was overheard, and, except in darkness, every movement scrutinized" (p. 4). What the telescreen misses, Big Brother—a fantasy image of the Freudian father-chief reinstated in the minds of the repentant sons[19]—relentlessly seeks out: "Always [his] eyes watching you and the voice enveloping you," thinks Winston. "Asleep or awake, working or eating, indoors or out of doors, in the bath or in bed—no escape" (p. 28).

Oceania is the paradoxical world of the subrational mind where opposites unite (WAR IS PEACE, FREEDOM IS SLAVERY, IGNORANCE IS STRENGTH [p. 17]) and, perhaps more significantly, where temporal planes are so collapsed that past and future are fused with the present, beginnings and ends merged. Dedicated to the "future or to the past," Winston's diary provides clues to the sexual desires and anxieties that, somehow linked to the past, burden him in the present and contribute to his ultimate fate. Looking at the book's paper, "creamy" and "yellowed with age," Winston recalls his "overwhelming desire to possess it," and while holding a "furtively" purchased pen over the paper, he feels a "tremor . . . through his bowels" (pp. 7–8). The book is, we learn, a lady's album—its "cream laid" paper a kind not "made" for at least fifty years (p. 94).

For Winston, memory and present reality are one: the very act of setting pen to paper becomes the symbolic re-creation of a fearful sexual adventure out of the personal, and mythic, past, a past still alive in his soul. The earliest entries in his diary reveal traces of the primal crime and its consequence, the continuing tension between anarchic impulse and prohibition, in the new owner's mind. With "childish handwriting," Winston describes a filmstrip in which a middle-aged woman and a small boy—the latter clasping the woman's body as though *"trying to burrow into her"*— are blown to bits, presumably by Oceanian bombs, while crouching in a lifeboat. This scene, with its violent primal violation of the maternal figure, indicates Winston's struggle between the craving to possess the mother and the certainty that such a longing is punishable. And when, a moment later, his pen sliding "voluptuously" over the page, Winston writes "DOWN WITH BIG BROTHER" (pp. 9–10, 19), we suspect that he is expressing conformity as much as defiance. The rebellious son's verbal assault against Big Brother, the father-chief, is simultaneously the attempt of a later son, one in whom the father-chief's punitive power has revived, to suppress the primal brothers' rebelliousness.

Even though living in the 1980s, Winston is still tied to this mythic past. Oppressed by thoughts of the Party's official anti-sexuality and his own impotence with his wife, Winston describes in his diary the terrified revulsion he once experienced when, just before intercourse with a whore, he discovered her not to be a garishly painted girl but an aged woman who, like the paper from the lady's album on which he is recording the event, was *"fifty years old at least"* (p. 69). In writing about the personal present,

Winston inadvertently conjures up the ancient curse of primal crime and primal taboo.

Reflecting on his rebellion against the Party, Winston thinks:

> What was happening was only the working-out of a process that had started years ago. The first step had been a secret, involuntary thought; the second had been the opening of the diary. . . . The last step was something that would happen in the Ministry of Love. . . . The end was contained in the beginning. But it was frightening . . . it was like a foretaste of death. (p. 160)

To grasp the implications of this foreboding, we must examine closely Winston's relationship with Julia.

In a dream, Winston sees his mother and sister, who, like the woman and child in the film, are in a boat sinking "from sight forever"; and he is overcome with anguish at the thought that now, in the hate-filled world of Oceania, he is cut off from the protective maternal love existing in that "ancient time," the historical past and his personal childhood. Abruptly the dream-image of the longed-for mother yields to a vision of the Golden Country, where elm trees sway gracefully in the breeze, "their leaves . . . like women's hair," and where, in a nearby stream, fish swim in pools. In this setting, which reminds one of the forest scene in *Coming Up for Air* and the jungle of *Burmese Days*, appears the woman who dramatically casts aside her clothes, a gesture belonging to the "ancient time" (pp. 30–32).

The Golden Country is the mother's body—partly the personal mother retained in the memory, but more importantly those traces of a once-intimate closeness to nature, to some primitive condition of vitality and serenity perhaps still hidden entirely somewhere in the mind—the possession of and by which is linked to the dreamer's present a sense of loss, isolation, and impotence. To some extent, Julia is the longed-for mother. She too boldly throws off her clothes, and she and Winston have sex in a forest setting that, with its masses of leaves stirring like "women's hair" and its archetypally evocative pool of fish, is a near copy of the dream vision. Later Winston associates their customary trysting place, a room over an antique shop in the proles' quarter, with his mother's bedroom. This lovers' hideaway awakens in Winston an "ancestral memory" of once having sat in a similar "room," "utterly alone, utterly secure, with nobody watching you, no voice pursuing you" (p. 96). Here, fed by Julia and, when terrified by the appearance of a rat, protectively enveloped by her naked body, Winston feels that he has regained an intrauterine serenity, that he has transcended the world of historical time, of physical and moral decay. The womb is the glass paperweight that Julia holds out toward him. It is a link with the remote past, a "tiny world" that, magically engulfing the bedroom, leaves him and Julia "fixed in a sort of eternity at the heart of the crystal" (p. 48).

There exists in Orwell's works a tension between wholeness and fragmentation. His characters' consciousness violated by feelings of guilt the
origin of which they only dimly apprehend, they vainly attempt to regain
some Edenic condition of peace and innocence. In *1984*, Orwell indicates
more forcefully than in his earlier works the obstacles that prevent the
return into the interiorized past, the "ancestral memory." The longing for
sister and mother, the female, is the opening act of a mythic (largely
Freudian) drama, more precisely a melodrama of lust and violence, in
fantasy if not in fact. In keeping with the melodramatic nature of the
protagonist's inner conflicts, Orwell uses the heavy, crudely exaggerated
style of the comic postcard to convey the terrifying atmosphere of a child's
nightmare still remembered by the adult. The intrusion of police-state
terrorism into the individual's private existence is the political expression
of an inner violation resonating beyond the realm of political experience,
the primitive instinctual self violated by that sense of evil that forces the self
to wander in the fallen world of historical time.

Oceania is a haunted house where "some person you . . . believed dead
long since would make a ghostly reappearance at some public trial and
implicate hundreds of others" (p. 46). Charrington, the antique dealer from
whom Winston rents the bedroom for himself and Julia, is also a revenant
from the "past," the all-powerful father alive inside the mind. Years before,
we are told, Winston's father had simply "disappeared"; and as Winston is
engaged in renting the bedroom over Charrington's shop (the symbolic
assertion of a determination to regain the maternal past), the fragile old
proprietor is dematerialized, fading "out of existence" (p. 138), as though
obliterated by the boldness of Winston's rebellious deed.

At first Winston is no more disturbed by Charrington's warning that the
bed, eventually to be used by the lovers, might be "cumbersome," than he
is by the shopkeeper's picture of an old church, which reminds Winston of a
line of childhood verse, *"here comes a chopper to chop off your head"* (pp.
97–98). Yet it is more than coincidence that from behind Charrington's
picture emerges a rat, an animal particularly horrifying to Winston; nor is it
accidental that this picture conceals the telescreen through which Charrington, really a member of the Thought Police, orders the couple's arrest
while repeating the line about the mutilating chopper. During the arrest,
Charrington, once a bent, feeble, almost disembodied old man, suddenly
becomes young and powerful and threatening.

This alarming reappearance of the father indicates that the conflict in
1984 cannot be described simply as the triumph of an immoral state over
the individual's conscience, as several critics have suggested.[20] Instead it
appears that the police-state apparatus is itself an objectification of the
triumphant Freudian superego, a force deeply embedded in the psyche.

Thwarting Winston's quest for the Golden Country, for some primitive source of peace and wholeness, is the feeling that the quest itself is a punishable erotic transgression. Consequently, the means by which Winston seeks to reach his ultimate goal—the female—becomes an object of terror. In the Ministry of Truth, where Winston works, are a number of chutes, called "memory holes," into which are dropped records destined for annihilation. However, it has been pointed out that the proper name for these devices is oubliette, not memory hole, a misnomer hinting at a connection between the mother and destruction. Not only is *mem* an Indian corruption of "ma'am" (which the Anglo-Indian Orwell would have known) but also it is linked to a cluster of childhood terms for mother ("mum," "mummy," and so on). In addition, *memory* is phonetically connected to *mammary*.[21] It is, therefore, not surprising that Winston, embraced in prison by an amorous old crone who suggests she may be his mother, gloomily agrees to the possibility of this while anticipating a truncheon beating (pp. 231–32).

But a much more dire punishment menaces Winston. As the narrative progresses, it becomes increasingly clear that beneath his conscious anxieties lies the primitive fear of sexual mutilation that, appearing in several guises, receives its most sensational form in the cageful of rats that O'Brien threatens to fasten onto Winston's face. Several times in the narrative we get the impression that Winston's archetypally criminal affair with Julia, his primally criminal liaison with a Party female supposedly devoted to the service of Big Brother, will result in an archetypal punishment. At one point, Winston, cautiously going to meet Julia in a crowded square dominated by a phallic column that supports a statue of Big Brother, pushes his way between what he thinks is a married couple, an intrusion that expresses a sexual transgression and its punishment: "For a moment it felt as though his entrails were being ground to pulp between the two muscular hips" (p. 116). Later, after chasing away the rat that has frightened Winston, Julia states that rats have been known to attack unattended babies: "It's the great huge brown ones that do it. And the nasty thing is that the brutes always—" (p. 145). The "nasty thing" is never made explicit; but this disgust, coming as it does from the hypersexed Julia—"with Julia everything came back to her own sexuality" (p. 134)—must refer to the infants' genital mutilation. Also pertinent is Winston's recollection of being tightly hugged by his mother, an embrace "somehow connected with the never-mentioned thing that was about to happen" (p. 162).

In *1984*, castration has a dual significance, standing both for the specific fear of punishment responsible for civilized man's alienation from the past and for the loss of his sense of wholeness and spontaneity. By its very presence, the mutilation anxiety suggests a tipping of the scales away from animal vitality toward death. The institutional structure of Oceania reflects such an inner condition. Newspeak, with its thought-constricting vocabulary, is the projection of that process of self-dismemberment through which the civilized mind has blotted out from consciousness large and important areas of experience. It is Winston's incomplete repression, the persistent and disturbing intimation of a primitive, libidinally rebellious self, that moves O'Brien, the cruel champion of civilization, to "cure" his patient's "defective memory" (p. 249).

Winston's cure involves a further narrowing of consciousness. At one point in the narrative, we learn of his suspicion that the Party is arrogant enough to demand belief in the proposition that two plus two are five. After being tortured, Winston proves the extent of his cure, his conversion, by accepting this absurdity. However, this final test of belief is curiously different from Winston's expectation. O'Brien holds up four fingers, and Winston must literally see five—which, for an instant, he does (p. 261). For a brief moment, Winston no longer realizes, and, therefore, no longer cares, that an extremity, an organ, is missing. In other words, loyalty to the Party and the civilization that it defends means that in addition to being cut free from his identity as a sensual creature, he must not even be aware that such an excision has occurred. If repression is to be complete, he must not remember that any part of him has had to be removed. And although the cure is not yet complete—he is still dimly aware that something has been "burnt out"—his apathy toward Julia at their final meeting is a sign that his consciousness has been radically altered (pp. 292–95).

Linked to Winston's return to the Party is his loss of faith in the proles, who, sensual and fecund and seemingly timeless, for a while appear to be the only element of sanity in Oceania. The proles are the Orwellian common folk whose style of life conforms to ancient patterns: "They were born, they grew up in the gutters, they went to work at twelve, they passed through a brief blossoming period of beauty and sexual desire, they married at twenty, they were middle-aged at thirty, they died . . . at sixty" (p. 71). Libidinally free, untainted by the guilt and hatred afflicting the more self-conscious members of the Party, they exist in a world apart. Carrying on their "swarming life of the streets" in almost total indifference to the enemy bombs falling in their quarter, the proles would seem to represent for Winston that commitment to this world, to endurance and survival despite the harshness of life, with which Orwell identifies Shakespeare's Fool in "Lear, Tolstoy and the Fool."

The curious circumstance that the tyrannical restrictions imposed by the Party on its members do not fall upon the proles, and that, as O'Brien states, there is absolutely no danger of the proles overthrowing the state, are less puzzling when we realize that in terms of the novel's fictive world they have no sociopolitical identity. Insofar as Oceania is meant to be a real, externally existing society, the proles cannot be a threat, for they are timeless figures to whom the sociological categories of realism simply do not apply. The proles exist as the mythical inhabitants of a slum-Eden, inhabitants of the country of the imagination. "Like cattle turned loose on the planes of Argentina" (p. 71), they stand for a primal state of unself-conscious unity with the cycle of nature. And the fact that they represent a condition of being animallike in its ignorance of personal evil and decay means that they cannot function at a realistic narrative level as members of a recognizable social class, for the degree of consciousness required by such a role would be incompatible with their identity as the collective embodiment of a myth: "*Until* [the proles] *become conscious they will never rebel*," Winston writes in his diary, "*and until after they have rebelled they cannot become conscious*" (p. 70). The circumstance that the doors of their houses are "suggestive of rat holes" (p. 82) indicates that Winston's own internalized sexual taboos, not the externally imposed political restrictions, prevent him from discovering in himself the untroubled capacity for living and dying at one with nature as do the proles. For him this dream, this " ' opeless fancy" that a matronly prole sings of in the yard below Julia and Winston's window, seems to be a goal made unattainable by the civilized mind's self-conscious awareness of guilty sexual rebelliousness; for at the moment of the couple's arrest the woman below—fifty years old, like the whore and the paper of Winston's diary—is abruptly silenced by the police (p. 223).

If, as Winston foresees, the end is contained in the beginning, the beginning is likewise contained in the end. Time forward is simultaneously time backward. Once firmly in the grip of the Party, Winston becomes not only O'Brien's victim and patient but also his dependent child: "For a moment he clung to O'Brien like a baby, curiously comforted by the heavy arm round his shoulders" (p. 254). And as though swept along by the death instinct, which, according to Freud, reduces organisms to their "primaeval, inorganic state," Winston continues to regress.[22] In a mirror he sees a "bowed, gray-colored, skeletonlike thing. . . . He had gone partially bald. . . . Here and there . . . were the red scars of wounds, and near the ankle the varicose ulcer was an inflamed mass. . . . But the truly frightening thing was . . . his body. . . . The curvature of the spine was astonishing. The thin shoulders were hunched forward so as to make a cavity of the chest, the scraggy neck seemed to be bending double under the weight of the skull" (pp. 274–75). If Winston sees in the mirror a bent old man, historical man scarred by the world's violence and his own participation in its guilt, Winston sees also a vision springing from the need to escape his historical identity: for this reflection—with its shrunken, curved torso and drooping, out-sized head—is that of a fetus curled up in the womb.

Winston's gazing at the reflection of his dual self surely represents

Orwell looking into the mirror of his own works. In *1984*, he is confronting those private obsessions that in the earlier narratives are much less clearly defined probably because Orwell was less able to examine them closely— the guilt, the anxiety, the escapist tendencies, the ambivalence toward women, the affinity for violence, and the disgust at the flesh. The novels of the thirties are to some extent the expression of Orwell's double need to make use of his private feelings and experiences for artistic purposes and, what seems the stronger impulse in the novels, to deny his inner complexity.

During the forties, however, the external world of violence and irrationality could not be avoided, and as a result Orwell's exploration into the darker areas of the psyche, his own as well as those of his contemporaries, was bound up with the need to define the relationship between himself as creative writer and the political realities of the age. Recognizing that the inner self could not for long remain insulated from the world's atavistic brutality and dementia, Orwell the novelist was more consciously aware of the necessity to close the gap between private obsession and public history.

Given the nature of the psychological complexities hinted at in the earlier narratives, it is not surprising that in *1984* Orwell uses psychoanalytic, primarily Freudian, formulations. Such an approach enabled him not only to tighten the connection between power hunger and sexuality but also to place both in a broader context, the development of civilization itself. The organization of society demands an ever-increasing renunciation of Eros, of the life-supporting sexual instinct; and this instinctual renunciation goes hand in hand with the growing power of a destructively aggressive instinct, which, in carrying out its mission within the minds and bodies of all people in societies past and present—of which Winston Smith, as his common surname suggests, is an emblem—may have grave consequences in terms of the individual's existence. Discussing the self-destructive tendencies of melancholiacs, Freud points out that within such people the inward-directed force of the superego has become too strong; the balance has tipped so much in its favor that "what is now holding sway . . . is . . . a pure culture of the death instinct" that may drive the "ego into death." And just as within the socialized individual there is an uneasy tension between an egoistic impulse toward sexual gratification and an aggressive instinct partly turned inward to control the sex drive, so too civilization as a whole is seen by Freud as a macrocosmic field of tension between sexuality and aggressiveness, with the latter becoming increasingly more dominant.[23]

To a great extent, Orwell's narrative is a re-enactment of the Freudian myth, including the development of the superego, which, becoming uncontrollable, might bring about the dissolution of the ego. Because Winston's personal crisis reflects and embodies the condition of civilization in general, in which mounting frustration and unhappiness is the price exacted by society, his desire to alleviate the painfulness of existence (the longing to have his aging and ulcerated flesh healed and made young, his quest to regain the mother whose sudden disappearance years ago he associates with a childhood scene in which he had selfishly deprived his hungry sister of a piece of chocolate) comes to be associated with a need to escape historical time itself. For history, the development of civilization, is a consequence of the primal crime, the Original Sin still existing below the mind's surface. And it is as though in *1984* Orwell is revealing the discoveries he has made in regard to his own interests as a novelist, his obsessive concern with the past and the dangers attendant upon too bold an exploration into it. Thus the first thing Winston sees on opening a "children's history book" is the frontispiece bearing the menacing image of Big Brother (p. 80).

Much has been made of Winston's efforts to thwart the Party's falsifying of history and his desire to discover exactly what has happened in the past. However, a closer look reveals that actually Winston is trying to move beyond history. As an employee in the history section of the Ministry of Truth, where his job is to falsify records, Winston had once come across a decade-old clipping indicating the presence of three Oceanians at a Party function in New York on the date when, on the basis of later records used to convict them of treason, they were accused of attending a conspiratorial meeting in an enemy country. For Winston, this discovery is important enough to bring down the Party: " . . . this was concrete evidence; it was a fragment of the abolished past, like a fossil bone which turns up in the wrong stratum and destroys a geological theory" (p. 78). But whatever may be Winston's conscious aim, his figure of speech betrays a subconscious compulsion not so much to reconstruct human history along objectively truthful lines as to make contact with a prehistorical reality. It is this distaste for historical time, with its tormenting consciousness of guilt and deterioration, that makes Winston uncertain as to whether the current year is 1984 and that produces the escapist daydream of enclosure within a womblike crystal paperweight, where "time could be arrested" (p. 152). Also, if Winston's expressed intention of establishing the innocence of the three supposed traitors indicates by extension a vain wish to exonerate the historical process itself, the geological simile hints at an even deeper hankering to prove untrue the mythical betrayal, the primal transgression, the guilt of which blocks a spiritual passage back into the "ancient time" of his fantasies.

The Party's manipulation of history, like O'Brien's efforts to cure Winston's "defective memory," is necessary since the suppression of mankind's primally criminal past, its ancient lust and prehistoric violence, is crucial to the process of civilization. The shrieking telescreen that interrupts Winston's dream of the Golden Country, of the female whose violation sets the historical process in motion, and awakens him into the tormenting real world of discipline and decay, is a reminder that to dream is dangerous. The journey inward down the twisting labyrinth of ancestral memory may lead to the Minotaur's den, to an intolerably direct confrontation with that prehistoric crime that all of Oceania, of civilization, is organized to suppress and conceal.

The hunger for power does not exist in a vacuum. Taking the ultimate form of mastery over the human mind, it represents, paradoxically, the runaway force of the civilized, aggression-driven conscience that, instead of sustaining life, endangers it by mounting increasingly more intense assaults on the individual's sensual identity. The presence of an insatiable power hunger indicates that the civilizing process is triumphing over the individual. And this unequal struggle is waged throughout society. In the same way that Winston's conscious guilty memory of having taken candy away from his sister masks a more ancient transgression demanding a curative punishment, in the great world a victory supposedly won over the enemy Eurasians, whose seemingly lustful Mongoloid features merge with the image of Goldstein on the telescreen, is linked to a reduction in the chocolate ration (pp. 15, 17).

We should, however, take note of what appears to be another paradox in *1984*. Although individuals are driven by a death wish, there is no incompatibility between the dominance of the aggressive instinct and the survival of the Oceanian state. In fact, the distinction between the individual's tenuous hold on life and the state's apparent immortality are necessary complements, a contradiction dialectically resolved in Orwell's visionary revelation of the dream at the center of human history.

The novel opens with Winston's longing to escape from the flux and decay of time, from the "swirl of . . . dust" that whips around him in the "vile wind" and closes with his certainty that escape is at hand. Instead of being a heroic if futile defiance of Oceania, Winston's joyful anticipation of release derives from an acceptance of Oceania's aims. With its thought control, its constant state of war that alters nothing, its stable ruling class and static proles, Oceania is itself outside of history. Having no past, no future, and no sociopolitical transformations, it is a timeless condition, an absolute and unchanging essence at the core of the civilizing process. In Goldstein's historical monograph, Oceania appears as the most recent stage of civilization's history, but within the narrative proper this society represents a logical end, the potential that is implicit within civilization at all moments.

Oceania is the macrocosmic expression of that primitive conflict between desire and taboo that, as Freud claims, first goaded man into history and now burdens him with a sense of guilt and deterioration. But Oceania is, as perhaps Winston ultimately realizes, much more than this. It is also an emblem of what Freud calls the "oceanic feeling," that timeless condition of unity, wholeness, and oneness with the universe, that state in which there is no distinction between self and other, ego and non-ego, child and mother.[24]

Although Orwell's narratives are often the disguised expression of Oedipal tensions, the sexual guilt associated with this condition is itself a mask for another feeling—frustrated power hunger. When O'Brien points out that the lone individual is weak, powerless, he is only restating a truth implicit in Orwell's earlier writings and in his criticism of the Edwardian myth of the independent man. But from the reality of isolation and frailty springs the dream of power: the power to be gained, or regained, from the restoration of oceanic oneness, the return to the womb. What arouses the anxiety of Orwell's characters is not simply the presence of the incestuous fantasy but also, and more basically, the suspicion that the fantasy of return cannot be realized.

The sado-masochistic perversities that Orwell found in the novels of James Hadley Chase become in *1984* an expression of man's latent rage at history, and, therefore, at himself: rage at history's failure to actualize the dream of wholeness and power, rage at history's violation of that dream. Certainly in many of Orwell's writings we can detect sado-masochistic violence, suffering, hatred, and humiliation. We can also sense that Orwell expressed his personal rage in the sado-masochistic pattern of self-assertive aggressiveness and passive victimization (for example, the brutal Ellis, Mrs. Creevy, and the pig Napoleon, and, on the other hand, the masochistic Flory, Dorothy Hare, and farm animals).

However, this opposition implies a unity; the rage for strength and wholeness binds aggressor and victim together into a symbiotic closeness. Although I do not know if Orwell was familiar with the writings of Erich Fromm, there are passages in his *Escape from Freedom* (1941) that are not only strikingly similar to Orwell's "Notes on Nationalism" but also suitable as a gloss on *1984*. Fromm points out that consciously or unconsciously the participants in a sado-masochistic relationship are seeking to escape the conflict within themselves between personal autonomy and a fear of the "powerlessness," "insignificance," and "aloneness" that may accompany the individual's independence. Both sadist and masochist resort to pain, physical or mental, to join with something else, to merge their identities as individuals into some greater whole.[25]

Viewed as a realistic novel, *1984* can be interpreted as an exposure of the way in which a totalitarian society lends itself to sado-masochistic relationships. However, for present purposes it is more important to note that the world existing in 1984, with its brutalities and humiliations, is the embodiment of an enduring wish, the collective expression of man's dream of wholeness, totality, as the term *totalitarian* implies. Its endless wars a

massive outburst of sado-masochistic rage, the indestructible state symbolically represents not the historical fulfillment of the dream, since history is
the record of the dream being frustrated, but rather mankind's struggle to
abolish the historical self. The sado-masochistic violence is the dream of
unity dramatized on the stage of history. The ruthless control the Party
elite exercises over its submissive followers is the echo of mankind's inner
yearning for oceanic oneness, as is Winston's mixed response to Julia, the
fantasy of ravishing her and the desire to be passively contained in her
maternal embrace.

The obsessive need to protect the dream from the contingencies of the
historical process explains why one of the frenzied participants in a Hate
Week session, seeing an image of Goldstein on the telescreen while the
room is abuzz with rumors of his disturbing book, hurls a Newspeak
dictionary at the arch-heretic (p. 15); for Goldstein's monograph on the
development of Oceania as a political phenomenon represents the opera-
tion of the historical consciousness, a mode of awareness that, disrupting
the dream, is incompatible with the Oceanian drive toward the diminution
of human consciousness. As we have seen in *Animal Farm*, the knowledge
of and implicit involvement with evil is tied in with the assumption of a
historical identity. Winston's deep-seated craving to break free from time is
thwarted by his conscious obsession with historical facts. Likewise his
"historical" relationship with the sexually provocative Julia stands in the
way of his quest for the womb. Consequently it is the harsh cure administered by O'Brien that holds out the promise of salvation from one's frustrating temporal existence. "You will be lifted clean out from the stream of
history," claims Winston's tormentor and savior (p. 257).

I have been arguing that totalitarian Oceania is both a surrealistic representation of the final repressive stage toward which the civilizing process
tends by its own inner logic and, at the same time, a latent imperative
toward some static condition of wholeness unaffected by the contingencies
of history. By the same token, we can view Oceania as a vast emblem of
religious experience stripped to its essence. Winston's ego-extinguishing
drive wombward is a radically religious act that, as O'Brien promises, will
gain the initiate an impersonal immortality.

Although several critics have pointed out the Christian symbolism in this
novel, such as the worship of Big Brother and the religious dogmatism of
the Party ideology, the assumption is that these elements are ironically
intended, satirical devices emphasizing: the perversity of modern secular
religions.[26] Perhaps more instructive is the opinion that apart from the
satire there exists in *1984* a clearly religious level of meaning set forth in
terms of the "age-old symbolic structure, and even phraseology, of resistant man's breakdown and conversion to . . . God."[27] While disputing the
claim that this reflects an unconscious attitude in Orwell, William Empson

agrees that the motif of religious conversion is to be taken literally, not metaphorically:

> Surely Orwell made very clear that he considered it the ultimate shame for a man to hand over his conscience either to Stalin the Big Brother or to . . . God the Father. . . . Surely the conception of a Ministry of Love, whose towering office hagrides the city because each citizen believes it has calculated for him the torture he would find most unbearable, corresponds to nothing in Communism and a great deal in the history of Christianity.[28]

Although less certain than is Empson that Christian submissiveness is being decried in the novel, I am convinced that however much Orwell may have feared and hated the transformation of secular ideologies into surrogate religions during the twentieth century, the religious experience dealt with in *1984* lies at the heart of Oceania. In fact, the state's hostility toward any manifestation of the individual's self-assertive pursuit of pleasure is quite similar to the antihumanistic and otherwordly attitude that in "Lear, Tolstoy and the Fool" Orwell attributes to both Lear and Tolstoy, and to which Orwell may well have been drawn, at least unconsciously.

The monotheistic worship of Big Brother is grounded in that fear of and dependent longing for the father that later attaches itself to the individual's double view of God as a threatening being who must be appeased and a providential deity who, by holding out the promise of an eternal reward, offers mankind consolation for its painful renunciation in this life.[29] This, however, only partially explains the religious significance of the novel. In *1984*, the ultimate reward, a collective immortality, involves something much more extreme than the renunciation of pleasure: the Party demands the renunciation of self. For the intimation of Oceanic oneness to become a total experience, the individual must be stripped of all that makes him an individual. De-eroticized, de historicized, de-humanized, the person is reduced to a state of pure being. The terminal point of this reductive process is the elimination of consciousness, a collapsing of the ego back into the instinctual life of the unconscious. The return to the unconscious is an entry into immortality; for as Freud claims, the energy within the unconscious is a force of total assertion, and by its very nature this energy insists on the organism's eternal existence.[30] It is just such a movement toward the nirvana of sheer being untroubled by the awareness of death that O'Brien has in mind as he gives Winston a brief history lesson: "The command of the old despotisms was 'Thou shalt not.' The command of the totalitarians was 'Thou shalt.' Our command is *'Thou art'* " (p. 258). Likewise the chorus of Party faithful mindlessly and blissfully chanting the initials of the leader's name is an image of the promised collective unconscious asserting its immortality: the hypnotic "B-B! . . . B-B!" is a fiat cry of "BE! BE!" (pp. 17–18).

Fromm describes the sado-masochistic striving for power and wholeness as a sort of cannibal feast, the sadist symbolically "swallowing" the willing masochist (p. 158). Analogously, the loss of individuality involves a swallowing, the unconscious devouring the conscious self (thus Winston's conscious terror of hungry rats). The religious nature of such a swallowing becomes more apparent if we extend the meaning of the image to signify a descent into the womb. Discussing the genesis of Christianity, Jung states that basic to the idea of religious rebirth is man's need to become free from the emotionally divisive effects of guilt and from the fear of death by a return to the regenerative womb. But this Ur-longing is complicated by the same incest anxiety that has spurred mankind forward into history. To evade this anxiety, Christianity has sublimated the original pagan desire for renewal through the sexual act into a symbolic return to the womb—the waters of baptism taking the place of the physical woman—that results in a spiritual rebirth. Yet despite this sublimation the primitive craving for the sexual re-entry into the maternal body lingers beneath the idealized surface of Christian symbolism:

> If one has once received an effectual impression of the ancient cults, and if one realizes . . . that the religious experience . . . was understood by antiquity as a more or less concrete coitus, then truly one can no longer fancy that the motor forces of a religion have suddenly become wholly different since the birth of Christ. Exactly the same thing has occurred as with the hysteric who at first indulges in some quite unbeautiful, infantile sexual manifestations and afterwards develops a hyperaesthetic negation in order to convince everyone of his special purity. Christianity, with its repression of the . . . sexual, is the negative of the ancient sexual cult. The original cult has changed its tokens.

Since the development of Christianity and post-Graeco-Roman civilization is directly linked to the "veiling over of the actual facts" about man's primal urges, Jung expresses no surprise at the fierce opposition to any attempt to discover the disturbing sexual roots of modern religion and society.[31]

Similarly in *1984* a consciousness that is too expanded may lead to the subversive realization that underlying even the official anti-sexual fanaticism of the Oceanian worship of Big Brother there exists a phallic cult that must remain hidden. This is demonstrated by the arrest of a poet who has indiscreetly allowed "God" to rhyme with "rod" (p. 234).

The development of Orwell as man and writer appears in the various levels of meaning in *1984*—on the one hand, the Freudian family drama shaping modern political institutions, and on the other hand, the Jungian view of the impulses secretly operating within Christianity. Orwell's career progresses from an uneasy preoccupation with rather narrowly Oedipal fixations to a more expanded self-awareness allowing him to deal with the cultural implications of his obsessions. From this self-examination evolves a criticism of those progressivist and even utopian assumptions that he and his contemporaries inherited from their Edwardian past—beliefs tragically inadequate as a means to understand the barbarism of the mid-twentieth century. Another development is the shift in Orwell from an involvement with the secular world of political history to an increasingly serious interest in spiritual matters, as indicated by his thoughts on the weakening of ancient pieties, the difficulty of satisfying mankind's longing for immortality, and the importance of keeping one's moral integrity inviolate. In his last novel, the key elements in Orwell's vision of reality—the Oedipal anxiety, the dream of regaining the feeling of oceanic wholeness, the view of history as embodying both mankind's rage at its failure to actualize the dream and our struggle to renounce the weak and isolated historical self—take on a special urgency because of Orwell's worsening tubercular condition. Confronted by the possibility, if not the certainty, of imminent death, he stubbornly probes into the psyche to uncover the primal dream of immortality that asserts itself against the fact of biological death.

Looking back from the perspective of *1984*, we are better able to understand why in Orwell's works there is such a tense and uneasy relationship between his extremely self-conscious protagonists and their social environment. If the development of human consciousness, individualized and aware of its loneliness in historical time, is implicit in the concept of civilization, there exists in the civilizing process a counter imperative toward the abolition of the individuated self (the "autonomous individual" Orwell claims is passing from the scene) and the restoration of a primordial wholeness, the merging of the self into the totality of the group. Orwell's characters know that they must shed their genital identity; for conscious sexual longing, being a form of self-assertion, becomes an obstacle in the search for wholeness. This may explain why bitterness and a sense of failure so frequently characterize the sexual lives of Orwell's characters. When sexual intimacy does take place, it emphasizes the disparity between the dream and the reality; one feels that the conscious frustration of those characters deprived of sexual contact conceals an unacknowledged sense of relief.

As evidence that the connection between sexual renunciation and the escape from time is more than just Orwell's private and subjective view, we might turn to an essay by the psychoanalyst Gregory Zilboorg that appeared about ten years before the publication of *1984*. Tracing the belief in immortality back to a need to evade the guilt of the primal crime by converting the patricidal urge into a loving wish that the slain parent will live forever, Zilboorg points out that a commonly accepted precondition for rejoining one's parents and ancestors in an endless afterlife is the rejection of genitality.[32] The individual's conscious attempt to silence the death anxiety produced by his sense of guilt has its macrocosmic counterpart in social and cultural institutions, traditions, and aspirations, all of which result from the "perennial tragedy of incest, murder, and blood-guilt" (pp. 198–99). Even more psychologically primitive than the fantasy of personal immortality is the utopian vision of society's unlimited extension into the future: "Here the object of our interest becomes depersonalized and the goal less immediate and less specific—an obviously deeper regression. The philosophic Utopias . . . born on this level and the . . . development of the technical achievements of civilization . . . all point to a strong pregenital drive and intrauterine fantasies" (p. 187). Similarly Orwell's Oceania represents the atavistic underside to the shining liberal vision of a triumphant secular man, proud of his individuality and confidently imagining that he can guide history into a future of limitless accomplishment.

As a civilized man cut off from the past, Winston can regain a primal wholeness only after being de-sexualized. The nakedness of the dream woman is a sign that the womb is there, open and waiting. But before entry, he must undergo a purificatory rite. Early in the novel, we see that the potentially regenerative female is, in terms of Winston's civilized mind, too closely linked to the physical temptress. Asked by a neighbor's wife to come to her apartment to unplug her "sink," a vaguely suggestive summons associated with the husband's absence, Winston approaches his task with distaste: "The kitchen sink was full nearly to the brim with filthy greenish water which smelt worse than ever of cabbage." Since in the dreamworld atmosphere of the novel manual dexterity can be regarded as a sign of disturbing sexuality, Winston goes about his job with reluctance: ". . . he hated using his hands." Carnal awareness still stands between him and the waters of rebirth: "disgustedly" he removes the "clot of human hair" blocking the pipe, the woman's pipe, and immediately washes his hands. But this cleansing is not enough, for at that moment the woman's son snarls, "Up with your hands!" What stains this experience with the sin and guilt is the presence in Winston of a punitive Christian conscience. It is not without significance that the physically, but not spiritually, absent husband—the smell of whose sweat still fills the apartment—is a Party zealot named Parsons (pp. 21–23 passim).

The severed hand Winston sees after a bombing raid and the bone-crushing handshake inflicted on him by O'Brien suggest the sexual uneasiness that motivates his washing of his hands after making the first diary entry (pp. 29, 84, 179). But Winston is still too attached to his familiar self to regard the descent into the ancestral past, into the "cavernous blackness" of the aged whore's "mouth" (p. 69), as anything else than a frightening loss of identity. The ritual act of purification that will prepare Winston for the descent and the loss involves a redirecting of the terror toward the sexual urge itself. One stage of the eradication of the genital self takes place in a cell where Winston is locked up with an inmate whose battered, ratlike face suggests the cinematic device of merging images surrealistically to lay bare the unconscious mind—in this case, Winston's secret desire to reject his genital identity. The prisoner's beaten-in face, its "mouth . . . swollen into a shapeless cherry-colored mass with a black hole in the middle" (p. 239), is a fantasy image of the bloodied pudendum and its violator's sexual mutilation. Moreover the bloody mouth is the promise that the initiate will soon be swallowed up into the oceanic womb.

The final stage of Winston's initiation into a de-eroticized condition takes place in Room 101, an image of what he has sought. For as Kornbluth states, Room 101 is the uterus. It is an underground chamber in the pyramidal Ministry of Love; it is apparently the first room in a series, the "starting place"; and these numerals "displayed on a page constitute a naive sketch of the female genitalia seen from below" (p. 93). And here, as the rat cage comes nearer to his face, Winston, realizing that there is only *"one* body" he can "thrust between himself and the rats," begs his tormentors to expose Julia, not himself, to this horror (p. 289). Opposites unite at the moment when, saving himself from physical mutilation by betraying his sexual partner, he symbolically sacrifices his ego-burdened historical identity. Rejected as a physical lover, Julia becomes the maternally protective *"one* body" within which Winston will find oneness.

With the trumpet call that announces a great victory over the enemy ringing in his ears, Winston, now cured, is totally reconciled with the father: the once-rebellious son, the prodigal returned from the fragmenting world of historical experience, has moved from guilt to remorse to purification, a reverse rite of passage backward into the Golden Country. Fittingly, in the final scene (p. 300) the contradictions of man's historical identity are resolved. The once-oppressive sense of personal mortality becomes a dream image of a "long-hoped-for bullet . . . entering his brain"; what the conscious self has perceived as Big Brother's hostility is now revealed to have been love (the "smile . . . hidden beneath the dark mustache"); the final androgynous image of the childlike Winston restored to Big Brother's "loving breast" suggests the collapsing of all dichotomies—threatening patriarch and beckoning mother, self and non-self, history and timelessness—into oceanic oneness.

Chapter X

Conclusion

In the essay "Good Bad Books" (1945), Orwell discusses various works that, although making no claim to great literary merit, have managed to survive, to remain readable and popular after more pretentious writings have fallen into comparative neglect. One mark of the good bad book—the phrase is Chesterton's—is a certain naiveté, an apparently unintended crudity that creates an effect of sincerity and emotional truth. Orwell implies that the artistic meticulousness of the well-written novel is not necessary for the production of an emotionally moving one. For instance, "Dreiser's *An American Tragedy* . . . gains something from the clumsy long-winded manner in which it is written; detail is piled on detail, with almost no attempt at selection, and in the process an effect of terrible, grinding cruelty is slowly built up" (4. 21).

Turning to the novelists themselves, Orwell suggests that what differentiates the serious artist—such as Meredith, Woolf, George Moore, and Wyndham Lewis—from the good bad writer is the presence in the latter of a "sort of literary vitamin," by which he might mean an imaginative vitality and spontaneity that results in rough-hewn but memorable books. One such work is *Uncle Tom's Cabin*, an "unintentionally ludicrous book, full of preposterous melodramatic incidents . . . but deeply moving and essentially true" (4. 22).

In this essay, it is hinted that there is a negative relationship between intellectual sophistication and the crude artistic vigor of the good bad writer. In some cases, Orwell claims that "intellectual refinement can be a disadvantage to a story-teller." There is no necessary connection between the ability to think logically and clearly and the capacity for literary creativity: "The existence of good bad literature—the fact that one can be amused or excited or even moved by a book that one's intellect refuses to take seriously—is a reminder that art is not the same thing as cerebration" (4. 21).

Whether or not "Good Bad Books" reflects Orwell's uncertainty regarding his place in the literary establishment, these remarks do tell us something about his aims as a novelist. The foregoing study should clarify my belief that from *Down and Out in Paris and London* to *1984* his novels are, in one fashion or another, so constructed as to convey subjective visions of reality. Even those documentary features that one ordinarily associates with a naturalistic presentation are used, with varying degrees of skill, to embody certain mental states, to make concrete and visible the emotional and moral dilemmas in the souls of the central characters, and possibly within the author too. This is not to say that from first to last Orwell's fictional works are narrowly surrealistic, with phenomenal reality constantly distorted into the psychic jungle of a Max Ernst painting. It is more accurate to say that they are loosely surrealistic in the sense that as a rule their fictional location is somewhere along the interface connecting the recognizable external reality of the realistic novel with the phantasmagoric world of dream and fantasy. As I have pointed out, there are times when Orwell does disrupt the surface texture of probability or in some other way jolt the realistic plot about in order to satisfy obscure subsurface imperatives. And it is at such moments that we become aware of the main flaw in his novels, the disturbing presence of internal stresses resulting from what is sometimes an uncoordinated treatment of different modes of experience—the private and the public.

In the longer narratives of the thirties, the reader is frequently left puzzled as to the connection between the personal experiences and feelings of the central figures and the condition of the society in terms of which we expect these characters, including their inner lives, to be defined. In what way, one might ask, does the obsession with antisensuality throw light on the economic exploitation witnessed by Orwell the dishwasher and tramp; what does John Flory's futile attempt to gain spiritual regeneration through Elizabeth Lackersteen tell us about the culturally deleterious effects of colonialism; where are we to find a connection between the sexual anxiety of Dorothy Hare and Gordon Comstock and their experiences with a godless, money-worshipping society? There seems to be a cleavage between those themes and stylistic devices usually associated with, on the one hand, Orwell the socio-political writer (realism, documentary detail, the individual's involvement with historical events and public realities) and, on the other hand, Orwell the psychological allegorist (nonrealistic techniques, the stress on primitive, irrational, and even neurotic motives, and the rejection of historical time).

Since Orwell explicitly discussed his own works so rarely and briefly, one cannot state with absolute certainty to what degree, at any one point in his career, he was aware of this flaw and was consciously attempting to correct it. There are, however, some indications that over the years he was becoming increasingly intent on investing the personal dilemmas of his fictional protagonists with a more far-reaching significance. We can detect signs of this newer type of character in a rather crude larval stage in *Aspidistra*, where Orwell tries to change Gordon Comstock from isolated poet-rebel-misanthrope into a more common and familiar type, the lower-middle-class "cit."—a transformation that, although not entirely convincing, does at least point in the direction of a character whose psychological condition might reflect the constraints a society would impose on its members. It is probably indicative of Orwell's sharpened consciousness of his responsibility as a writer to deal with the menacing political situtation of the late-thirties that in *Coming Up for Air* he stresses, perhaps with greater urgency than artistic skill, the social and cultural implications of the protagonist's inner devitalization. George Bowling's moral and emotional deterioration—his alienation from the past, the dispiriting awareness of his physical degeneration, his potentially self-destructive apathy and nihilism—is meant to show what is happening to a once-vigorous people.

During the 1930s, Orwell made use of themes and techniques that were borrowed from writers such as Joyce, T. S. Eliot, and Dostoevski to become free from the constraints of nineteenth-century realism and naturalism. Also, having embraced the modernists' tragic sense of life he was implicitly rejecting his own Edwardian past with its naively progressivist outlook on history. In the 1940s, however, Orwell's interests took a somewhat different turn. Confronted by a world of political madness and atavistic brutality, he shifted toward the literature of the grotesque, as found in Swift, Poe, Dickens, and later writers like London and Zamyatin, whose works reveal the savagery and primitive irrationality existing just below the surface of civilized life and the civilized mind. Furthermore, in control of his own imaginative powers, Orwell began to examine the interiorized past within himself, resurrecting the childhood vision of reality that he considered the source of artistic creativity. This inward look revealed a private world as strange and even barbaric as that of contemporary society.

Although Orwell's encounter with the irrational, whether in the world at large or in the depths of his own psyche, is alarming, it is also liberating: it freed him to use other literary forms better suited to conveying the primitive and hallucinatory qualities of the totalitarian age—the beast fable-fairy tale (*Animal Farm*) and the visionary fantasy (*1984*). And if during the early and middle forties Orwell's interest in psychology broadened into an examination of modern history, the essays of his last years, with their emphasis on those arcane motives and impulses at work within historical man, anticipated the final stage of Orwell's development—the meta-historical vision in *1984* of mankind's collective longing to wrench itself loose from the fallen world of historical experience; to escape from the human condition of frailty, solitude, and mortality; and to regain a state of oceanic oneness with the universe.

There is, I am convinced, a fairly close relationship between the expansion of Orwell's horizons as a writer and his increasing willingness to exploit nonrealistic devices, such as the broad, cartoonlike strokes used to flatten the events and characters of *Animal Farm* into a primitively simple emblem of innocence and betrayal, or, in *1984*, the surrealistic transformation of protagonist and setting into a camera obscura wherein we observe an archetypal struggle between desire and taboo. Along with the increasingly explicit concern with mass psychology that appears in Orwell's essays is a more deliberate employment in his fiction of techniques and styles designed to reveal those elements constituting a more or less common substratum beneath men's conscious behavior and feelings. The child's view of reality, the melodramatic effects of the good bad book, the cinematic devices for conveying the special atmosphere of fantasy and dream, the connotative value of sounds, the symbolic landscapes, the mythic patterns, and archetypal conflicts—all these are used, especially in *1984*, to conjure up those irrational forces restlessly stirring below civilized humanity's conscious life.

Although many of Orwell's longer narratives lend themselves to psychological interpretation, expressing as they do emotional complexities and tensions, these works show signs of artistic maturity only when Orwell makes sustained use of nonrealistic, sometimes even crude and vulgar, expedients. As we have seen, such contrivances do appear in the early works. But the difference between these and *1984* is that the former are for the most part realistic enough to raise the expectation that phenomenal reality—the world physically present outside the protagonist—will be treated as an independently existing entity, as something more than a projection of a mental condition. In *1984*, the surrealistic atmosphere is much more pervasive, the conflicts more firmly grounded in the depths of the psyche, than in Orwell's previous narratives; for this reason we are less likely to feel our expectations disappointed. Here Orwell's tendency to reduce milieu to inner space, to play fast and loose with the stuff that the naturalistic novel is made of, produces no glaring disunity of effect.[1]

Discussing what he calls the "ideology of being English," Bernard Bergonzi states that his countrymen are going through a crisis brought on by the knowledge that the traditions and norms of British life are not fixed and imperishable absolutes but rather values that, inherited from a more stable past, may no longer last in a world geared to rapid change. In the British literature of the last thirty years or so, especially in the novel, he detects a double reaction to the fear that a changed England is an England bereft of its identity—nostalgia for an earlier, more placid, less complicated age, and a nightmarish vision of what the future holds in store.[2] As examples of works reflecting the obsessive desire of Britishers to "escape the present by looking back to the era before the First World War," Bergonzi cites *Coming Up for Air* and *1984*, both of which exhibit that "alternation between nostalgia and catastrophe that has been evident in the work of later English novelists" (p. 150).

Bergonzi's remarks call to mind Orwell's description of one category of good bad books, escape literature. Such books "form pleasant patches in one's memory, quiet corners where the mind can browse at odd moments, but they hardly pretend to have anything to do with real life" (4. 20). A feature common to these works is that of flight, the attempt to reject certain disturbing experiences, to escape from the consciousness of time and anxiety and guilt. In Orwell's works of the early and middle thirties, the longing for peace and the escapist diminution of consciousness by which this yearning is to be satisfied—John Flory's suicide, Dorothy Hare's amnesia and drudgery, Gordon Comstock's rejection of his identity as tormented poet—are extremely private reactions, singular and eccentric. At times, we suspect either that Orwell was not sufficiently in control of his material in order to explore the cultural implications of the characters' moral and emotional problems or that the material is being manipulated to prevent such an exploration.

On the other hand, it is only fair to recognize that Orwell's literary career involved a constant tug-of-war between personal obsessions and a more or less conscious determination to deal with more general issues concerning society, culture, and the human condition. The various stages of Orwell's artistic liberation result not from a rejection of the private self, the irrational fixations inherited from the earlier Blair, but rather from an exploration into this interiorized past. Orwell's works bear out the truth that writing is an act of self-discovery—and for that matter self-creation. The succession of novels and essays suggests Orwell's growing awareness that those elements that are so discordantly intrusive in the earlier works—the characters' sexual anxieties, the displays of hatred and violence, the self-destructive behavior, the grotesqueness and sensationalism—are in fact central to his vision of reality. What Orwell's writings reveal is that if Cassandra is his muse, Caliban is his creative demon.

I believe that Orwell's novels are less effective when the psychodramatic weight of the narrative muffles the resonance of the characters' adventures. Conversely, the fiction is most rewarding when its psychologically dense nucleus flashes out and irradiates a whole cultural landscape. But even when flawed, the novels—and the essays, for that matter—possess a crude, compelling energy. Although the specific historical conditions that produced the Orwellian sensibility may change, one need not worry that the distinctive intensity of the Orwellian vision of reality will soon loosen its hold on the imaginations of his readers.

Notes

Notes to Chapter I.

1. *A Reader's Guide to George Orwell*, p. 159. Page references to cited works are parenthesized in the text whenever no confusion might result.
2. Ibid., p. 13.
3. George Woodcock, *The Writer and Politics*, p. 124. See also Laurence Brander, *George Orwell*, pp. 30–32, and Philip Rieff, "George Orwell and the Post-Liberal Imagination," *Kenyon Review (KR)*, pp. 49–50.
4. T. A. Birrel, "Is Integrity Enough?" *The Dublin Review*, p. 50. Orwell's opposition to centralized government, imperialism, industrialism, and capitalism, coupled with his nostalgia for a pre-modern Christian and agrarian society, leads Geoffrey Ashe to label him a Tory radical. See his "A Note on George Orwell," *Commonweal*, p. 191.
5. John Mander, "George Orwell's Politics: I," *Contemporary Review (ContempR)*, p. 35.
6. "*Homage to Catalonia*," *World Review*, p. 51.
7. Bertrand Russell, "Symptoms of Orwell's *1984*," in *Portraits from Memory, and Other Essays*, pp. 221–27 passim; Phillip Rahv, "The Unfuture of Utopia," *Partisan Review (PR)*, p. 745; Richard J. Voorhees, *The Paradox of George Orwell*, p. 87; Orville Prescott, "The Political Novel: Warren, Orwell, Koestler," in his *In My Opinion*, p. 29; Gaylord C. LeRoy, "A. F. 632 to 1984," *College English (CE)*, p. 135.
8. John Mander, *The Writer and Commitment*, p. 72.
9. Richard Rees, *George Orwell: Fugitive from the Camp of Victory*, pp. 51–52; Raymond Williams, *George Orwell*, pp. 16–18, 22.
10. Tom Hopkinson, *George Orwell*, p. 7.
11. Alan Dutscher, "Orwell and the Crisis of Responsibility," *Contemporary Issues*, pp. 312–13; Isaac Deutscher, "*1984*—The Mysticism of Cruelty," in *Russia in Transition, and Other Essays*, p. 244; Mander, *Writer and Commitment*, p. 100.
12. "Why I Write," in *The Collected Essays, Journalism and Letters of George Orwell*, ed. Sonia Orwell and Ian Angus, 1:5. Unless otherwise indicated, references to Orwell's shorter works are taken from this four-volume source. For his fiction and nonfiction I shall indicate only the year of either publication or, in the case of letters, composition. More precise dates are provided when needed.
13. Alexander Trocchi, "A Note on George Orwell," *Evergreen Review*, p. 152; Keith Alldritt, *The Making of George Orwell: An Essay in Literary History*, pp. 128–29.
14. Rees, *Fugitive from the Camp of Victory*, p. 85.
15. John Atkins, *George Orwell: A Literary and Biographical Study*, p. 27.
16. John Wain, "Orwell," *Spectator*, p. 632; Cyril Connolly, *Enemies of Promise*, p. 81; Brander, *George Orwell*, p. 23.
17. Richard H. Rovere, "The Importance of George Orwell," in *The American Establishment, and Other Reports, Opinions, & Speculations*, p. 171; Irving Howe, "George Orwell's Novels," *The Nation*, p. 110; B. T. Oxley, *George Orwell*, p. 13; Atkins, *A Literary and Biographical Study*, p. 269.
18. George Woodcock, *The Crystal Spirit: A Study of George Orwell*, p. 63.
19. Rovere, "Importance of George Orwell," p. 178.
20. David Lodge, *The Modes of Modern Writing: Metaphor, Metonymy, and the Typology of Modern Literature*. The following summary is based on parts 1 and 2 passim.
21. Tony Tanner, "Orwell: Death of Decency," *Time and Tide*, p. 871; Mander, *Writer and Commitment*, p. 77.

22. George P. Elliot, "A Failed Prophet," *Hudson Review (HR)*, p. 154.

23. Frederick R. Karl, "George Orwell: The White Man's Burden," in *A Reader's Guide to the Contemporary English Novel*, pp. 154–60 passim. In line with this criticism are Atkins's claim that Orwell had only a superficial knowledge of human nature (*A Literary and Biographical Study*, p. 278), Rees's statement that Orwell was uninterested in "psychology or in subtleties of character" (*Fugitive from the Camp of Victory*, p. 28), and Anthony Quinton's conclusion that "as explorations of human nature . . . [Orwell's] novels are without much interest." See Anthony Quinton, "A Sense of Smell," *Listener*, p. 213.

24. For example, see Frank W. Wadsworth, "Orwell as a Novelist: The Early Work," *University of Kansas City Review (UR)*, pp. 93–99, "Orwell as a Novelist: The Middle Period," *UR*, pp. 189–94, and "Orwell's Later Work," *UR*, pp. 285–90; Joseph Slater, "The Fictional Values of 1984," in *Essays in Literary History: Presented to J. Milton French*, ed. Rudolf Kirk and C. W. Main, pp. 249–64; Emanuel Edrich, "Naivete and Simplicity in Orwell's Writing: *Homage to Catalonia*," *UR*, pp. 289–97; Stephen Jay Greenblatt, *Three Modern Satirists: Waugh, Orwell, and Huxley*, pp. 37–73; Robert A. Lee, *Orwell's Fiction*.

25. For instance, see Christopher Hollis, *A Study of George Orwell: The Man and his Works*; Samuel A. Yorks, "George Orwell: Seer Over His Shoulder," *Bucknell Review (BuR)*, pp. 33–43; Anthony West, "George Orwell," in *Principles and Persuasions: The Literary Essays of Anthony West*, pp. 164–76; and Atkins, *A Literary and Biographical Study*.

26. Mander, *Writer and Commitment*, pp. 72–73.

27. Kingsley Amis, "The Road to Airstrip One," *Spectator*, p. 292.

28. Hopkinson, *George Orwell*, p. 6.

29. Deutscher, *"1984,"* p. 243, note 2.

30. D. J. Dooley, "The Limitations of George Orwell," *University of Toronto Quarterly (UTQ)*, p. 293; Yorks, "Seer Over His Shoulder," pp. 33–43; West, "George Orwell," pp. 164–76; Amis, "Road to Airstrip One," p. 293.

31. Rayner Heppenstall, "Memoirs of George Orwell: The Shooting Stick," *Twentieth Century (TC)*, p. 371; Dwight Macdonald, "Varieties of Political Experience," *The New Yorker (NY)*, p. 142; Gerald Fiderer, "Masochism as Literary Strategy: Orwell's Psychological Novels," *Literature & Psychology (L & P)*, pp. 3–21 passim; W. D. Smith, "George Orwell," *ContempR*, p. 283; Wyndham Lewis, "Orwell, or Two and Two Make Four," in *The Writer and the Absolute*, p. 183; Hopkinson, *George Orwell*, p. 17.

32. LeRoy, "A. F. 632 to 1984," *CE*, p. 137; Robert Hatch, review of *1984*, *New Republic*, p. 24; Edmund Fuller, "Posthumous Orwell Reissues," *Saturday Review (SatR)*, p. 19.

33. Sean O'Casey, *Sunset and Evening Star*, pp. 137–38; Brian Way, "George Orwell: The Political Thinker We Might Have Had," *Gemini*, p. 16; Fredric Warburg, *An Occupation for Gentlemen*, p. 234; Rayner Heppenstall, "Orwell Intermittent," *TC*, p. 480.

34. John Wain, "Here Lies Lower Binfield: On George Orwell," *Encounter*, p. 72; Henry Popkin, "Orwell the Edwardian," *KR*, p. 141.

35. T. R. Fyvel, "Orwell and the Elephant," *Tribune*, p. 16; Popkin, "The Edwardian," p. 141.

36. George Orwell, "War-time Diary" (17 June 1940), 2:350.

37. Peter Stansky and William Abrahams, *The Unknown Orwell*, p. 257.

Notes to Chapter II.

1. Hakan Ringbom, *George Orwell as Essayist: A Stylistic Study*, p. 52.

2. Berel Lang, "The Politics and Art of Decency: Orwell's Medium," *South Atlantic*

Quarterly (SAQ), pp. 426–28.

    3. Peter Stansky and William Abrahams express doubts about the autobiographical accuracy of "A Hanging." As assistant superintendent of police at Insein (near Rangoon), the location of the prison where the execution would have taken place, Blair had no official reason for attending an execution (*The Unknown Orwell*, pp. 192, 195–96). Mabel Fierze, a close friend of the Blairs, informed the biographers that Eric Blair once denied ever having attended a hanging (p. 264). Agreeing that we cannot establish for certain the truth of "A Hanging," David Lodge treats it as a self-contained verbal construct. Lodge's discussion of the essay (*The Modes of Modern Writing: Metaphor, Metonymy, and the Typology of Modern Literature*, pp. 9–17, 107–8, 113–15) is incorporated into my own analysis.

    4. Jacintha Buddicom, *Eric and Us: A Remembrance of George Orwell*, p. 38.

    5. *Down and Out in Paris and London*, p. 16.

    6. John Mander, *The Writer and Commitment*, pp. 105–10 passim.

    7. Jack London, *The People of the Abyss*, p. 14. Orwell read this work sometime during his late teens (*The Road to Wigan Pier*, p. 172).

    8. Laurence Brander, *George Orwell*, p. 58; Christopher Hollis, *A Study of George Orwell: The Man and his Works*, pp. 50–51.

    9. Jenni Calder, *Chronicles of Conscience: A Study of George Orwell and Arthur Koestler*, pp. 37–38.

    10. Introduction to the French edition of *Down and Out*, 1:114. This edition appeared in 1934.

    11. "Seldom can a book set in the lower depths of Paris have had so little to do with sexuality. Given its autobiographical nature, however, and given Blair's limited experience of women, it could hardly be otherwise. Before 1932 his closest relationships with women seem to have been with his mother and sisters, or with mother- and sister-surrogates" (Stansky and Abrahams, *The Unknown Orwell*, p. 267). Orwell's reference to some passage that his publisher, fearing negative reactions from circulating libraries, wanted Orwell either to alter or omit indicates the less restrained quality of the earlier version (Letter to Leonard Moore [1932], 1:84).

    12. Kieth Alldritt, *The Making of George Orwell: An Essay in Literary History*, p. 52; Brander, *George Orwell*, p. 60.

    13. Mander, *Writer and Commitment*, p. 80.

    14. Concerning Orwell's careful preparation for entering the world of vagabondage to collect additional material, see Stansky and Abrahams's discussion in *The Unknown Orwell*, pp. 266–78 passim.

Notes to Chapter III.

    1. For the background of the events dealt with in *Burmese Days* see Maung Htin Aung, "George Orwell in Burma," in *The World of George Orwell*, ed. Miriam Gross, pp. 19–30; and Peter Stansky and William Abrahams, *The Unknown Orwell*, pp. 170–75. A helpful survey of the changing attitudes toward colonialism in the East as reflected in British fiction from the late nineteenth century to the mid-twentieth can be found in Allen J. Greenberger, *The British Image of India: A Study in the Literature of Imperialism, 1880–1960*; of special relevance to *Burmese Days* are pp. 83–176.

    2. *Burmese Days*, p. 147.

    3. For this distinction between colonial Burma and the natural environment I am indebted to Jeffrey Meyers, "The Ethics of Responsibility: Orwell's *Burmese Days*," *UR*, p. 86.

    4. Robert A. Lee, *Orwell's Fiction*, pp. 3–5.
    5. Christopher Gillie suggests that the egoistic and physically masterful Verral is both Matthew Arnold's aristocratic Barbarian and a foreshadowing of the totalitarian man (*Movements in English Literature*, p. 135).
    6. Charles I. Glicksberg, "The Literary Contribution of George Orwell," *Arizona Quarterly (ArQ)*, p. 235; Christopher Hollis, *A Study of George Orwell: The Man and his Works*, p. 34.
    7. Frank W. Wadsworth, "Orwell as a Novelist: The Early Work," *UR*, p. 93; Stephen Jay Greenblatt, *Three Modern Satirists: Waugh, Orwell, and Huxley*, pp. 52–53.
    8. Terry Eagleton, "George Orwell and the Lower Middle-class Novel," in his *Exiles and Émigrés: Studies in Modern Literature*, pp. 78–85 passim.
    9. Gerald Fiderer, "Masochism as Literary Strategy: Orwell's Psychological Novels," *L & P*, p. 13.
    10. A man who knew Blair in Burma doubts that he had much to do with women during his years as an imperial policeman. This acquaintance saw no sign of Blair having lived with any Ma Hla May of his own (Stansky and Abrahams, *The Unknown Orwell*, p. 190).
    11. The phallic significance of eyes and the symbolic relationship between castration and phobic blindness, as well as other eye ailments, are discussed in Sandor Ferenczi's "On Eye Symbolism," in his *Sex in Psychoanalysis*, trans. Ernest Jones, pp. 270–76, and Ernest Jones's "The Theory of Symbolism," in *Papers on Psycho-Analysis*, p. 183.
    12. Sigmund Freud, *Totem and Taboo*, in *The Standard Edition of the Completed Psychoanalytical Works of Sigmund Freud*, ed. and trans. James Strachey, Anna Freud, Alix Strachey, and Alan Tyson, 13:132. Further references to Freud's works are from the *Standard Edition*. Also see Anny Katan, "The Role of 'Displacement' in Agoraphobia," *International Journal of Psycho-Analysis*, p. 43; Samuel R. Lehrman, "Psychopathology in Mixed Marriages," *Psychoanalytic Quarterly*, pp. 80–81; and Karl Abraham, "Ueber neurotische Exogamie. Ein Beitrag zu den Uebereinstimmungen im Seelenleben der Neurotiker und der Wilden," in *Psychoanalytische Studien zur Charakterbildung und andere Schriften*, ed. Johannes Cremerius, pp. 383–84.
    13. Freud mentions the tendency of repressed wishes to return as anxiety in "Repression," 14 (1957):157, and "On the Universal Tendency to Debasement in the Sphere of Love," 11 (1957):183. As Bernard C. Meyer states, "Whereas occasionally devices aimed at creating 'distance' lead to felicitous relationships, often enough unions composed of conspicuously exogamous elements end in sexual maladjustment and highly unstable marriages. Nor should it be difficult to understand such failures, for the very urgency of including an exogamous ingredient only emphasizes the compelling attraction of its opposite—the incestuous object. Flight into exogamy may therefore be but a chimera, and that which is so strenuously avoided is at the same moment the secret object of an unconscious pursuit" (*Joseph Conrad: A Psychoanalytic Biography*, p. 113).
    14. Freud, "A Special Type of Object Choice Made by Men," 11:172–73.

Notes to Chapter IV.

    1. Letter to Brenda Salkeld (1934), 1:140.
    2. Letter to Eleanor Jaques (1932), 1:104.
    3. John Atkins, *George Orwell: A Literary and Biographical Study*, p. 267; Laurence Brander, *George Orwell*, pp. 93–95; Jenni Calder, *Chronicles of Conscience: A Study of George Orwell and Arthur Koestler*, pp. 87–89; Christopher Hollis, *A Study of George Orwell: The Man and his Works*, p. 68; Frank W. Wadsworth, "Orwell as a Novelist: The

Early Work," *UR*, p. 98; Jeffrey Meyers, *Reader's Guide to George Orwell*, p. 80.

4. Letter to Brenda Salkeld (June 1933), 1:121.

5. Letter to Brenda Salkeld (December 1933), 1:126–28.

6. Ibid., p. 128.

7. Letter to Brenda Salkeld (1935), 1:150.

8. Letter to Brenda Salkeld (1933), 1:127.

9. Letter to Brenda Salkeld (1934), 1:139.

10. Letter to Leonard Moore (November 1934), 1:143.

11. Dorothy's amnesia is clearly an exaggerated form of forgetting, which, as Freud claims, results from the forcible repression of unconscious motives (*Totem and Taboo*, 13[1955]:30). Wilhelm Stekel describes the case of a girl whose eight-day wandering away from home he interpreted as a flight from an unconscious incestuous fixation on her father (*Peculiarities of Behavior*, trans. James S. Van Teslaar, 1:67–68).

12. "Review: *Tropic of Cancer*" (November 1935), 1:155.

13. C. C., review of *A Clergyman's Daughter*, *SatR*, p. 21. This view of the narrative may in some degree answer Calder's criticism that Dorothy is a weak fictional creation who "seems to fade into the detailed background" (*Study of Orwell and Koestler*, p. 87). It is more correct to say that in order to express a psychic drama Orwell collapses the distinction between the central character and the physical setting.

14. Jacintha Buddicom, *Eric and Us: A Remembrance of George Orwell*, p. 136.

15. "Clink" (written in 1932), 1:88.

Notes to Chapter V.

1. Max Cosman, "George Orwell and the Autonomous Individual," *Pacific Spectator*, p. 78; Richard J. Voorhees, *The Paradox of George Orwell*, pp. 34–35; Robert A. Lee, *Orwell's Fiction*, p. 65; Christopher Hollis, *A Study of George Orwell: The Man and his Works*, pp. 75–76; Lionel Trilling, "George Orwell and the Politics of Truth," in his *The Opposing Self: Nine Essays in Criticism*, p. 162; David L. Kubal, *Outside the Whale: George Orwell's Art and Politics*, pp. 91, 93; Nicholas Guild, "In Dubious Battle: George Orwell and the Victory of the Money-God," *Modern Fiction Studies (MFS)*, pp. 51–53, 56.

2. Dorothy Van Ghent, review of *Keep the Aspidistra Flying*, *Yale Review (YR)*, p. 463; John Wain, "Here Lies Lower Binfield: On George Orwell," in *The World of George Orwell*, ed. Miriam Gross, p. 76.

3. Stephen Jay Greenblatt, *Three Modern Satirists: Waugh, Orwell, and Huxley*, pp. 56–57; Philip Toynbee, review of *A Study of George Orwell* by Christopher Hollis, *Observer* (London), 2 September 1956, p. 9

4. John Wain, "In the thirties," in *The World of George Orwell*, ed. Miriam Gross, p. 81.

5. Keith Alldritt, *The Making of George Orwell: An Essay in Literary History*, p. 33.

6. *Keep the Aspidistra Flying*, pp. 53–54.

7. Terry Eagleton, "George Orwell and the Lower Middle-class Novel," in his *Exiles and Émigrés: Studies in Modern Literature*, p. 96.

8. Orwell's personal feelings were a mixture of optimism and foreboding at this time, as indicated by several letters written to Rayner Heppenstall in the autumn of 1935, while Orwell was writing *Aspidistra*. On the one hand, Orwell is elated at the prospect of marriage to Eileen O'Shaughnessy the following year—"the nicest person I have met for a long time" (1. 153)—and an increased income. But "on the other hand by next year we may all have been blown sky high. I was down at Greenwich the other day and looking at the river I thought what

wonders a few bombs would work among the shipping" (1. 154).

9. Anthony West, "George Orwell," in his *Principles and Persuasions: The Literary Essays of Anthony West*, p. 166.

10. Although in psychoanalytic thought money is most commonly regarded as a symbol of feces and therefore linked to the retentive phase of the anal-sadistic stage of development, Freud, with whom this idea is most closely associated, notes a connection between the giving and receiving of money and erotic, specifically incestuous, fantasies ("Two Lies Told by Children," 12 [1958]:306–7). Otto Fenichel states that "there are . . . men to whom money signifies their [sexual] potency, who experience any loss of money as a castration, or who are inclined, when in danger, to sacrifice money in a sort of 'prophylactic self-castration' " ("The Drive to Amass Wealth," in his *The Collected Papers of Otto Fenichel*, p. 99.)

11. The association of the aspidistra with the punitive restraint on impulse is implied by the scene in *Burmese Days* where Flory finds his path through the jungle "blocked by large ugly plants liked magnified aspidistras, whose leaves terminated in long lashes armed with thorns" (p. 58).

12. Frederick R. Karl, "George Orwell: The White Man's Burden," in *A Reader's Guide to the Contemporary English Novel*, pp. 161–62.

13. Alex Zwerdling, *Orwell and the Left*, pp. 155–59 passim.

14. The origin and growth of Mass-Observation is described in Samuel Hynes's *The Auden Generation: Literature and Politics in England in the 1930s*, pp. 279–97.

15. "Bookshop Memories" (November 1936), 1:242–46.

16. Letter to Henry Miller (August 1936), 1:229.

17. Letter to George Woodcock (1946), 4:205.

18. Alldritt, *Making of George Orwell*, p. 36; David Lodge, *The Modes of Modern Writing: Metaphor, Metonymy, and the Typology of Modern Literature*, p. 190.

19. Jeffrey Meyers, *A Reader's Guide to George Orwell*, p. 85.

Notes to Chapter VI.

1. Letter to Jack Common (26 September 1938), 1:352.

2. Letter to Herbert Read (March 1939), 1:386.

3. Letter to Jack Common (December 1938), 1:367–68.

4. "Inside the Whale" (1940), 1:527.

5. Letter to John Sceats (October 1938), 1:358.

6. Jeffrey Meyers, *A Reader's Guide to George Orwell*, p. 112.

7. John Wain, "Here Lies Lower Binfield: On George Orwell," *Encounter*, p. 79.

8. "Inside the Whale," 1:521.

9. *Coming Up for Air*, p. 91.

10. Kingsley Amis, "Road to Airstrip One," *Spectator*, p. 292.

11. Letter to Julian Symons (1948), 4:422. In *Wigan Pier* (p. 172), Orwell states that by the age of seventeen or eighteen he had read all of Wells's published works, which would have included *Polly*.

12. H. G. Wells, *The History of Mr. Polly*, p. 58.

13. Robert A. Lee, *Orwell's Fiction*, p. 95; Ruth Ann Lief, *Homage to Oceania: The Prophetic Vision of George Orwell*, p. 106.

14. Similarly, the vague guilt Bowling feels at picking roadside "primroses" just prior to his decision to visit Lower Binfield moves him to throw the flowers away and pretend to be buttoning up his pants as motorists drive past (p. 196).

15. "The Rediscovery of Europe" (1942), 2:200.

16. Roberta Kalechofsky, *George Orwell*, p. 92.

17. Richard Rees (*George Orwell: Fugitive from the Camp of Victory*, p. 80) calls Bowling a "convincing and agreeable symbol of the fundamental goodness and sanity of the common man." More inclined to regard him as a prefabricated character are Wain, "Here Lies Lower Binfield," p. 78; John Mander, *The Writer and Commitment*, p. 75; and David L. Kubal, *Outside the Whale: George Orwell's Art and Politics*, pp. 119–20.

18. Letter to Julian Symons (1948), 4:422.

19. Ibid.

Notes to Chapter VII.

1. "Boys' Weeklies" (1940), 1:465–66.

2. "Such, Such Were the Joys" (1947), 4:357.

3. "Rudyard Kipling" (1942), 2:186.

4. "Boys' Weeklies," 1:464–65.

5. "Raffles and Miss Blandish" (1944), 3:213.

6. "Riding Down from Bangor" (1946), 4:246.

7. *Homage to Catalonia*, p. 223.

8. "The Lion and the Unicorn: Socialism and the English Genius" (1941), 2:63.

9. "Raffles and Miss Blandish," 3:223.

10. "Boys' Weeklies," 1:477.

11. "The Art of Donald McGill" (1941), 2:158–59.

12. "Boys' Weeklies," 1:472–73.

13. T. R. Fyvel, "Orwell and the Elephant," *Tribune* (London), 3 November 1950, p. 16.

14. "Politics and the English Language" (1946), 4:137.

15. "Writers and Leviathan" (1948), 4:409.

16. "The Prevention of Literature" (1946), 4:65.

17. "Writers and Leviathan," 4:408.

18. "Inside the Whale" (1940), 1:518–19.

19. "Writers and Leviathan," 4:412.

20. My remarks on *Homage to Catalonia* are partly based on Emanuel Edrich's "Naivete and Simplicity in Orwell's Writing. *Homage to Catalonia*," *UR*, pp. 289–97. Edrich stresses the importance of the persona's almost childlike attitude toward the political events in Barcelona as an earnest that his interpretation of communist treachery represents an honest, unbiased judgment. My approach emphasizes Orwell's struggle to remain uncontaminated by the atmosphere of political treachery and violence in Spain.

21. Robert A. Lee (*Orwell's Fiction*, pp. 76–77) points out that in the description of the battlefront Orwell makes frequent use of animal imagery. Remembering the function of the animal world of the jungle in *Burmese Days*, we can more easily understand the connection in *Homage* between human decency and life at the front.

22. *Animal Farm*, p. 112.

23. "The Lion and the Unicorn," 2:77–78.

24. "War-time Diary" (1940), 2:345.

25. "Toward European Unity" (1947), 4:370–71.

26. "Notes on the Way" (1940), 2:16.

27. "Catastrophic Gradualism" (1945), 4:17–18.

28. Introduction to *British Pamphleteers: From the Sixteenth Century to the French Revolution*, ed. George Orwell and Reginald Reynolds, p. 10.

29. "Raffles and Miss Blandish," 3:222.

30. Review of *The Freedom of the Streets* by Jack Common (1938), 1:336.

31. "Patriots and Revolutionaries," in *The Betrayal of the Left*, p. 238.

32. "My Country Right or Left" (1940), 1:539–40.

33. "Looking Back on the Spanish War" (1942), 2:266.

34. Introduction to *British Pamphleteers*, ed. Orwell and Reynolds, p. 10.

35. "The Lion and the Unicorn," 2:75.

36. "James Burnham and the Managerial Revolution" (1946), 4:179.

37. A. E. Dyson, "Orwell: Irony as Prophecy," in his *The Crazy Fabric: Essays in Irony*, p. 206; Christopher Hollis, *A Study of George Orwell: The Man and his Works*, p. 151; Laurence Brander, *George Orwell*, p. 170; Max Cosman, "George Orwell and the Autonomous Individual," *Pacific Spectator*, p. 81; Stephen Jay Greenblatt, *Three Modern Satirists: Waugh, Orwell, and Huxley*, p. 65; Lee, *Orwell's Fiction*, p. 109.

38. The fact that Orwell never fathered a child suggests a connection with Ben and Boxer, neither of whom seen to have offspring.

39. "As I Please" (April 1944), 3:132–33.

40. Alex Zwerdling, *Orwell and the Left*, pp. 92–93, 148, 175–77.

41. Jacintha Buddicom, *Eric and Us: A Remembrance of George Orwell*, p. 39.

42. Preface to the Ukrainian edition of *Animal Farm* (1947), 4:406.

Notes to Chapter VIII.

1. "As I Please" (1944), 3:231–32.

2. "War-time Diary" (1940), 2:440.

3. "As I Please" (1944), 3:230.

4. "As I Please" (1946), 4:240.

5. Review of *Power: A New Social Analysis*, by Bertrand Russell (1939), 1:376.

6. "Will Freedom Die with Capitalism?" *Left News*, p. 1684.

7. "Raffles and Miss Blandish" (1944), 3:222–23.

8. "Antisemitism in Britain" (1945), 3:340.

9. "As I Please" (1943), 3:57; "Will Freedom Die with Capitalism?" p. 1683.

10. Introduction to *British Pamphleteers: From the Sixteenth Century to the French Revolution*, ed. George Orwell and Reginald Reynolds, pp. 9–10.

11. "Looking Back on the Spanish War" (1943), 2:259–60; "Occupation's Effect on French Outlook," *Observer* (London), 4 March 1945, p. 5; "Inside the Whale" (1940), 1:515.

12. "Wells, Hitler and the World State" (1941), 2:143.

13. "As I Please" (1946), 4:249.

14. Letter to H. J. Willmett (1944), 3:149.

15. Letter to Frank Barber (1944), 3:292.

16. "As I Please" (1944), 3:275.

17. "The Prevention of Literature" (1946), 4:63.

18. Looking Back on the Spanish War," 2:252.

19. Ibid., pp. 256–57.

20. Ibid., p. 258.

21. "Writers and Leviathan" (1948), 4:412.

22. Review of *The Edge of the Abyss* by Alfred Noyes (1944), 3:100.

23. "As I Please" (1944), 3:103.

24. Review of *Power: A New Social Analysis* by Bertrand Russell (January 1939), 1:375.

25. Review of *Mein Kampf* by Adolph Hitler (1940), 2:14.

26. "As I Please" (1947), 4:305–6.
27. "A Nice Cup of Tea" (1946), 3:40–43.
28. "In Front of Your Nose" (1946), 4:125.
29. "No, Not One" (1941), 2:166–67.
30. "Pacifism and the War" (1942), 2:226–27.
31. "As One Non-Combatant to Another" (1943), 2:299–303.
32. Letter to the Reverend Iowerth Jones (1941), 2:111.
33. Review of *Beggar My Neighbour* by Lionel Felden (1943), 2:315.
34. Letter to H. J. Willmett, 3:149.
35. Letter to Julian Symons (1948), 4:417.
36. Because I have not been able to determine what edition of *Lear* Orwell may have had in mind, I have quoted from Horace Howard Furness's edition, in *A New Variorum Edition of Shakespeare*, 7th ed., vol. 5. The bulk of available evidence indicates that Orwell's recollection of the Fool dangling from the gallows at the conclusion of the play is false—a sort of Freudian slip of the memory. Of those eighteenth- and nineteenth-century commentators who have remarked on the phrase "poor fool," Furness lists three who think the Fool is the referent, twelve (including Furness himself) who choose Cordelia (pp. 345–47). As far as I can determine, between 1880 and the publication in 1947 of Orwell's essay, opinion is clearly on the side of Cordelia. For example, see George Brandes, *William Shakespeare: A Critical Study*, trans. William Archer and Diana White, 2:140; A. C. Bradley, *Shakespearian Tragedy: Lectures on Hamlet, Othello, King Lear, Macbeth*, p. 314; G. Wilson Knight, *The Wheel of Fire: Essays in Interpretation of Shakespeare's Somber Tragedies*, pp. 191, 223; Harley Granville-Barker, *Prefaces to Shakespeare*, p. 201; J. S. H. Branson, *The Tragedy of King Lear*, p. 179. Modern editions of *Lear* indicating Cordelia as the referent are *The Temple Shakespeare*, Series edition, 11:168; *The Arden Shakespeare: Five Plays*, ed. D. Nichol Smith, p. 182; *Shakespeare: A Historical and Critical Study with Annotated Text of Twenty-One Plays*, ed. Hardin Craig, p. 896; and *Sixteen Plays of Shakespeare*, ed. G. L. Kittredge, p. 1214. All but one of the editions of *Lear* I have examined print "fool" in lowercase, the exception—George Ian Duthie, *Shakespeare's King Lear* (1949), p. 353— appearing after Orwell's essay.
37. "As I Please" (1945), 3:313–15.
38. "As I Please" (1944), 3:73.
39. "Charles Dickens" (1940), 1:455, "Inside the Whale," 1:510.
40. "Charles Dickens," 1:455, 499.
41. "Inside the Whale," 1:495.
42. "Charles Dickens," 1:421–22.
43. "Rudyard Kipling" (1942), 2:195.
44. "Charles Dickens," 1:420–22.
45. "The Prevention of Literature," 4:71–72.
46. Review of *Great Morning* by Osbert Sitwell (1948), 4:446.
47. "Charles Dickens," 1:424.
48. "Politics vs. Literature" (1946), 4:222.
49. Letter to James Laughlin (1940), 2:34; "London Letter" to *Partisan Review* (1941), 2:54. In 1944 Orwell describes what he regards as the currently fashionable "highbrow-baiting" of such writers as Joyce, Proust, D. H. Lawrence, and T. S. Eliot by the spokesmen of the anti-intellectual British Establishment as an attempt to "castrate the past" ("Benefit of Clergy: Some Notes on Salvador Dali," 3:160).
50. "Inside the Whale," 1:523.

Notes to Chapter IX.

1. "As I Please" (1946), 4:249.
2. "The Rediscovery of Europe" (1942), 2:206.
3. "Raffles and Miss Blandish" (1944), 3:217.
4. "Prophecies of Fascism" (1940), 2:30–31.
5. Review of *We* by E. I. Zamyatin (1946), 4:74–75.
6. *Nineteen Eighty-four*, p. 218.
7. Irving Howe, *Politics and the Novel*, p. 238.
8. Michael Maddison, "*1984*: A Burnhamite Fantasy?" *Political Quarterly*, p. 78; Raymond Williams, *George Orwell*, pp. 78–79; Harold J. Harris, "Orwell's Essays and *1984*," *TC*, pp. 160–61; Howe, *Politics and the Novel*, pp. 247–48; Phillip Rahv, "The Unfuture of Utopia," *PR*, pp. 748–49.
9. Howe, *Politics and the Novel*, pp. 248–50; Isaac Deutscher, "*1984*—The Mysticism of Cruelty," in his *Russia in Transition, and Other Essays*, pp. 241–43.
10. C. S. Lewis, "George Orwell," *Time and Tide*, p. 43.
11. Frederick R. Karl, "George Orwell: The White Man's Burden," in his *A Reader's Guide to the Contemporary English Novel*, p. 149; Richard H. Rovere, "The Importance of George Orwell," in his *The American Establishment and Other Reports, Opinions, & Speculations*, p. 178.
12. Deutscher, "*1984*," p. 231; Harris, "Orwell's Essays and *1984*," p. 161; Wyndham Lewis, "Orwell, or Two and Two Make Four," in his *The Writer and the Absolute*, pp. 191–92; Richard Rees, *George Orwell: Fugitive from the Camp of Victory*, pp. 103–5; V. S. Pritchett, review of *Nineteen Eighty-four*, *New Statesman and the Nation*, p. 646; Julian Symons, "Power and Corruption," *Times Literary Supplement (TLS)*, p. 380.
13. According to Keith Alldritt, (*The Making of George Orwell: An Essay in Literary History*, p. 161), "all the notorious barbarisms described in the book appear less as possible phenomena in the external world and more as objects in the hero's psychological landscape." A similar view is stated in Langdon Elsbree's "The Structured Nightmare of *1984*," *TCL*, pp. 135–41.
14. For a detailed psychological study of *1984* see Marcus Smith's "The Wall of Blackness: A Psychological Approach to *1984*," *MFS*, pp. 423–33. Although many of my interpretations coincide with Smith's, our conclusions differ. Smith stresses the antagonistic relationship between the state and the individual, with the state finally unable to impose its rational control over a rebellious Winston, who refuses to abandon his irrational fixation on Big Brother as the Oedipal mother. As I shall point out, the apparent conflict between the state and Winston is in fact a process of salvation in which he and the Party are reconciled.
15. T. R. Fyvel, "Wingate, Orwell and the 'Jewish Question': A Memoir," *Commentary*, p. 142. William Steinhoff claims that in style and content Goldstein's monograph is more similar to James Burnham's *The Managerial Revolution* and *The Machiavellians* than to Trotsky's *The Revolution Betrayed* (*George Orwell and the Origins of 1984*, pp. 201–4).
16. This summary is based on the following works by Freud contained in *The Standard Edition: Totem and Taboo* (1955), 13:141–45, 156; *Civilization and Its Discontents* (1961), 21:128–33; *Moses and Monotheism* (1964), 23:81–82. Orwell could easily have read Freud, since translations of these and some of his other works were published in England years before the writing of *1984* (*Totem and Taboo* [Routledge, 1919, and Penguin Books, 1938]; *Civilization and Its Discontents* [Hogarth, 1930]; *Moses and Monotheism* [Hogarth, 1939]).
17. Howe, *Politics and the Novel*, pp. 238–40.
18. Freud, "On the Universal Tendency to Debasement in the Sphere of Love," 11:190. The first English translation of this essay was published by Hogarth in 1925.
19. Philip Rieff, *Freud: The Mind of the Moralist*, p. 236.

20. See George Woodcock, "Orwell and Conscience," *World Review*, p. 32; and Neville Braybrooke, "George Orwell," *Fortnightly*, p. 408.

21. C. M. Kornbluth, "The Failure of the Science Fiction Novel as Social Criticism," in *The Science Fiction Novel, Imagination and Social Criticism*, ed. Basil Davenport, pp. 93–94.

22. Freud, *Civilization and Its Discontents*, 21:118–19.

23. Freud, *The Ego and the Id* (1961), 19:53–57; *Civilization and Its Discontents*, 21:119–44 passim; *Moses and Monotheism*, 23:94, 99–100. The first English translation of *The Ego and the Id* was published by Hogarth in 1927.

24. Freud, *Civilization and Its Discontents*, 21:64–72 passim.

25. Erich Fromm, *Escape from Freedom*, pp. 151–58. William Steinhoff's study of works and writers influencing *1984* (*George Orwell and the Origins of 1984*) does not mention Fromm.

26. Alan Barr, "The Paradise Behind *1984*," *English Miscellany (EM)*, pp. 197–203; D. J. Dooley, "The Limitations of George Orwell," *UTQ*, pp. 297–98; Christopher Small, *The Road to Miniluv: George Orwell, the State, and God*, p. 206.

27. Richard Gerber, "The English Island Myth: Remarks on the Englishness of Utopian Fiction," *Critical Quarterly (CritQ)*, p. 41.

28. William Empson, "Correspondence," *CritQ*, p. 158.

29. Freud, *The Future of an Illusion* (1961), 21:19, 24. The earliest English translation of this work was published by Hogarth in 1928.

30. Freud, "Thoughts for the Times on War and Death" (1957), 14:289, 296. An English translation of this essay was published by Hogarth in 1925.

31. Carl Jung, *Psychology of the Unconscious*, trans. Beatrice M. Hinkle, pp. 250–57 passim. This translation was first published in England by Routledge in 1916.

32. Gregory Zilboorg, "The Sense of Immortality," *Psychoanalytic Quarterly*, pp. 194, 197.

Notes to Chapter X.

1. While working on the first draft of *1984*, Orwell described it as "in a sense a fantasy, but in the form of a naturalistic novel" (Letter to F. J. Warburg [1947], 4:329–30). The naturalistic elements—the decaying buildings and disgusting rations, the shabbiness and physical squalor of daily life in Oceania—produce a crudely surrealistic effect of human degradation in a way analogous to Orwell's description of Dreiser's *An American Tragedy*, in his "Good Bad Books," with its massing of details to create an atmosphere of "terrible . . . cruelty" (4, 21).

2. Bernard Bergonzi, *The Situation of the Novel*, pp. 57ff.

Bibliography

Part I contains only those works by Orwell mentioned in this study. The works listed in Part II are those secondary sources referred to by page number either in the text or in footnotes.

Part I

Orwell, George. *Animal Farm*. New York: Harcourt, Brace, 1946.
Orwell, George, and Reginald Reynolds, eds. *British Pamphleteers: From the Sixteenth Century to the French Revolution*. London: Allan Wingate, 1948.
――――. *Burmese Days*. New York: Harcourt, Brace, 1962.
――――. *A Clergyman's Daughter*. New York: Harcourt, Brace, 1960.
――――. *The Collected Essays, Journalism and Letters of George Orwell*. Edited by Sonia Orwell and Ian Angus. 4 vols. New York: Harcourt, Brace, 1968.
――――. *Coming Up for Air*. New York: Harcourt, Brace, 1960.
――――. *Down and Out in Paris and London*. London: Secker & Warburg, 1949.
――――. *Homage to Catalonia*. New York: Harcourt, Brace, 1952.
――――. *Keep the Aspidistra Flying*. New York: Harcourt, Brace & World, 1967.
――――. *1984*. New York: Harcourt, Brace, 1949.
――――. "Occupation's Effect on French Outlook." *Observer* (London), 4 March 1945, p. 5.
――――. "Patriots and Revolutionaries." In *The Betrayal of the Left*, edited by Victor Gollancz, pp. 234–45. London: Victor Gollancz, 1941.
――――. *The Road to Wigan Pier*. New York: Harcourt, Brace, 1968.
――――. "Will Freedom Die with Capitalism?" *Left News* 58 (1941):1682–85.

Part II

Abraham, Karl. "Ueber neurotische Exogamie. Ein Beitrag zu den Uebereinstimmungen im Seelenleben der Neurotiker und der Wilden." In *Psychoanalytische Studien zur Charakterbildung und andere Schriften*, edited by Johannes Cremerius, pp. 383–86. Frankfurt am Main: S. Fischer Verlag, 1969.
Alldritt, Keith. *The Making of George Orwell: An Essay in Literary History*. New York: St. Martin's, 1969.
Amis, Kingsley. "The Road to Airstrip One." *Spectator*, 31 August 1956, pp. 292–93.
Atkins, John. *George Orwell: A Literary and Biographical Study*. New York: Frederick Ungar, 1954.

Ashe, Geoffrey. "A Note on George Orwell." *Commonweal* 54 (1951):191–93.

Aung, Maung Htin. "George Orwell and Burma." In *The World of George Orwell*, edited by Miriam Gross, pp. 19–30. London: Weidenfeld and Nicolson, 1971.

Barr, Alan. "The Paradise Behind *1984.*" *English Miscellany* 19 (1968):197–203.

Bergonzi, Bernard. *The Situation of the Novel*. London: Macmillan, 1970.

Birrel, T. A. "Is Integrity Enough?" *Dublin Review* 449 (3d quarter 1950):49–65.

Bradley, A. C. *Shakespearian Tragedy: Lectures on Hamlet, Othello, King Lear, Macbeth*. 2d ed., 1905. Reprint, London: Macmillan, 1949.

Brander, Laurence. *George Orwell*. London: Longmans, Green, 1954.

Brandes, George. *William Shakespeare: A Critical Study*, translated by William Archer and Diana White. 1898. Reprint, New York: Frederick Ungar, 1963.

Branson, J. S. H. *The Tragedy of King Lear*. Oxford: Basil Blackwell, 1934.

Braybrooke, Neville. "George Orwell." *Fortnightly*, n. s., no. 1014 (1951), pp. 403–9.

Buddicom, Jacintha. *Eric and Us: A Remembrance of George Orwell*. London: Leslie Frewin, 1974.

C. C. Review of *A Clergyman's Daughter. Saturday Review*, 15 August 1936, pp. 20 21.

Calder, Jenni. *Chronicles of Conscience: A Study of George Orwell and Arthur Koestler*. Pittsburgh: University of Pittsburgh Press, 1968.

Connolly, Cyril. *Enemies of Promise*. 2d ed. rev. New York: Macmillan, 1948.

Cosman, Max. "George Orwell and the Autonomous Individual." *Pacific Spectator* 9 (1955):74–84.

Deutscher, Isaac. "*1984*—The Mysticism of Cruelty." In his *Russia in Transition, and Other Essays*, pp. 230–45. New York: Coward-McCann, 1957.

Dooley, D. J. "The Limitations of George Orwell." *University of Toronto Quarterly* 28 (1958–1959):291–300.

Dutscher, Alan. "Orwell and the Crisis of Responsibility." *Contemporary Issues* 8 (1956):308–16.

Dyson, A. E. "Orwell: Irony as Prophecy." In his *The Crazy Fabric: Essays in Irony*, pp. 197–219. London: Macmillan, 1965.

Eagleton, Terry. "George Orwell and the Lower Middle-class Novel." In his *Exiles and Émigrés: Studies in Modern Literature*, pp. 71–107. New York: Schocken Books, 1970.

Edrich, Emanuel. "Naivete and Simplicity in Orwell's Writing: *Homage to Catalonia.*" *University of Kansas City Review* 27 (1961):289–97.

Elliot, George P. "A Failed Prophet." *Hudson Review* 10 (1957):149–54.

Elsbree, Langdon. "The Structured Nightmare of *1984.*" *Twentieth Century Literature* 5 (1959):135–41.

Empson, William. "Correspondence." *Critical Quarterly* 1 (1959):157–59.

Fenichel, Otto. "The Drive to Amass Wealth." In his *The Collected Papers of Otto Fenichel*, translated by Alix Strachey. 2d series, pp. 89–108. New York: Norton, 1954.

Ferenczi, Sandor. "On Eye Symbolism." In his *Sex in Psychoanalysis*, translated by Ernest Jones, pp. 270–76. New York: Basic Books, 1950.

Fiderer, Gerald. "Masochism as Literary Strategy: Orwell's Psychological Novels." *Literature & Psychology* 20 (1970):3–21.

Freud, Sigmund. *The Future of an Illusion, Civilization and Its Discontents, and Other Works*. Vol. 21 of *The Standard Edition of the Complete Psychological Works of Sigmund Freud*, edited and translated by James Strachey, Anna Freud, Alix Strachey, and Alan Tyson. London: Hogarth, 1961.

———. *The Ego and the Id and Other Works*. Vol. 19 of *The Standard Edition*. London: Hogarth, 1961.

———. *Moses and Monotheism, An Outline of Psycho-Analysis, and Other Works*. Vol. 23 of *The Standard Edition*. London: Hogarth, 1964.

———. "On the Universal Tendency to Debasement in the Sphere of Love," in *Five Lectures on Psycho-Analysis, Leonardo da Vinci, and Other Works*. Vol. 11 of *The Standard Edition*, pp. 179–90. London: Hogarth, 1957.

———. "Repression," in *On the History of the Psycho-Analytic Movement, Papers on Metapsychology, and Other Works*. Vol. 14 of *The Standard Edition*, pp. 146–58. London: Hogarth, 1957.

———. "A Special Type of Object Choice Made by Men," in *Five Lectures on Psycho-Analysis, Leonardo da Vinci, and Other Works*. Vol. 11 of *The Standard Edition*, pp. 165–75. London: Hogarth, 1957.

———. "Thoughts for the Times on War and Death," in *On the History of the Psycho-Analytic Movement, Papers on Metapsychology, and Other Works*. Vol. 14 of *The Standard Edition*, pp. 275–300. London: Hogarth, 1957.

———. *Totem and Taboo and Other Works*. Vol. 13 of *The Standard Edition*. London: Hogarth, 1955.

———. "Two Lies Told by Children," in *The Case of Schreber, Papers on Technique, and Other Works*. Vol. 12 of *The Standard Edition*, pp. 305–9. London: Hogarth, 1958.

Fromm, Erich. *Escape from Freedom*. New York: Holt, Rinehart and Winston, 1941.

Fuller, Edmund. "Posthumous Orwell Reissues." *Saturday Review*, 18 February 1950, pp. 18–19.

Fyvel, T. R. "Orwell and the Elephant." *Tribune* (London), 3 November 1950, p. 16.

———. "Wingate, Orwell and the 'Jewish Question': A Memoir." *Commentary* 11 (1951):137–44.

Gerber, Richard. "The English Island Myth: Remarks on the Englishness of Utopian Fiction." *Critical Quarterly* 1 (1959):36–44.

Gillie, Christopher. *Movements in English Literature*. Cambridge: Cambridge University Press, 1975.

Glicksberg, Charles I. "The Literary Contribution of George Orwell." *Arizona Quarterly* 10 (1945):2341–45.

Granville-Barker, Harley. *Prefaces to Shakespeare*. London: Sidgwick and Jackson, 1933.

Greenberger, Allen J. *The British Image of India: A Study in the Literature of Imperialism, 1880–1960*. London: Oxford University Press, 1969.

Greenblatt, Stephen Jay. *Three Modern Satirists: Waugh, Orwell, and Huxley*. New Haven, Conn.: Yale University Press, 1965.

Guild, Nicholas. "In Dubious Battle: George Orwell and the Victory of the Money-God." *Modern Fiction Studies* 21 (1975):49–56.

Harris, Harold J. "Orwell's Essays and *1984*." *Twentieth Century Literature* 4 (1959):154–61.

Hatch, Robert. Review of *1984*. *New Republic*, 1 August 1949, pp. 23–24.

Heppenstall, Rayner. "Memoirs of George Orwell: The Shooting Stick." *Twentieth Century* 157 (1955):367–73.

———. "Orwell Intermittent." *Twentieth Century* 157 (1955):470–83.

Hollis, Christopher. *A Study of George Orwell: The Man and his Works*. Chicago: Henry Regnery, 1956.

Hopkinson, Tom. *George Orwell*. London: Longmans, Green, 1953.

Howe, Irving. "George Orwell's Novels." *The Nation*, 4 February 1950, pp. 110–11.

———. *Politics and the Novel*. New York: Horizon, 1957.

Hynes, Samuel. *The Auden Generation: Literature and Politics in England in the 1930s*. New York: Viking, 1977.

Jones, Ernest. "The Theory of Symbolism." In his *Papers on Psycho-Analysis*, pp. 154–211. London: Baillière, Tindall and Cox, 1923.

Jung, Carl. *Psychology of the Unconscious*, translated by Beatrice M. Hinkle. New York: Dodd, Mead, 1952.

Kalechofsky, Roberta. *George Orwell*. New York: Frederick Ungar, 1973.

Karl, Frederick R. "George Orwell: The White Man's Burden." In his *A Reader's Guide to to the Contemporary English Novel*, pp. 148–66. New York: Farrar, Straus, 1962.

Katan, Anny. "The Role of 'Displacement' in Agoraphobia." *International Journal of Psycho-Analysis* 17, Pt. 1 (1951):41–50.

Knight, G. Wilson. *The Wheel of Fire: Essays in Interpretation of Shakespeare's Somber Tragedies*. London: Humphrey Milford, 1930.

Kornbluth, C. M. "The Failure of the Science Fiction Novel as Social Criticism." In *The Science Fiction Novel, Imagination and Social Criticism*, edited by Basil Davenport, pp. 64–101. Chicago: Advent Publishers, 1959.

Kubal, David L. *Outside the Whale: George Orwell's Art and Politics*. Notre Dame, Ind.: University of Notre Dame Press, 1972.

Lang, Berel. "The Politics and Art of Decency: Orwell's Medium." *South Atlantic Quarterly* 75 (1976):424–33.

Lee, Robert A. *Orwell's Fiction*. Notre Dame, Ind.: University of Notre Dame Press, 1969.

Lehrman, Samuel R. "Psychopathology in Mixed Marriages." *Psycho-*

analytic Quarterly 36 (1967):67–81.

LeRoy, Gaylord C. "A. F. 632 to 1984." *College English* 12 (1950):135–38.

Lewis, C. S. "George Orwell." *Time and Tide*, 18 January 1955, pp. 43–44.

Lewis, Wyndham. "Orwell, or Two and Two Make Four." In his *The Writer and the Absolute*, pp. 153–98. London: Methuen, 1952.

Lief, Ruth Ann. *Homage to Oceania: The Prophetic Vision of George Orwell*. Columbus: Ohio State University Press, 1969.

Lodge, David. *The Modes of Modern Writing: Metaphor, Metonymy, and the Typology of Modern Literature*. London: Edward Arnold, 1977.

London, Jack. *The People of the Abyss*. New York: Macmillan, 1904.

Macdonald, Dwight. "Varieties of Political Experience." *New Yorker*, 28 March 1959, pp. 135–51.

Maddison, Michael. "*1984*: A Burnhamite Fantasy?" *Political Quarterly* 32 (1961):71–79.

Mander, John. "George Orwell's Politics: I." *Contemporary Review* 197 (1960):32–36.

———. *The Writer and Commitment*. London: Secker & Warburg, 1961.

Meyer, Bernard C. *Joseph Conrad: A Psychoanalytical Biography*. Princeton, N. J.: Princeton University Press, 1967.

Meyers, Jeffrey. "The Ethics of Responsibility: Orwell's *Burmese Days*." *University Review* 35 (1968):83–87.

———. *A Reader's Guide to George Orwell*. London: Thomas and Hudson, 1975.

O'Casey, Sean. *Sunset and Evening Star*. London: Macmillan, 1954.

Oxley, B. T. *George Orwell*. New York: Arco, 1967.

Popkin, Henry. "Orwell the Edwardian." *Kenyon Review* 16 (1954):138–44.

Prescott, Orville. "The Political Novel: Warren, Orwell, Koestler." In his *In My Opinion*, pp. 22–39. Indianapolis: Bobbs-Merrill, 1952.

Pritchett, V. S. Review of *1984*. *New Statesman and Nation*, 18 June 1949, pp. 646–48.

Quinton, Anthony. "A Sense of Smell." *Listener*, 4 February 1954, pp. 212–14.

Rahv, Phillip. "The Unfuture of Utopia." *Partisan Review* 16 (1949):743–49.

Rees, Richard. *George Orwell: Fugitive from the Camp of Victory*. London: Secker & Warburg, 1961.

Rieff, Philip. *Freud: The Mind of the Moralist*. New York: Viking, 1959.

———. "George Orwell and the Post-Liberal Imagination." *Kenyon Review* 16 (1954):49–70.

Ringbom, Hakan. *George Orwell as Essayist: A Stylistic Study*. Acta Academiae Aboensis, vol. 44, no. 2. Abo, Finland: Abe Akademi, 1973.

Rovere, Richard H. "The Importance of George Orwell." In his *The American Establishment, and Other Reports, Opinions, & Speculations*, pp. 167–81. New York: Harcourt, Brace, 1962.

Russell, Bertrand. "Symptoms of Orwell's *1984*." In his *Portraits from*

Memory, and Other Essays, pp. 221–28. New York: Simon & Schuster, 1956.

Shakespeare, William. *King Lear*. In *The Arden Shakespeare: Five Plays*, edited by D. Nichol Smith. Boston: Heath, 1917.

———. *King Lear. A New Variorum Edition of Shakespeare*, vol. 5, edited by Horace Howard Furness. 7th ed. New York: Lippincott, 1880.

———. *King Lear*. In *Shakespeare: A Historical and Critical Study with Annotated Text of Twenty-One Plays*, edited by Hardin Craig. New York: Scott, Foresman, 1931.

———. *Shakespeare's King Lear*, edited by George Ian Duthie. Oxford: Basil Blackwell, 1949.

———. *The Tragedy of King Lear*. In *Sixteen Plays of Shakespeare*, edited by G. L. Kittredge. New York: Ginn and Co., 1946.

———. *The Tragedy of King Lear. The Temple Shakespeare*, vol. 11. London: Dent, 1908.

Slater, Joseph. "The Fictional Values of *1984*." In *Essays in Literary History: Presented to J. Milton French*, edited by Rudolf Kirk and C. W. Main, pp. 249–64. New Brunswick, N. J.: Rutgers University Press, 1961.

Small, Christopher. *The Road to Miniluv: George Orwell, the State, and God*. London: Victor Gollancz, 1975.

Smith, Marcus. "The Wall of Blackness: A Psychological Approach to *1984*." *Modern Fiction Studies* 14 (1968–1969):423–33.

Smith, W. D. "George Orwell." *Contemporary Review* 189 (1956):283–86.

Spender, Stephen. "*Homage to Catalonia*." *World Review* 16 (June 1950):51–54.

Stansky, Peter, and William Abrahams. *The Unknown Orwell*. New York: Knopf, 1972.

Steinhoff, William. *George Orwell and the Origins of 1984*. Ann Arbor: University of Michigan Press, 1975.

Stekel, Wilhelm. *Peculiarities of Behavior*, vol. 1., translated by James S. Van Teslaar. New York: Liveright, 1924.

Symons, Julian. "Power and Corruption." *Times Literary Supplement*, 10 June 1949, p. 380.

Tanner, Tony. "Orwell: Death of Decency." *Time and Tide*, 25 May 1961, pp. 871–72.

Toynbee, Philip. Review of *A Study of George Orwell*, by Christopher Hollis. *Observer* (London), 2 September 1956, p. 9.

Trilling, Lionel. "George Orwell and the Politics of Truth." In his *The Opposing Self: Nine Essays in Criticism*, pp. 151–72. New York: Viking, 1955.

Trocchi, Alexander. "A Note on George Orwell." *Evergreen Review* 2 (1958):150–55.

Van Ghent, Dorothy. Review of *Keep the Aspidistra Flying. Yale Review*, n.s., 45 (1956):460–63.

Voorhees, Richard J. *The Paradox of George Orwell*. West Lafayette, Ind.: Purdue University Studies, 1961.

Wadsworth, Frank W. "Orwell as a Novelist: The Early Work." *University of Kansas City Review* 22 (1955):93–99.

———. "Orwell as a Novelist: The Middle Period." *University of Kansas City Review* 22 (1956):189–94.

———. "Orwell's Later Work." *University of Kansas City Review* 22 (1956):285–90.

Wain, John. "Here Lies Lower Binfield: On George Orwell." *Encounter* 17, no. 4 (1961):70–83.

———. "In the Thirties." In *The World of George Orwell*, edited by Miriam Gross, pp. 76–90. London: Weidenfeld and Nicolson, 1971.

———. "Orwell." *Spectator*, 19 November 1954, pp. 630, 632, 634.

Warburg, Fredric. *An Occupation for Gentlemen*. Boston: Houghton Mifflin, 1960.

Way, Brian. "George Orwell: The Political Thinker We Might Have Had." *Gemini* 3 (Spring 1960):8–18.

Wells, H. G. *The History of Mr. Polly*. New York: Press of the Readers Club, 1941.

West, Anthony. "George Orwell." In his *Principles and Persuasions: The Literary Essays of Anthony West*, pp. 164–76. New York: Harcourt, Brace, 1957.

Williams, Raymond. *George Orwell*. New York: Viking, 1971.

Woodcock, George. *The Crystal Spirit: A Study of George Orwell*. Boston: Little, Brown, 1966.

———. "Orwell and Conscience." *World Review* 14 (April 1950):28–34.

———. *The Writer and Politics*. London: Porcupine Press, 1948.

Yorks, Samuel A. "George Orwell: Seer Over His Shoulder." *Bucknell Review* 9 (March 1960):23–45.

Zilboorg, Gregory. "The Sense of Immortality." *Psychoanalytic Quarterly* 7 (1938):171–99.

Zwerdling, Alex. *Orwell and the Left*. New Haven, Conn.: Yale University Press, 1974.

Index

A

Abrahams, William, 8
Agamemnon, King, 65
Alldritt, Keith, 3, 6, 60, 72
Amis, Kingsley, 6, 85
Anti-Semitism, 96, 112
Aragon, Spain, 98, 99
Arnold, Matthew, 168n5
Atkins, John, 3
Aung, Maung Htin, 26, 39
Austria, 76
Autonomous individual, 77, 90, 109, 157

B

Barcelona, Spain, 76, 99, 171n20
Baron Charlus (*Remembrance of Things Past*), 65
Barrie, James M., 89
Bengal, India, 121
Bennett, Arnold, 89
Bergonzi, Bernard, 163
Billy Bunter (*Magnet*), 65
Blair family, 74
Blair, Thomas Richard Arthur (Orwell's grandfather), 74
Britain. *See* England
Buddicom, Jacintha, 11, 58, 110
Bunyan, John, 2
Burma, 24–33, 35–37, 51, 79, 98, 167n3, 168n10
Burnham, James, 104
Burton, Edward (pseudonym of Eric Blair), 58
Byzantium, 127

C

Caliban, 164
Camus, Albert, 2
Cape, Jonathan, 22
Capitalism, 72, 102, 165n4
Cassandra, 2, 164
Chamberlain, Neville, 76
Chase, James Hadley, 138, 153; *No Orchids for Miss Blandish*, 138, 140
Chesterton, G. K., 2, 160
Chicago, U.S.A., 114
Childhood vision of reality, 110, 127, 128, 129–35, 146, 163
Christianity, 115, 118, 119, 154–55, 156
Churchill, Winston, 6
Cicero, Marcus Tullius, 9
Circe, 107
Cobbett, William, 2

Cold War, the, 118
Collected Essays, Journalism and Letters of George Orwell, The, 140
Comfort, Alex, 120
Communism, 155
Conrad, Joseph, 2, 92, 121
Count Fosco (*The Woman in White*), 25
Czechoslovakia, 76

D

Daladier, Edouard, 76
Dali, Salvador, 137, 138; *The Secret Life of Salvador Dali*, 137
David Copperfield (*David Copperfield*), 127
Dickens, Charles, 2, 3, 5, 95, 125, 126, 127, 128, 131, 135, 138, 162; *A Tale of Two Cities*, 126
Dostoevski, Feodor, 5, 74, 112, 162; *The Possessed*, 4; *Notes from the Underground*, 74–75
Dreiser, Theodore, *An American Tragedy*, 160, 175n1
Dublin, Ireland, 45

E

Edwardians, the: Orwell influenced by literature of, 3, 4; Orwell's criticism of, 89–90, 137, 153; vulnerability of humanism of, 122; mentioned, 5
Electra, 43
Eliot, T. S., 5, 36–37, 40, 110, 125, 127, 162, 173n49; "The Hollow Men," 36; "The Love Song of J. Alfred Prufrock," quoted, 36; "Preludes," 36
Empson, William, 154–55
Engels, Friedrich, 95
England, 18–22, 31, 42, 44, 50, 56, 67, 71–73, 76–77, 85, 89, 96, 99–103, 114, 120, 174n16
English society. *See* England
Ernst, Max, 161
Etruscans, the, 127
Europe, 50, 77, 90, 100, 112, 114, 122. *See also* Western civilization
Ezra, 42

F

Fascism, 77, 96, 120, 121
Fierze, Mabel (friend of Blair family), 167n3
Fisher King, the, 92
Forster, E. M., 26, 27, 39; *Passage to India*, 39

France, 91, 114, 115, 125
Franco, Francisco, 76, 96, 99, 121
French Communist party, 115
French Morocco. *See* Morocco
Freud, Sigmund, 5, 7, 8, 38, 142, 144, 146, 150, 152, 153, 155
Fromm, Erich, *Escape from Freedom*, 153, 156
Fyvel, T. R., 96

G

Gandhi, Mohandas K., 3, 120, 121–22
Gem (boys' magazine), 95
Genghis Khan, 137
Germany, 76, 101, 114, 120, 121
Gerty MacDowell (*Ulysses*), 44
Gissing, George, 3
God, 34, 42, 56, 118, 154, 156
Goering, Hermann, 102
Grotesquery, literary. *See* Orwell, George

H

Hare, Frances (Orwell's paternal grandmother), 74
Helen's Babies (by John Habberton), 96
History: attempt to escape from in Orwell's novels, 55–56, 149, 151, 154, 159, 162; contemporary distortion and denial of, 115–16; involving tragic sacrifice, 132; rage at, 153
Hitler, Adolph, 76, 85, 93, 102, 103, 112, 121
Hornung, E. W., 95; *Raffles* novels, 138
Howe, Irving, 142
Hutten, Karl (American criminal), 114
Huxley, Aldous, *Brave New World*, 139

I

Ibsen, Henrik, 90, 92; *The Wild Duck*, 90
Imperialism, 24–25, 27, 28, 34, 39, 78–81, 112, 165n4
Industrial Revolution, 113
Iphigenia, 65
Irrationality. *See* Childhood vision of reality; Orwell, George

J

Jacobson, Roman, 4
James, Henry, 7
Jeremiah, 42
Jesus Christ, 156
Jews, the. *See* Anti-Semitism
Jonah fantasy, the, 83, 84. *See also* Psychoanalysis
Jowett, Benjamin, 9

Joyce, James, 5, 44–45, 58, 60, 74, 110, 118, 125, 127; *Ulysses*, 44–45, 49, 126; *A Portrait of the Artist as a Young Man*, 60, 74
Jung, Carl, 5, 156

K

Kafka, Franz, 2
Kali, 33, 34
Kent, England, 47–51, 54
Kipling, Rudyard: 28, 95, 126; *Stalky and Co.*, 28
Koestler, Arthur, 2, 139; *The Gladiators*, 139
Kornbluth, C. M., 159
Kremlin, the, Moscow, 103

L

Langland, William, 2
Lawrence, D. H., 92, 125, 127, 173n49; *Women in Love*, 82
Leopold Bloom (*Ulysses*), 44, 45, 49
Lewis, Wyndham, 160
Little Women (by Louisa May Alcott), 96
Lodge, David, 4, 5, 22, 72
London, England, 12, 15–16, 18, 22, 42, 46, 47, 49, 50, 51, 62, 71, 102, 117
London, Jack, 12–14, 16, 17, 138, 162; *The People of the Abyss*, 12–14, 16–17; *The Iron Heel*, 138

M

McGill, Donald, 137
Machiavelli, Niccolo, 137, 138
Magnet (boys' magazine), 95
Mander, John, 5, 12, 22
Mann, Thomas, 2; *The Magic Mountain*, 4, 82
Marcuse, Herbert, *Eros and Civilization*, 72
Marxism, 66
Marxist criticism, 126, 137
Mass-Observation, 71
Mayhew, Henry, 95
Memel, Lithuania, 76
Meredith, George, 160
Mexico, 127
Meyers, Jeffrey, 1
Miller, Henry, 52, 77–78, 83; *Tropic of Cancer*, 52
Montaigne, Michel de, *Essais*, 9
Montparnasse, Paris, 127
Moore, George, 92
Morocco, 76, 81, 82
Moscow, Russia, 115
Munich Agreement, the, 76
Murdstones, the (*David Copperfield*), 127
Mussolini, Benito, 76

N

Nationalism, 112–13, 119
Nazism, 120
New Jerusalem, 103

O

Obermeyer, Rosalind (Orwell's landlady), 7
Oedipal elements, 65, 69, 128, 156. *See also*
Orwell, George; Psychoanalysis; Sex
Oedipus, 43
Orwell, George (Eric Blair): influence of, 1;
regarded as sociopolitical novelist, 2;
criticized for sociopolitical naiveté, 2–3;
described in sociopolitical terms, 2, 6,
165n4; personal conflicts affecting works
of, 2, 10, 18, 22, 26, 34–35, 37, 39, 92–93,
169n8; psychosocial disunity in works of,
2, 14, 22, 35–36, 39, 44, 45, 57, 61, 69–70,
72–73, 75, 82–83, 91–92, 128, 161; regarded as literary naturalist and realist,
3–4; interest in psychology, 3, 7, 74,
83–84, 137–38, 162; pre-modern influences on, 3, 35–36, 86, 92, 170n11; antihumanistic tendency in, 3, 125;
psychoanalytic approach to, 5, 8; surrealistic elements in novels of, 5, 33–34, 37–38,
45–46, 58, 135, 140, 141–59 passim, 162–
63, 174n13, 175n1; modernist influences
on, 5, 36, 37, 44–45, 58, 60, 74, 75, 77–78,
162; interest in literary grotesquery, 5,
128, 134–35, 138, 162, 164; distorted
judgment of, 6; neurotic traits of, 6; bipolar
view of reality, 6–7, 21, 94–107 passim;
broadening sociopolitical interests of, 6–7,
162; literary craftsmanship of, 7; as essayist, 9; early writing career of, 11, 42, 71,
76, 98–99; creation of literary persona, 12,
21; psychoanalytic concepts and motifs in,
34, 38–39, 43, 46, 49–51, 53–56, 57, 65,
68, 75, 142–59 passim; religious disbelief
of, 42; teaching in Middlesex, 42;
sociopolitical pessimism of, 42, 53–54, 77,
78–80, 90–92, 97, 101, 113–14, 118, 119,
153; writing as self-exploration, 57, 92–93,
149–50, 156–57, 164; common man as protagonist for thematic unity, 61, 69–70,
78–79, 91–92; escape theme, 64, 122,
150–51, 154; in Spanish Civil War, 76,
98–99; literary ideas of, 77–78, 125–28,
134, 138–39, 140, 160, 163–64; criticism of
Edwardian beliefs, 89, 90, 113–14, 137,
157, 162; declining influence of modernist
writers on, 90–91, 110, 127; power motive,
96, 101, 104, 105, 112–13, 119, 138, 150,
153; on danger of politics to writer-
intellectual, 97–98, 116; ambivalence
about revolution, 102–3; on pacifists, 102,
120–22; on contemporary man's moral and
spiritual condition, 118–19; apolitical tendency of
—*Novels*: *Animal Farm* (1945), discussed,
100, 104–10; discrepancy concerning Ben,
100, 107–10; mentioned, 53, 120, 132,
154, 162; *Burmese Days* (1934), historical
background to, 24; discussed, 24–40;
psychological aspects of, 30–35, 37–39,
168n13; disunity of, 35–36, 39; literary influences on, 35–37; mentioned, 45, 60, 66,
110, 145, 170n11, 171n21; *Clergyman's
Daughter, A*, discussed, 42–58; psychological aspects of, 43–58 passim; disunity of,
44, 45, 57; literary influences on, 44–45,
58; mentioned, 60, 69, 74, 85–86, 91; *Coming Up for Air* (1939), historical
background to, 76–77; discussed, 82–87,
89–93; psychological aspects of, 83–84,
86–87; Orwell's criticism of himself, Edwardian, and modern writers, 89–91; mentioned, 76–78, 81, 109, 110, 120, 125, 145,
162, 163; *Keep the Aspidistra Flying*
(1936), discussed, 59–75; disunity of,
60–62, 72–73, 75; a transitional novel, 60,
69, 74–75; literary influences on, 60,
74–75; psychological aspects of, 63–66,
68–70, 75; mentioned, 91, 161; *1984* (1949),
literary influences on, 138–39, 140–41,
162; discussed, 139–59, 160–61, 162–63;
unity of, 141, 163; psychological aspects of,
141–59, 162–63; treatment of history in,
149, 151, 154, 159; mentioned, 1–4, 8, 53,
129
—*Other works*: "Art of Donald McGill, The"
(1941), 136–37; "As I Please" (1944), 111–
12; "Benefit of Clergy: Some Notes on Salvador Dali" (1944), 7, 137, 138; "Clink"
(posthumously 1968), 12, 17; "Decline of
the English Murder" (1946), 114–15;
Down and Out in Paris and London (1933),
10, 11–12, 14–16, 17–23, 30, 51, 64, 67,
68, 82, 97, 111, 125, 160; "Good Bad
Books" (1945), 160, 163–64; "Hanging, A"
(1931), 10–11, 22, 98, 167n3; *Homage to
Catalonia* (1938), 76, 98–100, 120, 171n21;
"How the Poor Die" (1946), 9, 132–34,
135; "Inside the Whale" (1940), 77–78, 83,
109; quoted, 125, 126; "Lear, Tolstoy and
the Fool" (1947), 123–25, 148, 155; "Lion
and the Unicorn, The" (1941), 96, 102,
103; "Marrakech" (1939), 81–82; "Notes on
Nationalism" (1945), 112–13, 153; "Politics
vs Literature: An Examination of *Gulliver's Travels*," quoted, 127, 128; "Raffles
and Miss Blandish" (1944), 7, 138, 140;

"Reflections on Gandhi" (1949), 121–22; *Road to Wigan Pier, The* (1937), 37, 96, 97, 101; "Shooting an Elephant" (1936), 9, 78–81, 98; "Some Thoughts on the Common Toad" (1946), 116–18; "Sometimes in the Middle Autumn Days" (1933), 41–42; quoted, 56; "Spike, The" (posthumously 1968), 12, 17; "Such, Such Were the Joys" (posthumously 1953), 6, 64, 129–32, 135; "Why I Write" (1946), 3, 39

O'Shaughnessy, Eileen (Orwell's first wife), 7, 99, 169*n*8

P

Pacifism, 103, 120–22
Paris, France, 11, 14–22, 51, 67, 111
Plato, "Symposium," 39
Poe, Edgar Allan, 5, 128, 131, 135, 138, 162
Polly, Mr. (*History of Mr. Polly*). *See* Wells, H. G.
Porter, William Sidney, 15
Potter, Beatrix, 58, 110; *The Tale of Pigling Bland*, 110
POUM (Partido Obrero de Unificá`cion` Marxista), 76, 99
Proust, Marcel: 5, 93, 173*n*49; *Swann's Way*, 68; *Remembrance of Things Past*, 82, 91
Psychoanalysis: Orwell's knowledge of, 7; castration, 34, 39, 65, 147–48, 159, 168*n*11, 170*n*10; incest, 38, 43, 46, 49–51, 56, 57, 65, 68, 86, 146–47, 153, 168*n*13, 169*n*11, 170*n*10; Oedipal guilt and anxiety, 43, 65, 69, 128, 156, 157; longing for womb, 53–56, 75, 83, 87, 116, 145, 149, 153, 158; primal crime, 142, 144–45, 151–52, 158; superego, 146, 150; death instinct, 150; oceanic feeling, 153, 155, 157, 159
Puritan Revolution, 113

Q

Quarterly Review, The, 125

R

Rangoon, Burma, 26
Red and the Black, The, by Stendhal, 4
Rees, Richard, 3, 5, 7
Religion: theme of society indifferent to, 42, 44, 52; secular substitutes for, 115, 119; attitude of modern man no longer associated with, 116; modern man without a soul, 118; psychological essence of, 154–56
Rome, Italy, 127
Roosevelt, Franklin D., 6
Russia, 100, 114

Russian Revolution, 102
Russo-German Pact, 115

S

St. George, 85
Sancho Panza, 136, 137
Sex. *See* Orwell; Psychoanalysis
Shakespeare, William, 123–24, 137, 148; *Macbeth*, 53; *King Lear*, 123–25, 173*n*36
Shaw, George Bernard, 89, 102
Sherlock Holmes, stories by Arthur Conan Doyle, 138
Solzhenitsyn, Alexander, 1
Spain, 98, 100, 111, 115
Spender, Stephen, 2
Stalin, Joseph, 6, 85, 102, 121, 155
Stansky, Peter, 8
Stephen Dedalus (*Portrait of the Artist*), 45
Sudetenland, Czechoslovakia, 76
Surrealism. *See* Orwell
Swift, Jonathan, 5, 127, 128, 131, 134, 135, 138, 162; *Gulliver's Travels*, 128
Symbolism. *See* Orwell; Psychoanalysis

T

Talboys, Mrs. Mervyn (*Ulysses*), 49
Tamerlane, 137
Tennyson, Alfred, "In the Children's Hospital," 133
Thibaw, King (Burma), 26
Third Reich, the. *See* Germany; Nazism
Thorez, Maurice, 115
Time and Tide, 118
Tolstoy, Leo, 3, 123, 125; *Shakespeare and the Drama*, 123–25
Trotsky, Leon, 102, 142

U

Uncle Tom's Cabin (by Harriet Beecher Stowe), 160
Utopia, 27, 53, 54, 106, 158. *See* History

V

Victorians, the, 3, 35–36

W

Wain, John, 59
Wells, H. G., 1, 3, 86, 87, 88, 89, 92, 93, 114, 122, 137, 138; *The History of Mr. Polly*, 86, 87–89, 92, 170*n*11; *The Sleeper Wakes*, 138–39
West, Anthony, 6, 63
West, the. *See* Europe; Western civilization
Western civilization, 6, 27, 29, 35, 50, 77, 78, 111, 112, 118, 136–37

Whitman, Walt, 77
Wilde, Oscar, 92
Woodcock, George, 3
Woolf, Virginia, 7, 160
World War I, 6, 84, 91, 95, 96, 127
World War II, 7, 101

Z

Zamyatin, Eugene, 5, 138–39, 162; *We*, 139
Zilboorg, Gregory, 157–58
Zwerdling, Alex, 69, 109